# CHEMICAL PROJECT ECONOMICS

# CHEMICAL PROJECT ECONOMICS

**(THIRD EDITION)**

**V.V. MAHAJANI**

**S.M. MOKASHI**

UNIVERSITY SCIENCE PRESS

(An Imprint of Laxmi Publications Pvt.Ltd.)

An ISO 9001:2015 Company

BENGALURU • CHENNAI • GUWAHATI • HYDERABAD • JALANDHAR

KOCHI • KOLKATA • LUCKNOW • MUMBAI • RANCHI

NEW DELHI

**CHEMICAL PROJECT ECONOMICS**



Printed and bound in India
*Typeset at* Shubham Composer, Delhi
First Edition: 2005; Second Edition: 2015, Third Edition: 2023
*ISBN* 978-93-5138-120-4



**Branches**

| | |
|---|---|
| Bengaluru | 080-26 75 69 30 |
| Chennai | 044-24 34 47 26 |
| Guwahati | 0361-254 36 69 |
| Hyderabad | 040-27 55 53 83 |
| Jalandhar | 0181-222 12 72 |
| Kochi | 0484-405 13 03 |
| Kolkata | 033-40 04 77 79 |
| Lucknow | 0522-430 36 13 |
| Ranchi | 0651-224 24 64 |

**PUBLISHED IN INDIA BY**

UNIVERSITY SCIENCE PRESS
(An Imprint of Laxmi Publications Pvt.Ltd.)
An ISO 9001:2015 Company
113, GOLDEN HOUSE, GURUDWARA ROAD,
DARYAGANJ, NEW DELHI-110002, INDIA
Telephone : 91-11-4353 2500, 4353 2501
www.laxmipublications.com
info@laxmipublications.com

C—00677/022/012
*Printed at* : Ajit Printing Press, Delhi.

# Preface to the Third Edition

This edition is updated with GST (Goods and Services Tax) concept as applicable to a Chemical Project. With reference to GST there are cosmetic revisions in the text where Sales and Excise taxes were mentioned.

In profitability analysis we have introduced the frequently used term **EBITDA** in the corporate world.

We acknowledge with thanks feedback from friends in industry, faculty members and students.

V.V. Mahajani

S.M. Mokashi

# Preface to the First Edition

Chemicals assume a unique position in the sustainable development of the human race. Consequently the study of chemical projects demands special attention. However, due to different dimensions of safety, health and environmental (SHE) issues associated with these projects, the society sometimes does not appreciate this position. This outlook can be changed by a proper selection of the site, an appropriate selection of the process or technology and timely implementation of chemical projects in order to produce products at an affordable price.

The success of a chemical project is generally measured by its sustained benevolence, nonetheless, the project owner measures its success from its sustained profitability. This, in turn, depends upon several factors beginning with building a right plant of a right size, for a right product, at a right location (site) and at the right time. Selection of a product to be manufactured, its technology, design, engineering, appropriate financing and construction to achieve social benevolence are the key issues which have considerable impact on the success of the project, irrespective of the size and type of the project.

This book is an introduction to chemical project economics. The objectives of the book are: to highlight the basic concepts used in the selection of process and site for the project, deal comprehensively with procedures frequently used for estimation of the project cost, and measuring the financial viability of chemical projects. We know that the economic success of a project is the function of place and time. The basic principles dealt with herein are universal in nature.

This book is developed in the following sequence bearing in mind the present Indian scenario.

The first chapter discusses the importance of the subject and the various types of projects. The selection of process (technology) and site are vital for the successful implementation of a project.

The second chapter discusses the social and economic factors dealing with selection of a process or technology.

Chapter 3 highlights the importance of the project site selection exercise and the methodology to select the plant site. The estimation of the project cost and the cost of production are basic pre-project engineering activities to determine project viability. In the fourth chapter, different types of estimates and error analysis of various estimate methodologies are dealt with comprehensively. Estimation of various components of project cost as per recommended practice by Indian Financial Institutes are projected in the fifth chapter.

As Plant and Machinery is the largest and hence the most important component of project cost, special attention has been paid to its estimation in the next chapter, while the important components of cost of production with methods of estimation are explained in Chapter 7. The sources of finance and the cost of finance (interest) are important for smart management of project and are covered in the next chapter. It gives a bird's eye-view of financing a chemical project. In Chapter 9 loan repayment schedule with interest computation is presented along with capitalised and annual cost concepts. The depreciation of fixed capital investment plays an important role in the profitability of a project. To understand the concept of depreciation and its significance a complete chapter (Chapter 10) has been dedicated to this. It discusses the importance of this concept in taxation and project profitability with methods relevant to projects in India.

Finally, since the success of a project is measured through its profitability, the critical appraisal of the project profitability is essential to implement the project. These aspects are covered in two subsequent chapters (Chapters 11 and 12) thus providing estimates of working results of the project and financial evaluation of project profitability. The pricing of a product is important for sustainability of a project. An overview of the pricing concept is presented in a separate chapter (Chapter 13).

The two important reports pertaining to projects, viz., feasibility report and annual report, are presented in the last two chapters (Chapters 14 and 15). These chapters give an overview of the reports; their importance with their brief descriptions of contents, apart from discussing their importance to engineers, technologists in production and in research and planning departments.

This book has been designed to assist not only students, but also professionals associated with chemical projects. It would help to accomplish pre-project activities such as site selection, process selection and preparation of detailed techno-economic feasibility report. The book would also help management students to understand what differentiate chemical projects from others.

This book has been developed on the course contents of Chemical Engineering and Technology courses of final year degree level at Mumbai University at the Institute of Chemical Technology, University of Mumbai, Mumbai, India where Dr Mahajani taught this course for many years.

Our sincere thanks are due to Dr M. Sriram, Mr P.G. Kane, Mr K.P. Chaudhari, Mr P.D. Vaidya, Mr V.M. Paradkar and Mr O.P. Goyal, who have read the manuscript at different stages and offered constructive suggestions to make it more comprehensive. Our sincere thanks are also to Professor J.B. Joshi, Director, Institute of Chemical Technology, University of Mumbai, Mumbai where this project was designed and executed. We also sincerely thank the staff and students of this Institute.

We wish to thank Dr O. P. Kharbanda and Mr Kannan of ICICI for their encouragement. We acknowledge with thanks a good gesture of Mr VK. Sood, Project Manager, Narmada Chematur Petrochemicals Limited, for providing data on Project Financing.

We appreciate the efforts taken by Ms Vasudha Kulkarni for acting as an interface between the handwritten and the electronic version of the manuscript. We sincerely thank her.

Last but not the least, we thank our family members for bearing with us during the preparation of this book.

V.V. Mahajani

S.M. Mokashi

# Contents

*Preface to the Third Edition* v
*Preface to the First Edition* vii

1. INTRODUCTION 1
   1.1 An Overview 1
   1.2 Pre-Project Activities 6
   1.3 Types of Projects 8
   1.4 Chemical Project Classification 11
   1.5 Price of a Product 13
   1.6 Project: Conception to Commissioning 13
   References 16

2. PROCESS SELECTION 17
   2.1 Introduction 17
   2.2 Viability Parameters 18
   2.3 Profitability Parameters 29
   2.4 Process Evaluation 39
   Suggested Readings 42

3. PROJECT SITE 43
   3.1 Introduction 43
   3.2 Site Selection 45
   3.3 Site Evaluation 58
   3.4 The Plot A at Given Site 62
   3.5 Site Data 64
   3.6 Site Clearances 67
   Reference 68

4. ESTIMATE 69
   4.1 Introduction 69
   4.2 Estimate Basics Revisited 71
   4.3 Types of Estimates 74
   References 76

5. PROJECT COST 77
- 5.1 Introduction 77
- 5.2 Elements of Project Cost 78
- 5.3 Land and Site Development 81
- 5.4 Building and Civil Works 87
- 5.5 Plant and Machinery 90
- 5.6 Know-how and Engineering 91
- 5.7 Expenses on Foreign Technicians and Training of Indian Technicians Abroad 99
- 5.8 Miscellaneous Fixed Assets 101
- 5.9 Contingencies 102
- 5.10 Pre-Operative Expenses 105
- 5.11 Preliminary and Capital Issue Related Expenses 113
- 5.12 Margin Money (Working Capital) 114
- 5.13 The Project Cost Schedule 122
- References 123

6. PLANT AND MACHINERY 124
- 6.1 Introduction 124
- 6.2 The Basis 127
- 6.3 Equipment Cost Estimate 129
- 6.4 Piping, Instrumentation and Electricals, Cost Estimate 139
- 6.5 OSBL Facilities Cost Estimates 145
- 6.6 Miscellaneous Items of the Plant and Machinery Schedule 148
- 6.7 Order of Magnitude (Quick) Estimate 152
- 6.8 Computer-Aided Cost Estimate 165
- References 165

7. COST OF PRODUCTION 167
- 7.1 Introduction 167
- 7.2 Elements of Cost of Production 169
- 7.3 Gross Cost of Production 177
- 7.4 Normative Cost of Production 178
- 7.5 Monitor this Way 178
- 7.6 The Schedule 179
- Suggested Readings 182

**8. PROJECT FINANCING** 183
8.1 Introduction 183
8.2 Greenfield Project 183
8.3 Add-On Project 192
8.4 Ongoing Business 192
8.5 Illustrations 193
8.6 Working Capital 197
8.7 Venture Capital 198
Suggested Reading 200

**9. INTEREST** 201
9.1 Introduction 201
9.2 Basics Revisited 202
9.3 Loan Repayment 205
9.4 Periodic Payments: Instalments 211
9.5 Annualised Cost 213
9.6 Capitalised Cost 215
References 218

**10. DEPRECIATION** 219
10.1 Introduction 219
10.2 Depreciation Concept in Chemical Project 221
10.3 Depreciation Methods 222
10.4 Appreciation of Depreciation Concept 226
10.5 Depreciation Rates 226
10.6 The Depreciation Schedule 227

**11. PROJECT PROFITABILITY** 231
11.1 Introduction 231
11.2 Estimate of Working Results 232
Suggested Readings 239

**12. PROJECT EVALUATION** 240
12.1 Introduction 240
12.2 Break-Even Analysis 242
12.3 Incremental Analysis 244
12.4 Ratio Analysis 246
12.5 Discounted Profit Flow Technique (DPF) 256
12.6 Illustration 263
Suggested Reading 266

**13. PRODUCT PRICING** 267
13.1 Introduction 267
13.2 Project Economics Considerations 267
13.3 Market Considerations 272
References 276

**14. FEASIBILITY REPORT** 277
14.1 Preamble 277
14.2 Contents 278
14.3 The Utility of the Feasibility Report 283

**15. ANNUAL REPORT** 285
15.1 Introduction 285
15.2 Contents Overviewed 286
15.3 Insight into an Annual Report 292

**Index** 299-305

# 1 Introduction

## 1.1 AN OVERVIEW

Chemical projects have a special status in sustainable development of our society because we need chemicals in several forms such as pharmaceuticals, textiles, dyes, soap, detergents, cosmetics, food preservatives, fertilisers, fuels, metals, synthetic fibre, plastics, and so on. Without chemicals our life may become primitive and so we need plants and units to manufacture chemicals. Chemical plants deal with physico-chemical transformation of raw materials into value-added products with the help of various resources such as manpower, energy, water, space and money. The entire chemical manufacturing process could be a judicious combination of various unit processes and unit operations. For instance, in a refinery, crude oil is separated into various fractions, such as liquefied petroleum gas (LPG), naphtha, gasoline (petrol), kerosene, high-speed diesel and so on, by a series of distillation columns (distillation as unit operation). On the other hand, during the conversion of naphtha into aromatics, namely, benzene, toluene and xylenes (*o*, *m* and *p*), we use aromatisation as a unit process, then extraction followed by distillation as unit operations to recover the aromatics.

Chemical projects differ from other projects such as an automobile manufacturing project, hydropower generation project, highway construction project, dam construction project, and so on. As mentioned chemical process plants are unique because they transform one substance into a totally different substance. For instance, natural gas (mainly methane) is converted into methanol, which is liquid at 30°C under atmospheric pressure. From any chemical project we get three streams. First stream contains the product(s). The second stream contains co-products or by-products. The third stream contains emissions, which are popularly known as effluents. It consists of unwanted materials in the form of gas, liquid and solid (Fig. 1.1). While products, co-products and by-products trigger sustainable development, effluents have a negative impact on the same. Thus, a chemical project involves the technical aspect of producing a product from the preferred raw materials selectively and efficiently. At the same time there are socially vital aspects associated with a project. They have a social impact because of the toxic and explosive nature of many chemicals, which may be the raw materials or the products, by-products or intermediates generated in the process.

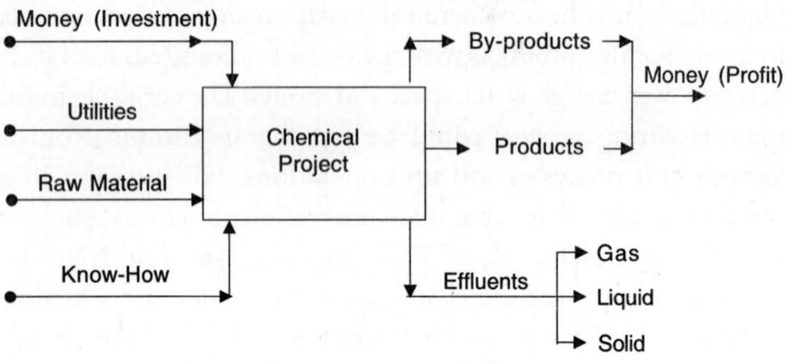


**Fig. 1.1** Chemical Project at Glance

Chemical plants often require large quantities of water in the production processes and for utilities like steam and cooling water. The water used in Chemical plants is rejected in the form of aqueous effluent stream, containing biodegradable and non-biodegradable complex molecules. These at times are even more complex than the original raw material (feedstock) or even the final product. If such waste streams are not treated properly to meet the stipulated local discharge standards, they can cause considerable social and economic problems downstream from the discharge point. Similarly, the discharge of gaseous emission into atmosphere can have a devastating effect on human health as well as plant and animal life. Thus, chemical projects have to be carefully designed taking into consideration their impact on social and economic life in the surrounding areas and towns. Environmental related issues associated with Chemical Projects are assuming tremendous cost and credibility dimensions as time progresses due to stricter emission standards pertaining to gaseous, liquid and solid pollutants to have a quality of life.

Chemical plants handle and generate flammable and explosive materials, sometimes as a fuel and at other times as plant chemicals in the production process. They are transported, received, unloaded, stored and handled again, at times under high pressure and temperature. In any of these processes, a leakage can occur either due to negligence or a faulty design. But the consequences may go beyond the plant and the plant personnel to the neighbouring towns, villages and life in general.

The scope of a chemical project, nowadays, is extended even to the power projects based on liquefied natural gas (LNG). Safety related issues arising out of huge shipment and storage of LNG might necessitate large allocation of areas for the project and relocation of villages, thereby having a direct social impact. Cryogenic fuel manufacturing is a chemical project related to our prestigious space programme. A nuclear power plant is a special case of a Chemical Project dealing with radioactive elements/compounds.

These considerations give a totally different dimension of Safety, Health and Environment (SHE) related issues to a chemical project. It will thus be seen that setting up a chemical plant requires the study of not only the technical and commercial aspects but also of the social requirements. This aspect needs a special attention in the setting up of chemical projects.

A study of chemical project economics has a unique significance in a sense that the chemical project should not only be economically viable but also socially acceptable and rewarding. Chemical project economics is, therefore, of considerable importance to the captains of industry, entrepreneurs, corporate planning managers, production engineers, research and technology development engineers and students of chemical engineering and technology as well.

Before we elaborate on chemical projects it is desirable to understand in a broader sense and perspective, the meaning of the words Engineering, Economics and Project Engineering.

### 1.1.1 Engineering

The word 'Engineer' has its origin in the French word *ing'nieure* which means an ingenious one. In a broader sense Engineering means doing things in ingenious ways and science is the very bedrock on which engineering is founded (Laithwaite, 1984). The effectiveness of engineering can be measured by the profit (money) generated. We consider all profit-making activities, ethical to us (as they are understood), are engineering activities. Bad engineering, design or operation or both, results in loss-making activities. Engineering is the product of our emotions with a desire to succeed. That is the reason plants engineered by different engineering contractors are never alike.

### 1.1.2 Economics

Noted economists like Keynes, Marshall, Robbins, Smith and others being social economists had a social perception in mind while defining and explaining the meaning of the word Economics. Dewett and Chand (1996) have presented a comprehensive account of various definitions as understood by social economists.

However, from engineering point of view, Economics is a perfect blend of the art and the science of production and distribution of wealth – generally quantified in terms of money (profit).

One can, therefore, appreciate that it is rather difficult to separate Economics from Engineering.

### 1.1.3 Project Engineering

By Project Engineering we mean the successful implementation of an idea into reality. Success is metered in terms of not only the profit generated over the period but also non-monetary returns the owner and the society gains during and after the implementation of a project. Loss on the other hand is a negative profit and it reflects failure.

Engineering of a chemical project consists of coordinated combination of technical and non-technical activities. Technical activities depend upon the type of the project. They are associated with the technology, scope of work, system engineering, equipment design, material selection and procurement and ultimately the coherent and comprehensive construction of all the plant components into a production unit (plant).

Non-technical issues include obtaining all the statutory clearances required from various authorities such as the Pollution Control Board, the State Electricity Board, the procurement of land or plot and lastly, the timely arrangement of the required finance to implement the project. These are important because the timely construction of the project is controlled by the availability of sufficient money as and when required. Delays often result in project cost overruns. The ability of a project to generate enough profit to return all the borrowed capital (money) for the project with interest to financial institutions and dividend to equity holders, has to be proven on paper *a priori*, with a detailed techno-economic feasibility report and risk analysis to avail of the finance whether from internal or external source.

Apart from financial aspects there are legal and statutory matters that are to be addressed and satisfactorily resolved. For instance, there may be legal matters pertaining to conversion of land into a non-agriculture plot, there may be public interest litigations against the project and so on. The site specific clearances are to be obtained before the construction activity begins.

Market forces often control the success of any business proposition. Very often the market has to be developed as in the case of speciality products such as detergents and toiletries, cosmetics, etc., during the project implementation. Hence it is to be watched and the project is to be modified in capacity and contents accordingly.

Time factor plays a very important role in the success of Chemical Projects for three principal reasons. First, long delays increase the interest on borrowings. Project extensions can change the market opportunities adversely. Delays increase the project cost and hence adversely affect the profitability. It should be noted that the entrepreneur is looking forward to generate profit through projects at a rate higher than that obtained from banks on fixed deposits.

It is thus seen that for chemical projects, engineering and economics are not separable. That is the subject of this book.

## 1.2 PRE-PROJECT ACTIVITIES

A project, whether chemical or otherwise has to be defined before steps are taken to implement it. Thus defining a project itself becomes a project. This basic requirement needs to be addressed mainly by the entrepreneurs or the managers engaged in corporate planning. They have to find answers to the following questions.

### 1.2.1 What to Produce?

This deals with the identification of a product or a series of products. Activities related to the project identification and conception requires an extensive foresight and market knowledge. In short, one needs entrepreneurship, as an individual or as an organisation at corporate level. If this step goes wrong then a lot of valuable time in the project is lost. Several project concepts have failed at this point.

### 1.2.2 How Much to Produce?

This decides the size of a project. This is determined by market share of the product and the economic plant capacity below which the price of a product is not attractive to consumers. In essence the market governs this decision. It may be easy for an established product but not at all so simple for a new product. There are examples where the market was found to be far below the expectation after the plant was established and also where the capacity of the plant had to be doubled in a few years to meet the overwhelming response from the market.

### 1.2.3 How to Produce?

This requires the selection of a technology. If one has the technology then the person may save the efforts of a technology search. Even then, it is advisable to find out answers to:

Is there any better technology available?

Is there a new technology under development?

This is necessary because before investing into a project it must be firmly and finally established that the project would not be technologically pushed into a dustbin. Remember, all future processes (technologies) must have built in

(a) Safety, Health and Environment (SHE) compliance, and
(b) Energy Conservation (ENCON) philosophy, resulting in Total Quality Management (TQM) operation.

When these basic questions are answered, then the more important questions about the project cost and financing will have to be addressed. The project cost and the working capital decide the total capital outlay of the project. The cost of production gives an idea about the day to day expenses. The important questions the owner has to answer himself and his financier are:

#### 1.2.3.1 What are Returns on the Projects?

The project owner may be looking for social returns on his project but eventually he has to show an income more than what he would get from the best investments elsewhere.

#### 1.2.3.2 Will the Project Survive Long Enough and Grow?

The returns on the project are possible only if the product is sold. This means that the product has a market and will withstand competition in the market from other manufacturers. Further, the market will allow growth in demand, which can be met and achieved through expansion of the presently planned capacity.

In subsequent chapters we shall deal with how best the above questions can be addressed.

## 1.3 TYPES OF PROJECTS

A chemical project can be broadly classified into two types of projects namely, Greenfield (Grassroots) project and Add-on project. Let us illustrate the above classification.

### 1.3.1 Greenfield (Grassroots) Project

A plant constructed from zero level and almost on a barren land, starting from land procurement and site development is referred to as a Greenfield project. For instance, the Gas cracker complex at Nagothane, Maharashtra, was built on a land that was partly agricultural and partly hilly and barren. The complex comprised a pipeline to bring in feedstock, namely, ethane and propane. Infrastructure to develop water and power resources, housing and educational facilities. However, every Greenfield project does not necessarily include development of the entire infrastructure. The complex at Nagothane was a large, stand-alone, mega-complex. A Greenfield project can also be located in an industrial area having developed infrastructure facilities.

### 1.3.2 Add-On Projects

Add-On projects essentially mean those projects that are built within an existing complex or built around the main project. Such a project could be an addition of a new facility, a backward or a forward integration, or altogether a new product line around existing or expanded infrastructure of utilities. For example, the waste stream of an existing plant may be treated to recover value-added products (wealth from waste) by designing a new recovery plant on the site. Further, one may use the products or the by-products of the existing plant to manufacture a value-added product, install a facility to manufacture the raw materials required for the existing products. In order to meet the extra demand of the product, without disturbing the existing plant, a duplicate plant can also be constructed. A situation may result wherein one may have the financial reserves to go into a new venture. All these projects fall into "Add-On Projects" category and are explained further.

#### *1.3.2.1 Battery Limit (B/L) Project*

A new project that is set up in an existing plant by using most of the available infrastructure facilities such as utilities, administration buildings, security, tank farm area, effluent treatment plant, and so on, is known as battery limit project. For example, a project to manufacture technical grade fumaric acid by scrubbing off gases from a phthalic anhydride plant (using *o*-xylene as a feedstock) is deemed as a battery limit project.

#### *1.3.2.2 Forward Integration*

A proposed project based on the product(s) of existing plant as raw materials is considered as a forward integration of the existing manufacturing activity. For instance, if a phenol manufacturer decides to set up a *bis*-phenol-A project based on phenol and the co-product acetone; the activity can be deemed as forward integration.

#### 1.3.2.3 Backward Integration

If the project owner decides to manufacture the raw materials for the existing project, then one can deem the activity as a backward integration. For instance, when diphenylcarbonate is being manufactured by using phenol and diethylcarbonate by an eco-friendly and safer technology and the owner decides to set up a plant to manufacture diethylcarbonate, the activity can be deemed as *backward integration*.

#### 1.3.2.4 Expansion Project

Addition of more capacity to existing facility can be deemed as horizontal integration. For example, adding a naphtha cracker to a cracker complex to enhance ethylene capacity is horizontal integration.

#### 1.3.2.5 Diversification

The project owner may totally diversify into altogether different product range. For example, a petrochemical producer (aromatics from naphtha) may diversify into power (electricity) generation not only for captive consumption but also for export to the state electricity grid.

#### 1.3.2.6 Debottlenecking

This may involve the addition or replacement of equipment and systems within the existing plant to increase the plant capacity. The project aims at revamping or refurbishing items that are limiting the plant performance in either quality or quantity. For example, the existing distillation tower with Pall rings as packing can be replaced with multifilament wire gauge packing having low pressure drop and lower HETP to get a product of better quality.

All these projects are known as 'Add-On' if they are built in and around existing units where land is available.

## 1.4 CHEMICAL PROJECT CLASSIFICATION

Chemical projects can be classified into different categories based on the following considerations:

- Price and size of a product; for example, basic chemicals, commodity chemicals and speciality chemicals.
- Capital outlay or investment in a project; such as a mega project, medium-size or a small-scale project.
- Nature of the product based on the industrial sector such as fertilizers, pharmaceuticals, etc.

We shall discuss this classification further in detail.

### 1.4.1 Price and Size of a Product

*Basic chemicals* are building blocks of the chemical industry. These are consumed in large quantities and by themselves they do not have any direct consumer applications. However, they control the end market. Therefore they are produced in bulk to meet the market requirements and to derive economic benefits of size. Thus they are low priced, high volume (weight) chemicals; for example, ethylene, propylene, benzene, sulfuric acid, etc. These projects need large investment the and the nameplate capacities are also very high, say in present context above 3,00,000 TPA for ethylene.

*Commodity chemicals* are produced in quantities in similar range in some cases but generally fewer than hundred thousand TPA capacities. These chemicals like ammonia, urea, phenol, methanol, poly vinyl chloride and acetic acid, have direct as well as indirect market. The market more often governs their prices, yet they have a firm price range.

*Speciality chemicals* are high value, low volume (weight) chemicals; for example, perfumery chemicals, toiletries, dye pigments and pharmaceuticals. The technical know-how is closely guarded. The plant capacities are also very low, typically in the range 1,000 to 10,000 TPA.

### 1.4.2 Project Capital Outlay

Based on project cost, projects can be broadly classified into mega, large, normal, medium- and small-scale project. (Table 1.1).

**Table 1.1** Classification of Projects

| *Project Size* | *Project Cost in ₹ Crore* |
|---|---|
| 1. Mega | Exceeding 10,000 (For example, refinery and ethylene cracker petrocomplex) |
| 2. Large | 1000 to 10,000 (For example, aromatic complex followed by polymer grade terephthalic acid (PTA) manufacture) |
| 3. Normal | 100–1000 (For example, oxo-alcohols) |
| 4. Medium | 25–100 (For example, formaldehyde from methanol) |
| 5. Small | Less than 25 (For example, fruit juice, canning, etc). |

*Note:* Lakh (Lac) = $1 \times 10^5$, Million = $1 \times 10^6$ and Crore = $1 \times 10^7$ ₹)

It is important to note that these cost related definitions are time dependent because the value of money changes with time and the market size. Therefore, the values given above will also change after a decade from now.

### 1.4.3 Industrial Sector

Based on the end uses and the fields of application, a chemical project can be grouped under various industrial sectors, some of which are listed here:

Petroleum refining, petrochemicals, fertilisers, heavy inorganic chemicals, dyes and intermediates, agrochemicals, (pesticides/

insecticides, etc.), pharmaceuticals, plasticisers, polymers, paints are some examples of the industrial sector.

## 1.5 PRICE OF A PRODUCT

It is important to understand the difference between price and cost as

$$\text{Price} = \text{Cost} + \text{Profit} \tag{1.1}$$

The equipment fabricator gives the price of, say, a heat exchanger, as ₹ 10 lakh while the project owner says the heat exchanger cost him ₹ 10 lakh plus statutory duties such as excise, sales tax (VAT), octroi and transportation.

Purely, based on the economic considerations one can have the price of a product as:

$$\text{Price (Transfer price)} = \beta\ \text{(Project cost)} + \text{Gross cost of production} \tag{1.2}$$

The constant, β, implies return on the investment (by way of fixed assets) in the project and other investment-related factors. While the gross cost of production means all operating expenses of the project.

## 1.6 PROJECT: CONCEPTION TO COMMISSIONING

As mentioned earlier, a project goes through various steps and sequences before it is fully implemented. Some of these take a long time and almost go to and fro before it is confirmed and the action, mainly of major commitments or expenditure, is taken. We shall introduce here significant stages or milestones in the journey of a project, that is, from its conception to commissioning so that readers will be able to comprehend the subsequent chapters in a more elegant and organised manner. Depending on the size of the organisation and resources available these steps are performed by the project owner himself or through consultancy agencies and project engineering companies.

### 1.6.1 Project Conception

The project can be conceived from business and market opportunities, new materials and technologies that available, consumer feedback, opportunities made available by global politics, or simply out of statutory compulsions such as to treat the waste of an existing unit. For instance, the government policy to make petrol lead free may lead to conceiving an idea of a project to manufacture ethyl tertiary butyl ether (ETBE) as an octane booster in place of tetraethyl lead.

### 1.6.2 Market Potential

A market potential needs to be established for the proposed product by way of a quick desk study. This has to be supplemented later with a more reliable field study when large expenses are to be incurred on the project.

### 1.6.3 Technology Search

It is desirable at this juncture to see whether technology is available to manufacture the product. This can be a desk study or an interaction with the project engineering organisation. Adequate technical data is to be obtained to evaluate profitability at least at the preliminary level.

### 1.6.4 Preliminary Feasibility Report

A preliminary feasibility report is prepared to aid the investment decision. If it is found worth going ahead, a detailed market potential based on desk study as well as field study may be commissioned.

### 1.6.5 Detailed Technology Search and Evaluation

With the help of a competent project engineering company, a detailed process or technology selection may be carried out. If need arises, memorandum of understanding (MoU) be executed at this stage with process know-how licensor and detailed engineering contractor.

### 1.6.6 Site Selection

The site for the proposed project needs to be selected after careful evaluation of various sites. For this purpose a competent project engineering company can be engaged to carryout this study.

### 1.6.7 Preparation of Detailed Techno-Economic Feasibility

This study results in what is known as a bankable document to obtain term loan from financial institutions. An attempt is made in this book, to cover these requirements in more details.

### 1.6.8 Statutory Clearances

Statutory clearances and approvals need to be obtained from the central government as well as from the state government, and local statutory bodies, such as Ministry of Environment, Ministry of Finance, Ministry of Forest, and so on with the help of Hazard analysis (HAZAN) and hazard operability studies (HAZOP) analysis, environmental impact assessment study, etc. The detailed techno-economic feasibility report may assist in obtaining statutory clearances for the project under implementation.

### 1.6.9 Contract for Know-how and Detailed Engineering

A contract should be signed with the process licensor for the supply of know-how. A contract should also be signed with the detailed engineering (project engineering) contractor to carry out the engineering of the project (or transformation of an idea into reality).

### 1.6.10 Project Financing

By and large the project is not totally financed by the promoter(s) by investing the entire capital. Hence a variety of methods are evaluated and then arrangements are made for financing the project under consideration.

### 1.6.11 Project Engineering

The project engineering involves detailed engineering, procurement, expediting and inspection services, followed by the construction of the plant (project).

### 1.6.12 Project Commissioning

After construction is completed, Mechanical commissioning of the plant is carried out. This is followed by process commissioning during which the guarantee runs are performed by the process licensor.

The project is then handed over to the production personnel to operate the same and to generate profit in years to follow.

After having understood the meaning of chemical projects, let us answer in more details issues pertaining to the subject of chemical project economics in chapters to follow, to aid successful implementation of a project.

## REFERENCES

Dewett K.K. and A. Chand, *Modern Economic Theory,* S. Chand and Co Ltd, New Delhi (1996).

Laithwaite E. *Invitation to Engineering,* Basil Blackwell Publisher Ltd., Oxford, UK (1984).

***Innovation is Anything that Produces Money.***

# 2

# Process Selection

## 2.1 INTRODUCTION

The long-time business success of any project greatly depends upon the selection of an appropriate sustainable process or technology. The routine financial calculations, such as return on investment, payback period, internal rate of return, and so on, are not adequate indices of success of any project that is being conceived. For instance, a project to manufacture ethyl tertiary butyl ether (ETBE) as an octane booster may be financially lucrative but its success over its lifespan will depend primarily upon availability of ethyl alcohol and isobutylene, as raw materials.

After having decided to go ahead with the project implementation based on preliminary feasibility report, a dilemma of selecting the most suitable process or technology arises. There may be more than one route available to manufacture the product under consideration. Also, after having selected the route, there may be more than one process licensor available for know-how. For instance, phenol can be manufactured in, at least, in following three different ways:

- Hydrolysis of chlorobenzene (Raschig process)
- Decarboxylation of benzoic acid obtained from toluene
- Alkylation of benzene with propylene to give cumene which further yields phenol (Cumene process)

At present, the last route known as the cumene route is popular among manufacturers of phenol. Due to the availability of propylene and benzene in ethylene complex based on naphtha cracker the cumene process route is popular. Even if we decide on raw materials, namely, benzene and propylene, the next question is about selecting the process licensor. Among others, we have UOP Inc., ABB Lummus Global Inc., Mitsui Ltd., as the process licensors. One may opt for two process licensors, namely, one for cumene technology (for instance, CD Tech, Houston) and the other for cumene to phenol technology (for instance, Lummus).

Thus selection of process (technology) is not a simple exercise, as it appears to be. In the text to follow the words process and technology are being used interchangeably. In fact, all discussions centred on process selection can be used for the selection of process licensor as well.

All commercial projects are essentially for earning monetary gains first, followed by social gains. One need to consider various parameters/factors while selecting a process. Not all the parameters are directly reflected in the profitability calculations. Some parameters are directly related to profitability and hence, are called *Profitability Parameters*. On the other hand, some parameters do not appear in profit computation but indirectly affect profitability and operation of the project considerably. Such parameters, as we define here for the sake of convenience, can be called *Viability Parameters*. It is always desirable to carry out profitability analysis only after the process is proved to be viable, as screened by industrial and social viability parameters. We shall discuss both the parameters in detail and present the methodology to evaluate them.

## 2.2 VIABILITY PARAMETERS

Viability parameters are directly related to success of the project and are indirectly related to the project profitability. Although difficult to quantify, as seen later, we may assign a risk or cost-value (notional) to all these parameters based on their relative importance. Thus, a pseudo quantitative method can be developed for their evaluation (please refer to Section 2.4.1). Let us now see the importance of various viability parameters.

### 2.2.1 Raw Materials

The sustainable and cheap source of raw materials is one of the important parameters of process selection. If a major raw material is imported, the import duty in future and currency exchange rate may cloud the viability of a project. The liberalisation of trade, or protection to local manufacturing via import duty depends upon political considerations. As a result of this, one has to be rather careful.

The import of raw materials may sometimes appear to be cheaper but in fact it will add to working capital requirements of the project. If the raw material is not up to the specifications, one needs to have the purification facility, thereby adding to the capital as well as operating cost. The facilities to receive and store at the port would definitely increase the project cost. Let us illustrate this point with some examples of relevance.

If a project is planned to manufacture polycarbonate grade *bis*-phenol-A from phenol and acetone, the port facilities for handling and storage need to be created if phenol is not available indigenously and, hence, would be imported, and if, no chemical terminal exists at the port.

If we are planning a project of 3,00,000 TPA polyvinyl chloride, based on ethylene and locally available chlorine, we need to import ethylene in case it is not available from any nearby petrochemical complex or ethane-propane gas cracker or ethanol dehydration unit. Ethylene is stored under cryogenic conditions ($C_2H_4$, bp 169.4K at atmospheric pressure). So if ethylene is imported, we need to have capital intensive facilities such as unloading arms, cryogenic atmospheric storage tank, compressors, cooling tower, electrical substation, firefighting facility, etc., at the port in addition to plant and machinery items at the manufacturing site. Expenses for land and site development, buildings and civil works, are also added, thereby escalating the project cost. The transportation of ethylene by road or rail tankers may pose safety-related issues. Therefore, if pipeline transport is envisaged, one needs to have gasification facility and booster compression station in between depending upon logistics involved.

For the project to manufacture 50,000 TPA acetic acid, we have three raw materials, namely, ethanol, *n*-butane and methanol. Though ethanol is manufactured from renewable raw material, the proposed project of this capacity may receive a setback, if sustained supply of alcohol is not guaranteed.

The other raw material *n*-butane is not readily available from Indian refineries. Recovery of *n*-butane from $C_4$ fraction to manufacture acetic acid might be cost-prohibitive at present.

The methanol-based route produces acetic acid via carbonylation of methanol. It means, we need carbon monoxide (CO). Methanol is manufactured via syn-gas (CO, $CO_2$ and $H_2$) which itself can act as a source of CO. After recovering CO (by pressure swing adsorption) the balance gas can be fed to methanol converter. Thus, for methanol manufacturer it is more convenient to set up a large-scale acetic acid project by taking into consideration economy of the scale.

Maleic anhydride can be manufactured based on benzene, *n*-butane and *n*-butenes. The more eco-friendly route based on butane or butenes could not be accepted, as these raw materials are not readily available like benzene.

So many examples could be given wherein potentially good projects were shelved due to non-availability of sustainable raw materials in adequate quantities. If restrictive suppliers from the overseas manufacture the raw material for the process then geo-political factors will overrule all other parameters.

### 2.2.2 Utilities

The chemical plant utilities are classified into basic and applied utilities. Water, power, air, fuels, refrigerant are considered as basic utilities, while steam, cooling water, heat transfer fluids, chilled water and glycol brine are considered as applied utilities.

Electricity (power) and water are the two minimum utilities required for any project. Due to industrialisation and increase in population, the demands for power and water have gone up. As a result, their availability has gone down.

The state electricity boards may not be in a position to meet the demand of power. Therefore, the project owner may have to put up his own captive power generation or co-generation facility within the project to meet the major demand of industrial power. In new refineries and petrochemical plants captive power plants are common. This alternative calls for extra capital and operating expenditure. It is not only the availability of power but uninterrupted continuous supply of power that is equally important.

The demand for water can be partly met by the novel concept of recycling water in the plant, after treating aqueous effluents. Some projects have already commissioned plants to recover good quality water from domestic aqueous effluents originating from the city. If the quality of water is not good (for instance, high silica, or high fluorides contents) a special treatment facility is required, which would definitely increase the project cost and to a small extent operating cost as well. Large projects particularly refineries located near seashore do use seawater as cooling water and may consider desalination of seawater as a possible source of water. This would also add to the capital and operating cost of the project.

### 2.2.3 Safety Health and Environment Compliance

The compliance towards safety, health and environment (SHE) is becoming mandatory for all projects. The awareness of society towards environment is growing fast. In many states, environmental impact assessment studies, environment audit, are now becoming mandatory for statutory clearance. Hazard analysis (HAZAN) and hazard operability (HAZOP) studies on the processes under evaluation can throw some light on the extent of damage, in case an accident take place. However, inherent process safety is gaining more and more importance. The inherent safe processes are now being preferred over traditional processes. For instance, in the manufacture of methyl methacrylate, isobutene is the preferred raw material. However, in another process cheaper acetone is used as the feedstock that needs to react with deadly hydrogen cyanide (HCN) to produce acetocyanohydrin, which when reacted with methanol and sulphuric acid and produces methyl methacrylate. The inherent safe process using isobutene, is preferred over the cynohydrin process.

To produce absolute alcohol, dehydration of alcohol by molecular sieve technique is nowadays preferred to the old process of using benzene as entrainer because of health related issues. Due the same reason butane-based maleic anhydride process is preferred to the process using benzene as the feedstock.

While selecting a process, one must also consider quality and quantity of effluent generated. Let us consider the manufacture of propylene oxide. The classical chlorohydrin route requires chlorine-handling facility. The plant generates large quantities of aqueous waste containing $CaCl_2$. This necessitates location of the project near seashore so that after removing COD/BOD to permissible discharge limit the saline waste containing $CaCl_2$ can be discharged into sea via deep-sea pipeline. The 'Oxirane' process, which uses iso-butane or ethylbenzene as the feedstock, provides answers to some of the above problems. It is a chlorine-free process and hence the waste stream is free from $CaCl_2$. Further advantage is that it produces valuable co-product, namely, *tert*-butanol if iso-butane is used or phenyl methyl carbinol if ethyl benzene is used as the raw material. The co-product *tert*-butanol is used to manufacture *iso*-butylene while phenyl methyl carbinol on dehydration yields styrene. Both are commercially important products. It is, therefore, obvious that for the manufacture of propylene oxide, the oxirane process would be a preferred choice in plants located in mainland away from seashore.

### 2.2.4 Simplicity of Process

It is always desirable to have a process involving minimal unit operations and unit processes. For instance, in the prevailing process of phenol manufacture, benzene and propylene are reacted and the product formed is recovered by distillation separately. According to the latest technology in cumene production a catalytic distillation unit is used wherein benzene and propylene are reacted (120–175°C) over a zeolite-based catalyst in a distillation column, and products are continuously removed from the reaction zone by distillation (Reactive Distillation). Thus reaction (unit process) and product separation by distillation (unit operation) are combined in a single operation known as *reactive distillation.* The product yield is claimed to be 5-6% higher than that obtained in a conventional cumene plant and if also saves energy.

Further by simplicity we mean less severe conditions of the plant operation. The Low Pressure Oxo (LP-Oxo) process has now replaced the old cobalt-catalysed high-pressure Oxo process for hydroformylation of olefins, which have terminal double bond (propylene, butene-1), into next higher aldehyde. This is the process for the manufacture of 2-ethyl hexanol from propylene. Apart from simplicity (low pressure operation) the LP-Oxo process reduces power consumption. The lower pressure reflects in lower capital investment in equipment and piping. The plant on stream-time is also increased.

Similarly, there is almost fivefold reduction in reactor pressure, during the manufacture of methanol thereby saving energy and capital investment. The reaction temperatures are also around 250°C as compared to the old technology wherein temperature was around 400°C.

The simplicity of the process is often reflected in less-stringent operating conditions (temperature, pressure), easy maintenance, controls and shutdown and start-up procedures, less number of steps, emissions, by-products and also less manpower requirement. All these factors ultimately reduce the capital investment and operating cost.

### 2.2.5 Backup of Manufacturing Facility

A process having back-up of manufacturing facility is always desirable. For speciality chemicals, pharmaceuticals, electronic grade chemicals, etc., where raw material and product prices are very high though the quantity produced is less than that of commodity chemicals. The process or technology could be a closely guarded secret. It is, therefore, desirable that such process licensor should have an operating plant (or product manufacturing experience) and marketing experience of the same. On the other hand, for the manufacture of commodity chemicals such as ammonia, urea, methanol, and so on, wherein the technologies are by and large matured, the process licensor need not have the manufacturing backup. Nonetheless, as seen in Section 2.2.6, proven track record is always desirable.

Some process licensors having a manufacturing facility of their own may offer to buyback products at an agreed price to meet local demands in the countries of their origin. This results in a plant of economy size despite low demand in domestic market. The brand name plays a critical role in speciality chemicals, at least in the early years of project functioning. For instance, if an item is already being imported from the process licensor's manufacturing site, it becomes easier to sell the same when produced indigenously under the technology transfer from the process licensor. For example, if a project is being set up to manufacture alkyl phenols based on the foreign know-how, it would be desirable to have a tie-up with the company whose products are already being imported. This would also facilitate market seeding during the period of construction.

It is absolutely essential that the licensor offer the process technology free of patent infringement. A patent dispute may result either in cancellation of the project or project cost overrun, which are undesirable and could be disastrous. If the licensor is exploiting the process, the assurance that the technology is free from patent infringement is obvious.

A manufacturer in developed countries, due to stiff competition tends to maintain a superior technology with real-time upgradation and innovations. The technology obtained from such a source is always better as there is access to process improvements. It is then easier to implement Total Quality Management (TQM) and Safety, Health and Environment (SHE) and Energy Conservation (ENCON) concepts in the proposed project.

Further, the state-of-the-art technology training to plant operators becomes much easier when there exists a manufacturing facility.

A process licensor willing to share upgradation of technology at a very nominal fee or no fee should get preference over others.

### 2.2.6 Proven Track Record

Many a times it is possible, that the process licensor may not have its own manufacturing facility, but has maximum working plants covering a wide range of production capacity. Such a licensor has better chance of being selected for know-how.

There are, however, cases wherein a really good engineering contractor of proven track record had lost the job to relatively, then, new upcoming engineering contractor purely on financial grounds. The result had been disastrous start-up for the project. The engineering contractor, who had lost the contract, in the first place was then called at 'higher fees' for rescuing the project.

The project owner can benefit from the experience and innovations of other manufacturing plants. Issues related to SHE and TQM could then be addressed in more elegant and meaningful ways.

### 2.2.7 Equity Participation

Equity participation (joint venture) by the process licensor gives the advantage of acquiring a good workable and, perhaps, the latest technology. As a result technologies which otherwise may not be available become a reality for the project owner. For example, in the project of Gujarat Chematur Petrochemicals Ltd, there is a participation in equity by Chematur AB of Sweden with GNFC. The project is for the manufacture of aniline and toluene diisocyanate (TDI). It should be noted that TDI technology is not easily available for commercialisation.

### 2.2.8 Valuable Intermediates/Co-Products

The process producing a valuable by-product or co-product is always preferred over others. For instance, for the manufacture of propylene oxide there are, at present, two proven routes available. The conventional process follows propylene chlorohydrin route (in India two plants exist based on this route) resulting in the large quantities of aqueous effluents containing calcium chloride. The other process known as 'Oxirane' is based on isobutane peroxide route resulting in a 'cleaner' technology producing *tert*-butanol as the co-product from which oxygenates such as methyl or ethyl tertiary butyl ether (MTBE, ETBE) could be easily produced. In petrol formulations, MTBE is replacing tetra ethyl lead as an octane booster. Of course, the profitability parameters would indicate a minimum capacity below which this technology is not profitable.

Contrary to the above, sometimes, the co-product becomes a nuisance or liability. For instance, there may be demand for phenol, but no demand for co-product acetone in the conventional benzene–cumene route. In such a situation, phenol process based on toluene–benzoic acid route would be a better choice.

Valuable intermediates are found to buffer adverse impact of market fluctuations. For instance, two different processes are available for production of vinyl acetate monomer (VAM). In one process, acetaldehyde and acetic anhydride are used as the raw materials; while the other process uses ethylene and acetic acid. Ethyl alcohol can be used as the feedstock in both the processes. One would appreciate difficulties in selling small quantities of ethylene in the market, should VAM plant be running under capacity or closed down. On the other hand, one would not face such difficulties in selling acetaldehyde or acetaldehyde-based products.

### 2.2.9 Catalyst Recovery

Various catalysts used in the chemical process industries are subjected to spent catalyst treatment process. This is done not only to address pollution-related problems but also to get an economic advantage. The recovery of the catalyst becomes economically mandatory particularly when noble metals are used as catalysts. For example, in many hydrogenation processes Pt, Pd, Ru, Rh, Re supported catalyst are used. In the case of ethylene oxide manufacture, silver-based catalyst is used. The latest LP Oxo-process, where propylene is hydroformylated, uses Rh catalyst to yield *n*-butyraldehyde, which is then converted to 2-ethyl hexanol. It becomes economically advantageous to recover such precious metal elements from the spent (used) catalyst. Therefore, a process licensor (or the catalyst supplier) agreeing to buyback spent catalyst and in return give fresh catalyst at an agreed differential price, is always preferred.

### 2.2.10 Backward and Forward Integration

The selected technology/process be such that it would make backward integration possible. It is desirable to have backward integration, as the raw material could be made available at cheaper price and in some cases even at the cost of production. The direction of integration depends on raw materials used and the final product for the market. The forward integration often results in value-addition.

Let us consider the manufacture of diphenyl carbonate from phenol and dimethyl carbonate. It is possible to carry out backward integration and produce dimethyl carbonate from methanol and carbon monoxide. Methanol can be considered as the raw material for propylene manufacture also via methanol to olefin (MTO) technology. It should be noted that phenol in turn could be manufactured using propylene and benzene. However, all these are commodity chemicals and require large-scale production to be competitive. Hence the manufacture of dimethyl carbonate can be forward integration for the owner of methanol project.

Similarly, setting up a nitric acid plant (project) to support ammonium nitrate manufacture can be deemed as backward integration.

### 2.2.11 Political Considerations

Sometimes even a good process licensor might not be considered if his origin is from the country with which buyer country has no trade relationship at all. Though this is considered the last parameter, it can become a deciding parameter. With globalisation of business, this parameter has lost the significance now. However, one never knows how geo-political issues would shape up in future and hence it is mentioned here.

After having seen viability parameters, we shall discuss profitability parameters. The methodology of evaluation of both the parameters would then be presented to aid process/technology selection.

## 2.3 PROFITABILITY PARAMETERS

It is possible to quantify profitability of the process (technology) through certain parameters affecting fixed capital investment and operating cost. Therefore, these parameters are known as profitability parameters. In its simple form, based on the economic considerations only, one can deduce a relation between selling price (Transfer price), project cost (Fixed capital cost) and gross cost of production (Operating cost) which is given as follows:

$$\underset{\text{(Sales)}}{\text{Price}} = \beta \underset{\text{(Fixed capital)}}{\text{(Project cost)}} + \underset{\text{(Operating cost)}}{\text{Gross cost of production.}} \quad (2.1)$$

The factor 'β' depends upon the desired rate of return (profit) on the capital deployed by the project owner. Through this return on investment (ROI) the project owner or entrepreneur takes care of the following components:

- Interest on term loan and working capital to financial institution & bankers
- Corporate tax to the Government
- Dividend to equity participants
- Loan repayment
- Reserves for future expansion, Replacement of worn out equipment, Research and technology development, etc.

The desired rate of return or return on investment varies from industry to industry. However, the desired rate of return for speciality chemicals project is obviously much higher than that for commodity chemicals. It is obvious that the desired return on investment has to be higher than the interest rate on fixed deposits in banks or interest on term loans.

In practice, the price depends on many factors. The introduction to pricing of a product is presented in Chapter 13.

The profit of any project could be expressed as gross profit:

$$\text{Gross profit per year} = (\text{Sales} - \text{Gross cost of production})/\text{year}. \tag{2.2}$$

$$\text{The rate of return} = (\text{Sales} - \text{Gross cost of production}) \text{ per year}/\text{project cost}. \tag{2.3}$$

At this juncture working capital borrowing in not to be much of a concern. In order to appreciate the meaning of the above terms, let us quickly review various elements of Gross Cost of Production and Project Cost, and then discuss the role of profitability parameters, in the exercise of the process selection.

### 2.3.1 Gross Cost of Production

All operating or recurring expenditures excluding interest on term loan, loan repayment, corporate tax, dividend and depreciation (as a notional cost) are clubbed under gross cost of production. Further, gross cost of production is sub-divided into administrative expenses (at admin. site) and cost of production at the manufacturing site.

The cost of production comprises raw material and utilities expenditure (about 60–80%), packaging cost, salaries and wages of plant personnel, followed by factory overhead. The administrative cost (admin. cost) includes administrative overhead expenses; salaries and wages of administrative people, selling expenses and other miscellaneous expenses, are not included in cost of production. As a rule of thumb, administrative cost could be 5–15% of cost of production. For details please refer to the Chapter 7.

For a given plant capacity, salary wages, packing cost, factory overheads and administrative cost and selling expenses will remain constant irrespective of technology or process selected. The major difference in all processes being screened would come from raw materials and utilities consumptions and are hence discussed here.

#### 2.3.1.1 Raw Material and Utility Consumptions

The latest processes will always be more efficient in terms of raw material as well as utilities consumption. For most chemical processes, except electro-chemical, the raw material cost is considerably higher than utility cost.

All process licensors give consumption of raw materials, chemicals and catalyst, if any, required as quantity required per unit weight of product. This information in turn would enable us to find out the monetary contribution of raw materials in the cost of production from their unit rates.

The consumption of basic utilities, mainly water and power are kept to be minimum by incorporating energy conservation (ENCON) concept or heat integration concept in the Basic engineering package (BEP). For example, in the latest generation methanol plant, power required for compressing syn-gas to reactor pressure and recirculating compressor is obtained by steam turbine running on superheated high pressure steam generated by carrying out ENCON measures around reformer.

In the latest technology of manufacture of phthalic anhydride by vapour phase oxidation of *o*-xylene, the energy integration is done in such a manner that the battery limit plant does not require any external power. The process is known as *zero-energy process*.

A radial flow catalytic reactor will result in lower pressure drop than that in a conventional axial flow-packed bed reactor. As a rule of thumb, in methanol plants having capacity greater than 1000 TPD, the radial flow reactor is preferred.

The utility consumption, like raw materials, is also presented in terms of utility consumed per tonne (*T*) of product. The consumption of steam is given as *X* tonnes (*T*) of steam (at a specified pressure, *P*) per tonne of the product. The excess or export steam is then given as (–), which means we get credit at steam price (₹/*T*) in the cost of production.

Thus by knowing consumptions of raw materials and utility one can easily estimate the cost of production. By and large administrative salaries, overheads and sales expenses do not cross 10% of the cost of production. Therefore, the gross cost of production is considered to be 1.1 times the cost of production.

## 2.3.2 Project Cost

A detailed discussion of the various elements of project cost component is given in Chapters 5 and 6. Here, we shall see how various processes affect these components and hence their overall impact on the project cost.

### *2.3.2.1 Land and Site Development*

The process licensor indicates the battery limit of the plant area. The area required for storage, utilities and effluent treatment plant (outside battery limit facilities, OSBL) is always significant and is site specific. It is always recommended that the area required for OSBL facilities be estimated. For instance, fumaric acid could be produced by fermentation of molasses as well as by isomerization of maleic acid which in turn is obtained by hydration of maleic anhydride. Area required for bioprocesses is always larger than that for the above chemical route. Further, in offsite and effluent treatment plants more area would be required for molasses as the feedstock.

The aqueous effluent treatment by modern wet air oxidation technology requires considerably lower area than that for conventional biotechnology.

Though the contribution of land and site development towards project cost is about 3–5% for petrochemical projects, the processes based on biotechnology may result in higher contribution.

#### 2.3.2.2 Building and Civil Work

The process licensor not only indicates building (if any) but also special precautions to be taken for storage of product/by-products and raw materials. For example, the storage of nitrophosphate fertilisers need very low humidity. Further, adequate information need to be generated for offsite facilities including storage of raw materials, intermediates, products and effluent treatment. Depending on storage requirements, such as seasonal availability, production campaign in multipurpose plant, offsite civil work, will vary. For instance, the manufacture of ethylene glycol from molasses involves of fermentation of molasses to yield alcohol, which is then dehydrated to obtain ethylene. Ethylene glycol is then obtained by conventional route wherein ethylene is oxidised to ethylene oxide followed by hydration to yield glycol. All processes mentioned are well established independently and are licensed by reputed process licensors. No major storage of ethylene and ethylene oxide is required. However, the storage of molasses is required to take care of seasonal availability of molasses.

A process employing rotary dryer has one set of requirement of building work compared to that having a fluidised bed dryer. For instance, in the manufacture of ammonium sulphate one can use rotary as well as fluidised bed dryer. In the production of ammonium sulphate from gypsum, the co-product $CaCO_3$ is separated by either decanter centrifuge in one process and by belt filter in the other process. The filtration process needs a different area than the centrifuge.

The relative contribution of this factor to the project-cost for petrochemicals project could be in the range 10–15% of cost of the project.

#### 2.3.2.3 Plant and Machinery

In the case of petrochemical projects, the contribution of plant and machinery component to the project cost could be in the range 40–60%. Thus by sensitivity analysis, one can say that this parameter dominates over any other parameter of profitability analysis. The detailed discussion of various components of 'Plant and Machinery' is presented in Chapter 6. This item is divided into two components, namely, the main plant (also referred as battery limit plant) and the outside battery limit facilities (OSBL) such as storage facilities, utilities and effluent treatment plant.

*Battery Limit Plant*

The process licensor offers the know-how that is meant for a battery limit plant only. The know-how fees are linked to the performance of technology (plant) to produce the desired products (by-/co-products) meeting the respective quality specifications. Therefore, the process licensor may insist on purchasing critical equipment (critical to performance of the technology) from the vendors of his choice, which means there is a need to import some equipment. For example, in the 'Zero-Energy' process of *o*-xylene to phthalic anhydride the process licensor may insist on importing the steam turbine if the same with identical efficiency is not available indigenously.

At times, some piping & instrumentation required may not be available in local market and hence out of necessity one is forced to import the same.

Thus, the battery limit plant and machinery item has indigenous as well as foreign exchange component. The imported items do attract project import duty. The finance ministry, every year decides on project import duty as some percentage of landed prices of equipment. Thus, by acquiring the imported component we not only lose precious foreign exchange but also the project cost goes up through duty structure.

With the liberalisation policy, the trend, as of today, is towards reduction in import duty. However, one cannot expect zero import duty. Exception to this being 100% export-oriented units.

A process having lower component of equipment, piping, instrumentation and electricals in the form of imported equipment, will always be preferred under otherwise equal considerations.

*Outside Battery Limit (OSBL) Facilities Storage*

While indigenous raw materials could be stored from one week to one month depending upon logistics involved, a larger storage facility is necessary for imported materials depending upon the size of shipment. This would change sizes of storage vessels.

*Utilities*

Normal and peak consumptions of utilities are given by the process licensor along with their specifications. This would enable design engineer to size utilities generation facilities.

If the process has built in 'Energy Conservation' concept, the utilities demand may go down thereby reducing the cost of production. Let us illustrate this concept by an example of a heat pump device used as an energy conservation device in a close boiling distillation system, say, styrene-ethyl benzene or propylene propane. The need of cooling water in a condenser and steam in a reboiler can, therefore, be totally eliminated leading to tremendous savings on both utilities. However, one needs a vapour compressor to compress vapours. While the operating cost is reduced, the capital investment associated with vapour compression system goes up. One of the process licensor may offer heat pump system while the other may rely on proven conventional system. The final decision then depends upon the cost of power, steam, cooling water and the rate of interest on borrowed capital.

In the latest methanol plant the energy consumption has reduced to half as compared to the first generation plant due to energy integration. This makes if economical in Indian conditions as well. Similar situation exists in the case of ammonia manufacture.

In order to have a zero-energy phthalic anhydride plant, one may have to import super efficient steam turbine and thereby increasing foreign exchange component in the Plant and Machinery cost.

A process requiring higher emergency power (HT and LT) would necessitate higher investment in stand by diesel generating (DG) set.

Thus, we see that there exists an economic trade off between capital cost and utilities consumptions when various processes (technologies) are available for the same product.

*Effluent Treatment Plant*

A process generating the least quantity of gaseous, solid and liquid effluents would be an obvious choice. If the liquid effluents are very less in quantity, they may exhibit very high Chemical Oxygen Demand (COD) and Biological Oxygen Demand (BOD). As a result, the conventional effluent treatment may not be possible. One may have to select between incineration (operating cost intensive) or wet air oxidation (capital cost intensive) technology.

As a result of conservation of water in the plant, the liquid effluents generated are concentrated in the so-called waste product. The latest trend is to recover the valuable chemicals from the waste (wealth from waste). For example, commercial technologies are available for recovering organic acids such as acetic acid, propionic acids, and so on, from the waste stream by solvent extraction method followed by stripping of acids. Such treatment facilities are bound to increase capital expenditure in plant and machinery cost but additional by-product recovery is going to increase annual sales as well.

The latest technology of wet air oxidation of the waste stream can become energy exporter if Chemical Oxygen Demand (COD) of the waste stream is more than 50,000 mg/l. The reactor being a bubble column type, it occupies less space. Further, with the *deep shaft technology* one can have this reactor below the earth surface. Not only low or medium pressure steam could be generated but also the treated waste stream produces water, which can be recycled back (after treatment for total dissolved solid (TDS) content by membrane technology) thereby reducing demand of water from the state industrial development corporation.

The effluent treatment plants are entitled to have 100% depreciation (again this depends upon the policy of the Government) and hence apparent higher capital expenditure need not be the sole criterion of selecting a technology.

#### 2.3.2.4 Know-how and Engineering

The process know-how with a basic engineering package (BEP) is provided by the process licensor. When the know-how is imported, licensing fees with a BEP need to be paid in foreign currency which entails tax payment in Indian Rupees. If the process-licensor is a manufacturing company and not a licensing company, it is easier and profitable to the licensor to engage an Indian Engineering Contractor to prepare the BEP.

For a very big project, the know-how fee also includes the fee for training of personnel and construction supervision. Detailed engineering of the project is generally, carried out by an Indian Project Engineering company. Contrary to the normal belief, the detailed engineering fee of the Indian Company is limited to the number of equipment involved, complexity of piping and electricals, intricacies of instrumentation, and is not to be derived as the percentage of project cost.

The contribution of this parameter to the project cost could vary from 15–25% the higher scale being for the latest and prized technology. Thus the process having lower know-how and engineering fees would have a better chance of selection with other parameters being equal.

#### 2.3.2.5 Expenses on Foreign Technicians and Training of Indian Technicians Abroad

The process licensor who is willing to do free-of-cost process commissioning and is willing to bear all training expenses of Indian technicians abroad, would be automatically preferred over others not offering the same.

#### 2.3.2.6 Miscellaneous Fixed Assets

There is no effect of different processes on this component of project cost.

#### 2.3.2.7 Contingencies

By and large these comprise 10% of all the above items. Hence the process selection would have that much effect on contingencies.

#### 2.3.2.8 Pre-operative Expenses

As will be seen subsequently, the interest during the period of construction contributes substantially (at times 75%) towards pre-operative expenses. By and large pre-operative expenses could be about 15% of project cost. The interest depends upon the capital expenditure schedule, term loan and equity component.

The participation by foreign process licensor in the form of equity would lessen the burden on foreign loan and interest. Similarly, the extent of foreign exchange component by way of imports in Plant and Machinery would also affect foreign loan and interest. It should be noted here through the agreement of bilateral trade between the respective governments. It may be possible for the process licensor to arrange for 'soft' loan. Therefore, while selecting a process, one should give adequate consideration to this factor also.

#### *2.3.2.9 Preliminary and Capital Issue Related Expenses*

Once project-financing pattern is finalised, there is little to choose among various processes while considering this parameter.

#### *2.3.2.10 Margin Money*

As a rule of thumb for petrochemical projects, the margin money is around 25% of the working capital. Inventories of raw materials, utilities, finished products, credit to buyers, and salary and wages of plant personnel are the main contributors to working capital. This factor is also not affected much by various technologies. However, working capital and hence margin money would be higher if raw material is imported.

Thus from the foregoing we note that the process choice has an influence on the capital outlay of the project (project cost).

After having examined various viability and profitability parameters in depth, let us see how we carry out 'evaluation' exercise leading to the selection process (technology).

## 2.4 PROCESS EVALUATION

The evaluation of process (technology) would ultimately depend upon both viability and profitability parameters.

### 2.4.1 Viability Parameters: Viability Coefficient (*V*)

The viability parameters listed are rather subjective. However, in order to take away 'subjective' element, a weighted average method of evaluation of viability parameters is proposed here. A numerical value is allocated to the parameter to signify its importance on a 1–10 scale. For instance, availability of raw materials and utilities being the most important viability parameters, are allocated an importance value 10. If process under consideration is not using noble metal catalyst, the catalyst recovery parameter can be considered to be having an importance value, say, 2. The same parameter, with noble metal catalyst, assumes the importance factor 10, and so on. After having listed all viability parameters with their importance coefficient, we go on assigning marks to a process (technology) under evaluation on that scale.

Table 2.1 presents a typical procedure. For every process, viability coefficient $V$ is calculated.

**Table 2.1** Viability Parameters Evaluation

| *Process Viability Parameter* | *Numerical Importance* | *Technology* | | |
|---|---|---|---|---|
| | | $T_1$ | $T_2$ | $T_3$ |
| $P_1$ = Raw materials | $X_1$ | $a_{11}$ | $a_{12}$ | $a_{13}$ |
| $P_2$ = Utilities | $X_2$ | $a_{21}$ | $a_{22}$ | $a_{23}$ |
| $P_3$ = Environmental | $X_3$ | $a_{31}$ | $a_{32}$ | $a_{33}$ |
| $P_4$ | $\vdots$ | | | |
| $\vdots$ | | | | |
| $P_n$ | $X_n$ | $a_{n1}$ | $a_{n2}$ | $a_{n3}$ |

Viability coefficient ($V$) is then calculated for each process (technology).

$$V = \frac{\sum_{1}^{n} a_j}{\sum_{1}^{n} X_i} \tag{2.4}$$

### 2.4.2 Profitability Parameters: Profitability Coefficient (*P*)

The profitability parameters can directly be quantified by means of projection of the profit generated by the project over its lifespan. For the sake of simplicity, we shall consider gross profit of the project under consideration. The term 'gross profit' is defined as

$$\text{Gross profit} = (\text{Sales} - \text{Gross cost of production}) \text{ per year} \quad (2.5)$$

The project life is assumed to be 10 years and the gross profit for the first year is computed by assuming 100% capacity utilisation (which is not the case in detailed techno-economic feasibility report). The gross profit thus computed for one year is then multiplied by project life (i.e. 10 years) to arrive at total gross profit in 10 years. Profitability coefficient (*P*) is then defined as

$$P = \frac{\text{Gross profit over lifespan of project (10 years)}}{\text{Project cost}} \quad (2.6)$$

The results will not change drastically if we neglect working capital borrowing. Strictly speaking, the word 'Project cost' should be replaced by project capital outlay involving project cost and working capital borrowing.

### 2.4.3 Process Selection Coefficient

After having seen how to arrive at the viability coefficient and profitability coefficient, we now know how to decide on the choice by computing process selection coefficient. The process selection coefficient (PSC) is then worked out as the product of both.

$$\text{PSC} = (P)\,(V) \quad (2.7)$$

The process having lowest PSC is eliminated. The processes having nearby PSC need second scrutiny, and may be, by more experienced person or manager. In case the highest PSC is substantially different from the others, in all probability, this is the process (technology) of choice.

## SUGGESTED READINGS

Hatch L.F. and Matar S., *From Hydrocarbons to Petrochemicals*, Gulf Publishing Company, Houston, Texas (1981).

*Kirk-Othmer Encyclopedia of Chemical Technology*, John Wiley and Sons, New York (All Editions).

Speight J.G. and Ozum B., *Petroleum Refining Processes,* Marcel Dekker Inc., New York (2002).

*Ullmann's Encyclopedia of Industrial Chemistry*. VCH, Weinheim Germany (All Editions).

Waddams A.L., *Chemicals from Petroleum* 2nd Edn. ELBS and John Murray, London (1970).

Weissermel K. and Arpe H.J., *Industrial Organic Chemistry*, VCH, Weinheim, Germany (1993).

Also readers should see monthly publication Hydrocarbon Processing, (Gulf Publishing Co.) wherein refining processes, petrochemical processes, and gas treating processes are briefly described indicating consumptions of raw materials, chemicals and utilities; and investment figures are presented.

***The Project Success Depends Upon Right Choice of The Process (Technology).***

# 3

# Project Site

## 3.1 INTRODUCTION

The Site Selection is a very important pre-project planning activity. The project is constructed only once and, therefore, the site has considerable impact on the performance of the project during its life cycle. The project profitability and productivity are site specific.

Sustainable development of a nation is realised through a well balanced, continuously growing agriculture and industrial sector. The setting up of an industrial project is a beacon of hope for many people because the project brings in social as well as economic change to the site (location). The infrastructure planning and industrial growth may not go hand in hand, in a vast developing country like India, due to complex interactions of variety of factors. The cluster theory may work well for the small European nations, but in a vast country like India it is the dispersal of an industry or those small clusters across the country that would be more meaningful for sustainable development. Too many projects clustering around one site precipitate some peculiar problems related to local infrastructure (such as housing, public transport, roads, rail links, pollution due to all types of vehicular traffic, water and power supply, treatment of domestic solid waste, liquid waste, and so on). Metro cities like Mumbai, Kolkata and Chennai could be the excellent examples of this aspect.

The successful implementation of a project without any project cost overrun also depends on the site selected, like other factors for instance, process (technology) selection (Chapter 2).

Location of a mega public sector industrial complex such as a refinery and petrochemical complex, power plants is often a topic of wide public discussions, and at times can even become a political controversy. In recent past, some projects were required to be relocated even after site development was over and equipments for erection were ready for installation at the site. The enormous delays caused due to relocation of the project not only affect the owner but also society at large that is indirectly deprived of the benefits. For instance, delays in selecting the site for a refinery is not only disadvantageous to the project owner but also to the society that is being deprived of raw materials for petrochemical complexes, transportation fuels (petrol and diesel), aviation fuel and domestic fuel (LPG). Further, more precious foreign exchange is required to be spent to meet domestic demands of the above products.

Electric power and water are the main utilities required for any chemical project. If adequate power is not available, a captive power plant becomes a necessity. Many refineries have their own power plant (captive power plant).

The majority of water used in chemical projects ultimately ends in liquid effluents. The liquid effluents, gaseous emissions and solid waste generated cause alarming environmental concerns among the neighbouring population.

The impact of a project on its neighbouring environment plays a key role for the project to sustain and enjoy 'healthy life' during the years to come. Issues related to Safety, Health and Environment (SHE) compliance vary from site to site. Unfortunately, such an important topic of site selection has not received much attention in the published literature. Though for a small part of project management, the site selection exercise is an equally important exercise as process or technology selection. As the demand for environmental management system grows, the organisation's commitment to responsible care through accreditation to ISO 14000 (2000) becomes a business house philosophy. Then the site selection becomes more and more relevant and important.

In this chapter a comprehensive treatment is presented for selecting the site based on a method that can assist in quantifying otherwise subjective parameters. Also, discussed are some important data required to be collected about site and its relevance in basic engineering and detailed engineering. Some important clearances to be obtained from the state and central governments have also been mentioned in brief.

## 3.2 SITE SELECTION

The entire site selection exercise can be divided into three main factors:

1. Prosperity factors: prosperity of nation
2. Profitability factors: profitability of the project
3. Productivity factors: productivity of the plant.

### 3.2.1 Prosperity Factors (Prosperity of Nation)

For large nation like India it is important to have a uniform industrial growth across the nation. On the eve and dawn of independence, the industrial growth had been confined to already grown metro-cities like Mumbai, Kolkata, and Chennai and so on. However, during the last five decades, the government is also seeking growth in other parts of the country. The dispersal of industries, appropriate use of resources and national security are three important prosperity factors. We shall discuss these in brief and try to assess their impact on site selection.

#### *3.2.1.1 Dispersal of Industries*

Apart from the economic imbalance caused between the state and the rest of nation, the concentrated industrial growth near city centres like Mumbai, creates enormous problems for city managers. It adds tremendous pressures on public transport (bus/ train) system. Utility management, in order to meet demands of utilities like, water and power, becomes a very challenging job. The local municipal corporations are left with a major task of meeting social and environmental problems arising out of unplanned growth. The policy of dispersal of industry is reflected in identifying industrially backward area. The state and the central governments offer financial and tax benefits, lower tariffs for power and water as incentives for setting up a project in industrially notified backward area.

#### 3.2.1.2 Appropriate Use of Resources

Appropriate use of resources is of considerable importance to our vast country. The national railway network is under pressure for transportation of coal, kerosene, LPG, diesel, petrol, petro-products and fertilisers. The road network, we have, is yet to be near to that in the developed countries. The consumption of energy resources would be too high if products are not produced near the marketplace or the plant is not located near the availability of raw materials. This proximity factor has forced the government to consider use of pipelines for transportation of liquid products/ raw materials, gaseous products/raw materials. The north central part of India is thriving on agro-economy and there is good demand for fertilisers. It was, therefore, decided to have a HBJ gas pipeline from Hazira to Jagadishpur and have fertilisers plants set up along this pipeline. The fertiliser production now being in the doorstep of farmers, optimum use of fertiliser can be envisaged. Similarly, pipelines have been constructed or are under construction even for transportation of crude oil from the receiving port to the site of a refinery. The pipeline transportation of fuels such as natural gas, petrol and diesel to the site located nearby market has now become a reality.

#### *3.2.1.3 National Security*

In the past, the government preferred to have industries of strategic importance such as refineries, nuclear power stations, defence armaments production, and so on, to be away from hostile borders. Considering weapon development programme all over the world, risks are more or less, logistically, equal. Despite this fact sometimes to be on a safer side project site for the above-mentioned industries may be considered to be away from hostile borders. Private entrepreneurs may overrule this risk factor in favour of other site-specific benefits.

Thus while selecting a site for the proposed project, one has to consider emphatically prosperity factors in the interest of nation as well. The remaining two factors, namely, profitability and productivity are centred around the project. Thus once sites are selected based on 'prosperity factors' the final screening is done based on Profitability and Productivity factors.

### 3.2.2 Profitability Factors (Profitability of Project)

The factors, which directly figure in computation of profit and hence return on investment, are known as *profitability factors*. They have a direct bearing on the project cost as well as on the cost of production. Let us consider these one by one.

#### *3.2.2.1 Land*

The price of land (generally not leased) is directly reflected in the cost of project. Land contours, i.e. unevenness of land would have a direct bearing on the cost of site development. If a small culvert is passing through a plot, additional expenditure may be required to divert or build it around the plot. The small hill needs to be razed to make almost even level of the plot.

After the recent earthquakes seismic area mapping of the entire country has been revised. Seismic area classification of the site results in additional expenditure in buildings and civil works in case site is in 'active' area. The chemical projects have been constructed in 'active' area also. For instance, the world's first natural gas to gasoline project of New Zealand Synthetic Fuels Corpn. (NZSFC) designed to produce 14,500-bbl/day (lbbl=42 US gallons) gasoline is located at the footsteps of volcanically active Mt. Egmont. The plant has two trains of methanol plants each producing 2,000 TPD methanol. This would give an idea of the size of the project. Piles not only supported all major foundations but also large numbers of bore wells were constructed to maintain water table at a safe level so that soil liquefaction could be avoided during an eruption of volcanic activity of Mt.Egmont. Thus one can appreciate the site-specific cost escalation in the project cost. We know in India too, a refinery-petrochemical complex could withstand major earthquake without any major damage despite the fact that surrounding townships and villages underwent major damage. This was due to anticipated higher seismic activities during the design and construction stage of the entire civil work.

#### 3.2.2.2 Climatic Conditions

The climatic conditions at a given site have bearing not only on the cost of project but also on the operating cost. The climatic data are obtained from the meteorological department or the state industrial development corporation.

*Rainfall*

The average rainfall and intensity of rainfall have direct bearing on storm water drainage system. There are instances where the entire plant came to a standstill because storm water entered pump motors resulting in pumps failure. The inadequate drainage of the storm water at the peak intensity of rain was found to be a factor responsible for such a failure. The plant-building and other buildings should have the architecture inline with the rainfall. Similarly snowfall in northern India, Himalayas, would have an impact on the building and civil work for a project under construction in that area. If a site is in the area of cyclone-prone zone as in the eastern region, the project owner needs to spend more money on buildings and civil work; thereby again increasing the cost of project. If there is good amount of precipitation (rain and/ or snow) one would consider the feasibility of water-harvesting system.

*Humidity*

Higher rainfall is associated with higher humidity, at least, over a monsoon period. The relative humidity would have a bearing on cooling tower fixed cost and its operating cost. Some hygroscopic products need to be stored in dry and cool atmosphere, necessitating humidity control devices. This would have impact not only on the project cost but also on the cost of production.

*Temperature*

Maximum and minimum temperature at the plant site has an impact on the capital cost as well as operating cost. Design of cooling tower, air coolers and plant insulation is affected by temperature. This would have impact on the plant cost and operating cost as well. The buildings for plant administrative purpose, worker's amenities and control room may need air-conditioning depending upon the duration of hot periods. In case the plant is located in the footsteps of Himalayan mountain area, one may have to provide a central heating system during chilly winter season as in Europe. The large variation in temperature would result in loss of material through tank breathing. The cryogenic storage of ethylene, propylene, LNG, etc., at near atmospheric pressure is influenced by temperature at the site. If the plant site temperature is likely to dip below the pouring point of materials being stored, the provision for heating tanks as well as transfer lines, not only increases capital expenditure but also adds to utilities, steam or power consumptions, as the case may be, thereby increasing the cost of production. For example, eco-friendly boilers use low sulphur heavy stocks (LSHS) as the fuel having pour point in the range between 65–85°C depending upon the source of LSHS. The storage of some chemicals may need temperature as well as humidity control. This would then reflect in the capital as well as operating cost of air-conditioning system. While designing air coolers we have to consider highest temperature prevailing at the plant site.

It is always, therefore, recommended to list down climatic factors and assess their impact on plant and machinery cost and cost of production.

#### 3.2.2.3 Raw Material Source

If raw material supply sources are away from the manufacturing site, the inventories of raw materials and also those required for utilities such as LSHS, fuel oil, and so on, would naturally be higher. This would result in higher capital cost for storage tanks and warehouse. The working capital requirement would go up. If raw materials are imported, one may have to have 'unloading facility and storage facility' at the receiving port or pay some rent for using such facilities at common chemical terminal. Increased logistics means more freight charges adding to the cost of production. If raw materials are imported, it makes more sense to have a plant site near the coastal location.

In some cases, the project owner may be required to have a special dedicated fleet of trucks/rail tankers for the supply of raw materials thereby adding to the capital as well as the operating expenditure.

#### 3.2.2.4 Product Market

In order to satisfy 'Prosperity Factors' one may locate industry in a notified industrially backward district. In such a case, the market for product may be far away from the manufacturing site. In order to have sustained supply of products to the market, the project owner needs to have more inventories of finished products. This would not only increase the cost of offsites but also increase working capital requirement. In a competitive world, the market price being dictated by consumer/buyer, the project owner may have to bear transportation cost in dispatching product to the marketplace. This would then take away part of profit.

For some special products, for instance, ethylene glycol to be used in the manufacture of polyester fibre, the project owner needs to have a dedicated fleet of tankers to avoid any contamination. This would also add to the capital investment and operating cost.

For new planned projects, one would find if rather difficult to meet the demand of logistics of the above two parameters, namely, raw material source and market source simultaneously. In such a case, one needs to carry out evaluation very carefully. For example, carbon black is used in the manufacture of tyres. Therefore, one may be tempted to have a project site near the tyre manufacturing plants. However, the raw material for carbon black could be natural gas, refinery fuel gas or heavy oil which one would find to be expensive to transport by special gas pipeline or fleet of tankers for liquid feedstock from the refinery. As a result the project to manufacture carbon black is located near the raw material source.

#### 3.2.2.5 Water

Water is required for various purposes in a chemical project. For example, water is required as process water in plant, required for cooling purpose in cooling tower circuit, for generation of low, medium and high pressure steam depending upon the requirement. It is also required for general cleaning, for potable use in administration blocks, canteen, etc. Water is also required for fire-fighting and for the use in colonies. Depending upon the demand and quality of water, we need to provide water treatment plants incurring capital as well as operating cost. If there is a mismatch between the demand and supply of water (even after recycling, etc.) one need to drill bore wells. It means one should have knowledge about water table at the site selected. The bore well construction would result in capital expenditure and operating expenditure. One might think in terms of harvesting rainwater or water from melted snow. The capital intensive 'desalination' of seawater/brackish water could be a possible solution to meet the demand of good quality water for a mega project located near coastal area. If the state industrial development corporation supplies water, the charges are site-specific and hence one must consider water charges in cost of production under the heading 'utilities'.

#### 3.2.2.6 Power

Power (electricity) is the next basic utility after water. It is transmitted countrywide under high tension. The supply from the State Electricity Grid and requirement within the plant, will decide the size of power- receiving station. This would be reflected in plant and machinery cost. The power tariff is reflected in operating expenditure (as cost of production). If the power supply interruption is frequent at the site under consideration, one has to provide diesel power generating (DG set) set to take care of emergency power. This would then add to the capital as well as operating expenditure. Considering shortage of power, there is a trend to have a captive power plant as co-generation facility wherein steam produced could be used for heating purpose thereby increasing an efficiency of energy utilisation. A captive power plant in the refinery or petrochemical complex would add to the project cost and to the cost of production.

#### 3.2.2.7 Environmental Aspects

Environmental management systems (EMS) are site-specific. If the project owner decides to go for ISO 14000 (2000) the capital as well as operating expenditure could go up compared to when only local discharge standards are followed. The effluent (gaseous, liquid and solid) discharge standards are site-specific. For example, a more elaborate liquid effluent treatment is essential for a plant discharging aqueous effluent in a river located in central India say, river 'Ganga' than that required if the effluent were discharged to deep sea for a plant located on coastal area. Thus the site would influence environmental management system (EMS) by way of the capital and operating expenditure.

#### 3.2.2.8 Housing

A remotely located site needs housing for majority of plant personnel, if adequate infrastructure does not exist in a nearby township. For example, at Lote (Chiplun) in Ratnagiri district (Maharashtra State) a housing colony was required for all early projects due to inadequacy of flats in the nearby township Chiplun. This would then increase land and site development as well as building and civil works components in the project cost. Also operating expenditure would go up slightly due to consumption of water and power.

#### 3.2.2.9 Transport to Staff and Labour

If the project site is away from the residential township and is not connected well by public transport system (rail or bus), the owner needs to provide transport to people. Even in a city like Mumbai where public transport system is reasonably good, the plant personnel request organisations for transport. This means that the project owner has to have a fleet of buses adding to capital as well as operating expenditure. Alternatively, he can hire buses thereby incurring operating expenditure only.

#### 3.2.2.10 Equipment Transportation

The delivery of fabricated equipment at the site is generally excluded from the scope of manufacturers. Therefore, one needs to add this transportation cost. If heavy equipments are involved one may have to use multi-axle vehicles. If the site is away from national highway, the owner has to spend money in improving approach road as well as strengthening bridges on the way. All this would add to expenditure. This work is to be done in collaboration with local state industrial development corporation and public works department (PWD), etc.

#### 3.2.2.11 Statutory Duties and Taxation

Prior to introduction of Goods and Services Tax (GST) in July 2017, States used to offer subsidies, tax holidays, concession on Sales Tax etc. to attract industries. Many Pharmaceutical manufacturing units moved to Himachal Pradesh to avail such benefits. The other reasons are availability of water and electrical power at lower tariff. Now after introduction of GST, manufacturing units will be located purely on techno-economic considerations and not on consideration of tax holidays. However, the state Govt. may offer refund of the State GST (SGST) for the period of 5 to 10 years as the case may be. The states may offer other incentives like lower tariff for electricity and water and infra structure. For example, a Common Effluent Treatment Plant (CETP) installed and operated for benefit of a cluster of industrial units. Incineration facility might be available for hazardous waste treatment.

From the foregoing it is clear that the location (site) would affect the project cost as well as operating cost (cost of production). For mega projects, the additional capital expenditure can run into few crore of rupees. The effect of the above factors could be easily quantified. After seeing productivity factors, we can discuss methodology to be followed in evaluation of both the factors.

### 3.2.3 Productivity Factors (Productivity of Project)

Like profitability factors, certain factors cannot be quantified in terms of cost or profit and yet they can influence productivity of plant considerably. Since these factors are important for running a plant, their importance must not be underestimated.

Some important factors affecting productivity are discussed below.

#### *3.2.3.1 Communication*

Communication is the basic need of any business house. It becomes more important if the project site is located far away from metro cities keeping in line with prosperity factors discussed earlier (Government policy of dispersal of industry). During the project construction, the site manager is required to frequently communicate with his own office (Project Engineering Company), with vendors and with the project owner. By the word communication, we not only mean fax, phones and e-mails, etc., but also road, rail and air communication. Delays incurred in establishing the contact, informing the problem and then receipt of the solution would result in delays during construction. Accumulation of small delays can result in major delay in project implementation, thereby incurring project cost overrun and loss of production, which is not desired at all.

Thus communication becomes an important factor during project construction.

While the plant is operational, the communication to outside world may be equally important in connection with procurement of raw materials, catalysts, selling product, offering technical services on speciality products, calling special maintenance people, etc.

The 'Communication' parameter is thus not only important during the period of project construction but also equally important in operating the project.

#### 3.2.3.2 Industrial Infrastructure

An industrial infrastructure includes availability of welding facilities, cutting facilities, some workshops having lathes, cutting machines, drilling machines, etc. If such a facility is not available in nearby areas, one needs to have own facilities within a plant to look after day to day maintenance. This factor would have bearing on the sustained production activity.

#### 3.2.3.3 Reliability of Power and Water Supply

In order to run a plant smoothly, there should not be frequent power failures, because it affects plant productivity. Entire plant cannot be run on DG set. Similarly, economic consideration may result in non-availability of captive power plant.

Water supply is equally important. If adequate water is not supplied or is not available at the project site, the owner has to make alternative arrangements such as supply through road tankers. Strike by tankers resulting in sudden non-availability of water would adversely affect the productivity of the project. The other option would be to have bore-wells at the site. It is possible to have an effluent treatment plant for water recycle at the expense of higher capital investment and operating cost as discussed earlier.

#### 3.2.3.4 Housing/Hotels

If housing/hotels accommodations are not available at the site or nearby site for project construction team, one has to build the same before commencing project construction. Further, plant personnel are unlikely to stay in hotels with families. Therefore, housing needs to be provided by way of residential colony.

The logistics involved between place of work and place of residence can lead to adverse impact on plant productivity. For instance, in Mumbai many people spend at least two hours daily in commuting between the home and workplace. After hectic travel the productivity at works is bound to get affected adversely.

#### 3.2.3.5 *Civic Amenities*

The site chosen for a project should have various civic amenities such as schools for kids, high schools, colleges (preferably), hospitals, chemists shop; diagnostic centres, transport facility, cinema/drama theaters, entertainment clubs, good restaurants, and so on. These amenities help relieve work stress/family stress after hectic workload. The State Industrial Development Corporations due to lack of funds may not be in a position to build such facilities. The industries located at places short of these facilities have failed to attract good professionals despite attractive remuneration. For fresh graduates and unmarried/single people such places with practically no civic amenities if becomes difficult of sustain and the management finds it rather difficult to retain good professionals. As a result, plant productivity suffers because each time new people are required to be trained for plant operation.

It is possible to provide 'quality life' facilities by building a township. However, the expenses incurred are disproportionately high for small- and medium-scale projects. For very large projects under public or private sector, it may be possible to have its own township. For example, Gas Cracker Complex at Nagothane (Dist. Raigad, Maharashtra State) has such a township.

#### 3.2.3.6 *Labour*

Availability of the skilled labour and its stability has become, lately, an issue of major concern for industries located in notified backward districts. By and large, people employed as unskilled or semiskilled person in the project constitute 20–25% workforce. During farming and harvesting season, the absenteeism is very high. Frequent social and village functions trigger absenteeism. This affect productivity considerably. Further, the character of local labour, namely, hostile or docile has become a vital criterion for smooth running of a project, as seen in many parts of our country.

#### 3.2.3.7 Surface Transport

In surface transport we consider road transport, rail transport and sea transport. The ease of movement of raw materials, catalyst and other chemicals and finished products to and fro from the site is a very important factor. Road link is a must. Proximity to the national highway makes the site access rather easier. For the movement of large volume or tonnage of materials. the rail-link is really helpful. For example, for a plant producing fertilisers, rail-link is definitely advantageous. On the other hand, for a project to manufacture citric acid by fermentation, rail-link is not a must.

Proximity to seaport is an important consideration when raw materials are imported or finished products are exported. For example, to import LNG/LPG an all-weather port is essential.

#### 3.2.3.8 Airport

Proximity to airport facilitates movement of the key personnel. However, it is not as important as surface transport.

## 3.3 SITE EVALUATION

After having seen importance of various factors (parameters), which can influence the exercise of site for the proposed project, we shall now discuss how site evaluation exercise can be conducted with the help of prosperity, profitability and productivity factors. It is always desirable to form a team of two or three senior engineers having design and construction experience of a chemical project. Preferably one of them should be a civil engineer. A questionnaire can then be prepared to collect relevant information on all the above factors about various sites under considerations. A visit to the probable sites for the project under considerations by the team formed, as discussed above is essential. If the 'site' is not well known, it pays to drive on the road leading site to have a first-hand experience of road worthiness for transportation of very heavy and odd-size equipments from fabrication shop to the site location.

Having dialogues/interviews with local existing industries would reveal many site deficiencies. The local hostility towards chemical project could be gauged properly by interacting with the local civic bodies. There are cases when the potentially good sites for the project have been discarded/abandoned due to social/political pressures. In a democracy such happenings are quite common.

After having gathered all data about sites, the first step is to screen these according to the 'Prosperity factors'. Based on these factors potential sites can be shortlisted.

It is desirable to check and confirm with the State Industrial Development Corporation about the availability of land in an industrial estate.

### 3.3.1 Evaluation Based on Profitability Factors

A quick estimate of project cost is done for any one of shortlisted sites. This estimate is then deemed to be the base case. The project cost estimates for other sites are made and the differential cost is added or deleted from the base case. For example, the cost of effluent treatment plant can vary from site to site because of changes in specifications/qualities of discharged effluents.

For the sake of this exercise, we can consider return on equity to be the same as that interest rate of term loan. In fact, without doing so one can decide to have higher returns on equity also and then have a weighted average cost of the capital. The project capital costs are then multiplied by term loan interest rate of the term loan to have apparent annualised cost.

The profitability factors affecting operating cost/cost of production are listed and their contribution is tabulated. The total effect of profitability factor would then be the sum of the above operating cost and annualised cost arising out of capital expenditure. With reference to the base site, expenditure coefficient (EC) is then computed. The sites having the lowest or nearby EC are preferred. This aspect is illustrated in Tables 3.1 and 3.2 with the help of some fictitious figures.

**Table 3.1** Evaluation of Profitability Factors (Affecting Project Cost) (*Basis: At Site 'A', Project Cost: ₹ 900 Lakh*)

| *Factor* | *Project Site, Relative Cost : (₹ Lakh)* | | | |
|---|---|---|---|---|
| | *A* | *B* | *C* | *D* |
| 1. Land | | | | |
| Land and site development | – | – 45 | – 85 | – 130 |
| Building and Civil Works | – | – 57 | – 72 | 00 |
| 2. Climatic conditions | | | | |
| rainfall | – | 00 | – 05 | 10 |
| Air conditioning | – | 90 | 00 | – 100 |
| 3. Raw material source | – | 00 | 10 | 16 |
| 4. Product market | – | 00 | 05 | 11 |
| 5. Water treatment | – | 51 | 00 | 08 |
| 6. Power | – | – 54 | 18 | – 54 |
| 7. Environmental | – | 24 | 36 | – 30 |
| 8. Housing | – | 81 | 120 | 180 |
| 9. Transport of staff | – | 00 | 00 | 00 |
| 10. Transport of Equipment | – | 05 | 08 | 12 |
| 11. Statutory duties | – | 00 | – 10 | – 15 |
| Total Cost of the project: | 900 | 995 | 925 | 808 |

**Table 3.2** Evaluation of Profitability Factors (Operating Cost)

| *Factor* | *Project Site, (₹ in Lakh)* | | | |
|---|---|---|---|---|
| | *A* | *B* | *C* | *D* |
| 1. Water and power | 50 | 22 | 20 | 18 |
| 2. Water treatment | 12 | 16 | 12 | 24 |
| 3. Air-conditioning | 14 | 22 | 14 | 00 |
| 4. Raw material and product transport | 24 | 32 | 44 | 62 |
| 5. Effluent treatment | 18 | 24 | 27 | 15 |
| 6. Transport of staff | 58 | 36 | 22 | 08 |
| 7. Interest on capital At 12% | 108 | 119 | 111 | 97 |
| Total | 284 | 271 | 250 | 224 |
| Expenditure Coefficient | 1.0 | 0.95 | 0.88 | 0.79 |

### 3.3.2 Evaluation Based on Productivity Factors

The assessment based on productivity factors is trickier for it is rather subjective. Here we follow the method of weighted average, identical to that used in Chapter 2.

All the productivity factors are listed and are assigned importance value on the scale 1–10. The factor having importance value 10 is the most important factor. For instance, power and water supply factor would have an importance value 10. The proximity to airport would have an importance value 2 and so on. Based on the individual judgement the importance value may vary slightly and hence it is subjective depending upon the appraiser. After assigning the importance value, credit is given to the site under evaluation. The productivity coefficient is then obtained as

$$\text{Productivity coefficient (PC)} = \frac{\text{Sum of all credits}}{\text{Sum of a importance value}} \tag{3.1}$$

Once productivity coefficient is computed, the relative site productivity coefficient is then computed with reference to the reference (base) site. After havirg obtained relative expenditure coefficient and relative productivity coefficient, the site screening is done. Table 3.3 depicts the evaluation of 'Productivity Coefficient'. It is seen that the expenditure coefficient for site D is the least but its productivity coefficient is also the least. We make up our mind that any site having productivity coefficient less than, say 0.5 may not be acceptable. This in turn mainly depends upon policies of the State Government and project implementation time. Thus the site D satisfies our minimum criterion. Now the choice of the site will be made between sites C and D. The final choice of site would depend upon futuristic (near) policies of the State Government and intuitive feelings of the project owner.

**Table 3.3** Evaluation of Productivity Factors

| *Factor* | *Importance* | *Project Site* | | | |
|---|---|---|---|---|---|
| | | *A* | *B* | *C* | *D* |
| 1. Communication | 10 | 8 | 6 | 7 | 6 |
| 2. Industrial infra-structure | 9 | 8 | 7 | 6 | 4 |
| 3. Reliability of power and water | 9 | 7 | 7 | 6 | 6 |
| 4. Housing/Hotels | 8 | 7 | 7 | 6 | 4 |
| 5. Civic amenities | 7 | 7 | 6 | 6 | 4 |
| 6. Labour | 7 | 6 | 5 | 5 | 4 |
| 7. Surface Transport | 8 | 8 | 8 | 8 | 7 |
| 8. Airport | 2 | 2 | 1 | 0 | 0 |
| Total | 60 | 53 | 47 | 44 | 35 |
| Productivity Coefficient | | 0.88 | 0.78 | 0.73 | 0.58 |
| Relative Productivity Coefficient | | 1.0 | 0.89 | 0.83 | 0.66 |

*Note:* (All figures in Tables 3.1 to 3.3 are fictitious. Numerical values do not have any meaning but serve best to illustrate the methodology).

## 3.4 THE PLOT A AT GIVEN SITE

The above considerations facilitate the process of screening various possible sites for the proposed project. However, once the site is selected the location of the land for the proposed project becomes intrinsically important. The selection of the plot of land at the chosen site requires due consideration of the factors discussed here.

### 3.4.1 Location

A plot of land is considered more suitable if it has more than one access from the road. A corner plot or a plot between two roads gives you that benefit. This allows heavy transport vehicular traffic to be separated from the business or staff traffic. If river or culvert (seasonal) is flowing nearby then it is important to check that water level during flooding (if flood-prone) remains well below and away from the plot. Similarly, a high-tension electric line passing through the plot poses a permanent restriction on the plot layout and reduces land availability for buildings and tank farms.

### 3.4.2 Soil

The soil with high load-bearing capacity minimises cost of foundations. High water table means that water will rise up in rainy season. This hampers excavation and brings external pressures on underground tanks and drains.

### 3.4.3 Terrain

Uneven and hilly land should be avoided but a land with gradual slope is preferred because the slope facilitates self-draining process and storm water drains layout. Uneven land entails higher capital expenditure while constructing drainages.

### 3.4.4 Shape

A square plot is the best but it is not always possible and in that case a shape closer to a square is referred. A triangular plot wastes a lot of land hence should be avoided.

### 3.4.5 Facilities

A chemical plant depends on the source of water and power. Further, it also depends on the discharge point of effluent. While selecting a plot the power source location should be checked because sometimes a lot of money is spent on bringing HT power (electric) supply to the plot from the grid or an electric sub-station.

## 3.5 SITE DATA

The site-specific information is important to the process licensor as well as to the detailed engineering contractor who is going to construct the plant. Though the process licensor may not need all information about the site, it is desirable to give him this information as well, so that he can, wherever possible use the same in the preparation of Basic Engineering Package. For instance, the process licensor needs to know the cooling water inlet and exit temperatures to design the coolers accordingly. Otherwise, he may specify that at battery limit cooling water temperature be say, 15°C, which may or may not be possible at the proposed site. The detailed engineering contractor needs to know the cooling water temperatures to size cooling water or procure the same as a module. We shall discuss some important site data parameters.

### 3.5.1 Geographical Location

The description indicating the plot number, the exact location (either village or industrial zone of the State Industrial Development Corporation, taluka or district), pin code number and the state, should be listed properly. The distance (approx.) from the national highway, the nearest port and the railway station should also be indicated. The location could be identified on a map of that area. The nearest post and telegraph office should be the contact number including telephone number, identified. Fax number and the e-mail address should be given to facilitate communication.

### 3.5.2 Soil Survey Report

A soil survey report from a competent authority is always desirable. Soil contour maps are required for site development. It is necessary to indicate seismic zone classification of the plot. Knowledge of soil-bearing capacity and seismic zone area classification is absolutely necessary for the building and civil work design. There are instances wherein project had been delayed because the storage tanks had sunk or tilted due to bad design of foundation. The design engineers in that case had not taken into account the bearing-capacity of the specific storage site. It is recommended, therefore, that once the plant layout is finalised, the exact locations of load-bearing equipment could be marked and then specific soil-bearing capacity data be collected. For instance, for pumps one can use general soil-bearing data because the load is not very high. On the other hand, the knowledge of soil-bearing capacity at the exact location is absolutely essential for compressors (centrifugal or screw) and turbines alone or coupled together where alignment is very critical.

### 3.5.3 Wind Velocity and Direction

The knowledge of maximum and minimum wind velocity, duration, and direction would help us carry out environmental impact assessment study with special reference to gaseous pollutants. Information on cyclones, hurricanes would assist the design of building and civil work.

Direction of wind plays an important role in designing plant layout. For instance, in a petrochemical complex wind should blow from fired heater (furnace) to other plant equipment. This is because in case of leaks in the plant, vapour cloud should not travel to fired heater where there is a potential for igniting the same leading to the disaster. Wind velocity would give us an idea of convective heat transfer coefficient in an open area, which would help design insulation system very effectively.

### 3.5.4 Other Meteorological Data

The other meteorological data include rainfall (average and intensity), humidity and temperatures (minimum and maximum). The importance of all these factors has been discussed earlier in Profitability Factors under climatic conditions.

### 3.5.5 Quality of Water

The quality of water is judged by analysis of water from the source. The quality of water enables, utility-engineer or process engineer, to design raw water treatment units for boiler, cooling tower and process application. The data are generally available with the state industrial development corporations.

### 3.5.6 Power

In order to design the power-receiving station, one must have information on the power supply from the state electricity grid (33 kV or 22 kV). The reliability of power supply is also important.

### 3.5.7 Local Discharge/Emission Standards

The site-specific discharge standard with reference to gaseous emissions, liquid effluents, and solid waste are required not only to study environmental impact assessment, but also to design and operate environmental management system leading to ISO 14000 (2000) accreditation.

### 3.5.8 Local Design/Fabrication Standards

The detailed engineering contractor and process licensor need to know the standards followed during the design and fabrication stage.

## 3.6 SITE CLEARANCES

Here, we shall see various important clearances the project owner needs to seek before starting construction at the site. We shall not go into details of format of various clearances or letters of intent (LOI) but list the important clearances in general.

### 3.6.1 Environmental Clearance

For any site, an environmental clearance must be obtained from various statutory bodies of the state as well as the central Government. Environmental Impact Assessment Study is to be conducted by a competent and approved authority. Hazard analysis (HAZAN) and Hazard and Operability (HAZOP) study are must for the safe operation of any project. If possible, it is desirable to take into confidence local 'Green' lobbies while the site-specific clearances need to be obtained. This would avoid delays in project construction or startup due to litigations. 'Transparency' in the site-specific study is highly recommended.

### 3.6.2 Power

It is absolutely essential to have a clearance from the State Electricity Supply Board, in the form of a letter indicating that the required power for the project under consideration will be provided at a specified tariff.

### 3.6.3 Water

The State Industrial Development Corporation should give guarantee on continuous availability of raw water for the project by way of formal letter mentioning charges.

### 3.6.4 Port/Harbour

If a jetty is planned on a coastal area, appropriate clearance should be obtained from the Port Authorities to build and to operate the jetty.

### 3.6.5 Civil Aviation

If the project site is near the airport, a formal clearance must be obtained from the Civil Aviation Authority regarding the tall structures in the project.

### 3.6.6 Indian Railways

In case the raw materials, finished products and other items such as coal need to be transported by railways, appropriate clearances from the Railway Authority regarding loading and unloading facilities, rail track within a project, etc., need to be obtained.

The above are major site-specific clearances. Apart from the above mentioned clearances one need to have clearances for the project, depending upon the investment (project cost) from the respective ministries in the Government, Reserve Bank of India for foreign exchange transactions, Foreign Investment Promotion Board, Cabinet Committee on Foreign Investment and so on.

## REFERENCE

Rase, H.F. and Barrow, M.H. *Project Engineering of Process Plants*, John Wiley and Sons, New York, 1957.

*The Success in Life is Site Specific.*

# 4 Estimate

## 4.1 INTRODUCTION

In Chemical Project Economics, estimates play a very important role. The journey of project conception to implementation (construction) proceeds through the estimates made at various levels. For instance, let us see we have conceived an idea to manufacture 1,00,000 TPA propylene from methanol. The financial viability of this technically sound concept is always first checked by computing an order of magnitude estimate. We may obtain an estimate of plant and machinery items either from the journals or professional magazines, or by directly from the process licensor. Through appropriate location index escalation index and cost-capacity relationship, we arrive at an order of magnitude estimate of the cost of the project. Based on the consumption figures of the raw materials and utilities, we can estimate the total or gross cost of production. This would then result in quick estimate of profitability and, hence, financial viability of the project. After concluding worthiness of an idea, one needs pre-preliminary study to gauge seriousness of further efforts. This is further strengthened by preliminary feasibility study based on budgetary estimate. When we decide to go ahead with project implementation, a detailed techno-economic feasibility study, often known as a bankable document, is required to seek term loan from financial institutions. This study is based on reasonably accurate (near accurate) estimate of project cost (fixed capital investment) and gross cost of production (operating cost). Only while implementing or constructing the project, real costs involved become known. The pre-construction activities related to a project are thus based on an estimate only. Therefore, the importance of 'estimate' can never be underestimated in any project implementation.

An estimate is a prediction or assessment of the price of an item (price to vendor but cost to owner) or services under consideration. An estimate differs from a 'guesstimate' because an estimate has a reliable and historical database. The guesstimate by nature is an assumptive or intuitive estimate rather than a properly worked out estimate. The guesstimate has often a basis without analysis.

The estimate cannot be the final purchase price or cost incurred because the real price is always either a deviation or error-free, and by nature the estimate is not error-free. Thus an estimate is always associated with some positive or negative deviations from the real price.

Therefore, we have an estimate, ($E$), of an item that is always expressed as

$$E = R \pm d \tag{4.1}$$

Where $d$ is the deviation from $R$ – the real price.

From Expression (4.1) it is obvious that while there is no limit to positive deviation ($+ d$), there exists lower limit for negative deviation ($-d$) and this limit is $R$. In other words, negative deviation ($-d$) can be maximum $R$. This is because an item cannot have a negative price and in the limit it can be zero. Thus by this reasoning, we shall see all estimates can have higher positive deviations while negative deviations are on the lower side. Many estimation engineers often ignore this fact. Generally, deviations are expressed as some percentage (%) of the original value.

As we shall see later in Chapters 5 and 6, estimates of many components or constituents are added to have the final estimate of the project cost. Also many times, we may have to multiply two estimates of different quantities to arrive at the final estimate. To arrive at the estimate of the cost of a reactor, the estimate of weight of reactor is multiplied by the estimate of material and labour charges per unit weight. Thus, estimation engineer or reviewer is interested in knowing how accurate is his estimate after addition of all estimates. During the exercise of project cost estimate, positive deviation results in a conservative estimate. In reality if the cost is less than that estimated, the project becomes more attractive. The large negative deviations would result in lower project cost, which can become a real problem while implementing the project due to project cost overruns. Similarly, if we are bidding for a turnkey project or an equipment say reactor, heat exchanger, the offer based on unsound higher estimate may lead to a situation wherein the project owner may reject the offer. Thus too high or too low deviations are going to be detrimental to business. Therefore, it is desirable to have insight into various properties of estimate. Gore (1958) addressed this basic problem of estimate in a comprehensive manner. We shall overview the same here.

## 4.2 ESTIMATE BASICS REVISITED

An estimate $E$ consists of various components that can be expressed as

$$E = f(A, B, C, ...) \tag{4.2}$$

Where $f$ can be addition, subtraction, multiplication or division.

The deviations in $A$, $B$, $C$ .may be represented as $\pm a$, $\pm b$, $\pm c$ ... and so on.

The positive and negative deviations in $E$ can then be obtained as:

$$E + d = f(A, B, C...) + \{(df/dA)^2 (a)^2 + (df/dB)^2 (b)^2 + (df/dC)^2 (c)^2 + ...\}^{1/2} \tag{4.3}$$

and

$$E - d = f(A, B, C...) - \{(df/dA)^2 (-a)^2 + (df/dB)^2 (-b)^2 + (df/dC)^2 (-c)^2 + ...\}^{1/2} \tag{4.4}$$

In order to illustrate we shall restrict to two components A and B of an estimate $E$. The same methodology would then be applicable to more components also.

Thus we have two deviations namely,

$$+d = [(df/dA)^2 (+a)^2 + (df/dB)^2 (+b)^2]^{1/2} \quad (4.5)$$

and $$-d = -[(df/dA)^2 (-a)^2 + (df/dB)^2 (-b)^2]^{1/2} \quad (4.6)$$

### 4.2.1 Addition or Subtraction

Let us consider $E$ to be the sum of $A$ and $B$.

$$E = (A \pm a) + (B \pm b) \quad (4.7)$$

Therefore, $(df/dA) = 1$ and $(df/dB) = 1$ (4.8)

We, then, have

$$+d = [(+a)^2 + (+b)^2]^{1/2} \quad (4.9)$$

$$-d = -[(-a)^2 + (-b)^2]^{1/2} \quad (4.10)$$

Thus $$E = A + B \pm [(a)^2 + (b)^2]^{1/2} \quad (4.11)$$

And inaccuracy of an estimate (expressed as %) is then given by

$$= \{\pm [(a)^2 + (b)^2]^{1/2}/(A + B)\} \times 100 \quad (4.12)$$

#### *Illustration*

Let us illustrate the above method with the help of an example of estimation of the cost of $CO_2$ absorber in ammonia plant.

The cost of the column shell and dished ends = 150 ± 15 units

The cost of internals = 75 ± 11 units

(The above are coded costs)

The cost of the column = $[150 + 75] \pm [(15)^2 + (11)^2]^{1/2}$

= 225 ± 18.6 units

% Inaccuracy = (± 18.6/225) 100

= ± 8.3

Thus we see that during addition of components of estimates the deviation of an estimate is less than that of individual components.

Further, the deviation would depend upon the deviation of component having maximum or highest deviation for example,

If the cost of the column shell and dished end = 150 ± 25 units

The cost of internals = 75 ± 11 units

% Inaccuracy = (± 27.3/225) 100

= ± 12.1%

This property would be of greater significance to us while estimating components of project cost, and plant and machinery. Since project cost consists of addition of so many components along with 'Plant and Machinery' item, its accuracy (project cost) depends heavily on accuracy of estimate of Plant and Machinery item because its contribution to project cost is 40–60% (typical of petrochemical project).

### 4.2.2 Multiplication

Let us consider an estimate, *E*, to be product of two cost components namely *A* and *B* as

$$E = (A \pm a)\ (B \pm b) \tag{4.13}$$

Therefore, we have

$$(df/dA) = B \quad \text{and} \quad (df/dB) = A \tag{4.14}$$

$$+\, d = [B^2\ (+a)^2 + A^2(+b)^2\ ]^{1/2} \tag{4.15}$$

$$-\, d = -[\ B^2\ (-\ a)^2 + A^2(-b)^2\ ]^{1/2} \tag{4.16}$$

If (+ *a*) and (–*a*) are numerically identical,

$$E = (A)\ (B) \pm\ [\ B^2(a)^2 + A^2(b)^2\ ]^{1/2} \tag{4.17}$$

$$\%\ \text{Inaccuracy} = \pm\ \{[B^2(a)^2 + A^2(b)^2]^{1/2}/AB\}100 \tag{4.18}$$

#### *Illustration*

Let us illustrate this through an example.

The estimated weight of the reactor is, $A = 1 \pm 0.15$ T,

The estimated charges (material + labour)

$B = (2 \pm 0.20)$ Lakh/₹/T

Therefore, estimated cost of the reactor is = 2,00,000 ± 36,055 (₹)

The inaccuracy would be ±18%. Thus 15% inaccuracy in weight and 10% inaccuracy in charges result in 18% inaccuracy in the final estimate.

It is, thus, seen that during multiplication inaccuracy of individual variables gets amplified in the product. Therefore, extra caution needs to be exercised for such a situation.

For division, $A/B$, inaccuracy can also be estimated from the first principle. However, 'division' is not frequently encountered.

Enyedy (1997) has also presented a comprehensive account about accuracy of the estimate.

After having seen accuracy in the final estimate from the individual estimates, let us see various type of estimate.

## 4.3 TYPES OF ESTIMATES

Various types of estimates are required during the course of project conception to commissioning. When an idea is conceived, we need order of magnitude estimate of project cost to envisage whether to pursue the idea or not. To assess soundness of an idea, we need a very preliminary estimate to aid investment decision. A budgetary estimate would lead to investment decision. Once we have decided to go ahead with the project under consideration, we need a detailed definitive estimate to seek term loan from financial institution. The same estimate would also be useful in cost control of the project at a very early stage of implementation of project.

During project implementation, we would like to have a conservative estimate that means to have lower negative deviation. An estimate with very high negative deviation would lead to project cost overruns, which is not desired during project implementation.

In summary, we can have following types of estimates (see Table 4.1).

**Table 4.1** Type of Estimate

| *Estimate* | *Upper Limit (%)* | *Lower Limit (%)* |
|---|---|---|
| Order of magnitude | + 50 | – 30 |
| Preliminary | + 30 | – 20 |
| Budgetary | + 20 | – 15 |
| Detailed/definitive | + 10 | – 05 |

The above classification is similar to one recommended by American Association of Cost Engineers (AACE) as cited by Enyedy (1997).

Let us illustrate utility of above types of estimates with the help of an example of a project to manufacture 50,000 TPA, ethyl tertiary butyl ether (ETBE) as a petrol (gasoline) additive, in western Maharashtra. Based on the published information the project owner first prepares the order of magnitude estimate for the cost of the project. For this purpose, he might use the recent past data for a nearby capacity plant set-up in any country, say, USA. After having seen its economic viability, a preliminary estimate is prepared to justify further efforts. This is followed by a budgetary estimate with the help of in-house data for equipment, piping, electricals instrumentation, buildings and civil works, etc. At this stage, the owner may seek the help of project engineering company to aid investment decision. If the project under investigation is financially sound, a definitive or detailed estimate is prepared (generally by a project engineering organisation) resulting in detailed techno-economic feasibility report (see Chapter 14).

The project owner then uses this report to obtain all clearances required to implement the project. This report is used to make financial arrangements (term loan) also. In the early stage of the project, the definitive estimate prepared is used for controlling the cost.

If preliminary estimates and hence feasibility study indicates that the idea is not economically attractive, all efforts to prepare a detailed estimates could be saved.

From the foregoing, the significance of various estimates is obvious.

## REFERENCES

Enyedy G., *How Accurate is Your Cost Estimate, Chem. Engg* **104** (7) 106 (1997).

Gore W.L., *How to Improve Estimate Accuracy, Petroleum Refiner* 37 (6) 142 (1958).

***An Estimate is not a Guesstimate!***

# 5

# Project Cost

## 5.1 INTRODUCTION

Project cost includes all costs incurred while transforming an idea into reality by way of a plant constructed at the site and subsequent commissioning of the plant. This includes costs of tangibles in the form of land, buildings, plant equipments, instruments, electricals and piping, etc. Also included are costs of intangibles associated with services required to erect the plant and make it functional such as architects fees, know-how and engineering fees, expenses to obtain various statutory clearances, formation of a company wherever applicable and so on. The interest on term loan during construction period, cóst associated with management of public issue (shares) too are port of the project cost. All these costs eventually become Project Cost and hence 'capital item' in the balance sheet of a company under application of funds. The project cost is also known as project capital outlay or fixed capital investment.

The decision to implement or construct any project is based on 'Project Cost Estimate', and when the actual project is implemented we come to know the real cost of the project. If the difference between real cost (known at the end) and project estimate (known at the beginning) is positive, then it is known as project cost overrun. There could be several reasons for the project cost overrun. However, the owner of project and manager of project engineering company would like to have negative or zero-overrun or would like to keep the difference at least at the minimum. By and large, the project cost overrun is attributed to bad estimates or bad management of project implementation.

The 'Project Cost' is not only important to the entrepreneur (Project Owner) but also equally important to the project financier if the owner is borrowing money in the form of loan. The project cost decides financial viability of the project under consideration.

Different types of estimates of project cost are required when the project undertakes a journey from the conception to commissioning. For instance, an order of magnitude estimate is required when an idea is potentially attractive. This would then result in preliminary estimates to aid investment decision. Once the decision is made, a detailed techno-economic feasibility report is prepared wherein the project cost estimate has to be near realistic (+10%, –5%). Rarely, a project is rejected after the detailed project cost estimate leading to detailed techno-economic feasibility study (also known as bankable document). In Chapter 4, we have discussed the meaning of the word estimate and different types of estimates used at different levels of project conception to implementation journey.

## 5.2 ELEMENTS OF PROJECT COST

Let us consider how to invest money in a Greenfield project. In general, the project cost that is applicable to a Greenfield project is, with some omission, also applicable to a battery limit project. However, contributions of components of project cost may vary from zero to some finite value. For example, miscellaneous fixed assets may not be required for a battery limit project. For a Greenfield project, land is needed and the site needs to be developed for construction of a plant. The entire plant can be installed within a building or can be in open atmosphere as in the case of a petrochemical complex. The plant consists of not only equipments but also piping, instrumentations and electricals lumped together as plant and machinery item of the project cost schedule. The plant design construction and operation would be as per know–how given by the process licensor. Depending upon complexity of the plant, additional expenses may be incurred towards commissioning by process licensor and training of Indian plant operators on an overseas plant based on the same technology. There would be various fixed assets in the form of furniture, communication facilities, vehicles, etc., for smooth functioning of a project in the form of miscellaneous fixed assets. While a plant is being constructed various types of expenditure are incurred, such as salaries of project persons, legal disputes, interest during period of construction, start-up expenditure, etc., known as pre-operative expenses. If a project is large and funding is needed by way of public share issue, there is always some expenditure associated with managing this issue and this is clubbed under preliminary and capital issue related expenditure. Last but not least, an important aspect of the project is the need of working capital for running the project till sufficient cash to run the same is generated. A part of this working capital is capitalised in the form of margin money in the project cost.

The various elements/components of project cost in line with the norms prescribed by financial institutions such as ICICI and IDBI are listed in Table 5.1. While executing a project we may need foreign exchange to support know-how and import of plant and machinery items. In some cases we may need foreign exchange even to import raw materials. It is desirable to have a back-up in the form of Annexure or a table of foreign exchange required along with the exchange rate prevailing at the time of estimate. Many times it is referred as a currency basket. The relative contributions of these components to project cost for a typical Greenfield petrochemical project are presented in Table 5.1. The contributions are indicative in nature and should be used judiciously. The scenario for other projects, such as dyes, pharmaceuticals, polymers, detergents, etc., is not radically different from what is presented here. The difference occurs due to an open plant of a continuous process for commodity chemicals and in housed batch plant for speciality chemicals such as dyes, pharmaceuticals products.

**Table 5.1** Elements of Greenfield Project Cost

| *Element* | | *Contribution (%) to Project Cost (Typical Petrochemical Project)* |
|---|---|---|
| 1. Land and Site Development | : | 3–5 |
| 2. Buildings and Civil Works | : | 5–10 |
| 3. Plant and Machinery | : | 40–60 |
| 4. Know-how and Engineering | : | 15–25 |
| 5. Expenses on Foreign Technicians and Training of Indian Technicians Abroad | : | 1–3 |
| 6. Miscellaneous Fixed Assets | : | 2–5 |
| 7. Pre-operative Expenses | : | 15–20 |
| 8. Contingencies | : | 8–10 |
| 9. Preliminary and Capital Issue Related Expenses | : | 1–2 |
| 10. Margin Money | : | 3–6 |

In general, the contribution of the plant and machinery is the highest to the project cost followed by know-how and engineering, pre-operative expenses and so on. On the other hand, the contribution of the miscellaneous fixed assets and the preliminary and capital issue related expenses is not as significant. It means the estimates of plant and machinery component need to be more realistic and maximum time should be spent on its estimate rather than time being spent on miscellaneous fixed assets. Therefore a separate Chapter 6 is devoted. To appreciate intricacies of estimates and their impact. A common mistake is made that 95% of estimation resources are spent on things of 5% importance. In the project management this trend needs to be reversed.

We shall, now, discuss the meaning and procedure for estimating various project cost components. The 'Plant and Machinery', being the most important component of Project Cost, shall be dealt with extensively in Chapter 6. To make this entire exercise more practical, wherever possible, we shall follow guidelines of financial institutes, such as ICICI and IDBI.

## 5.3 LAND AND SITE DEVELOPMENT

For implementing any chemical project, land is the prime requirement. The land is required for the main plant, i.e. battery limit (B/L) plant and for all supporting facilities known as *outside battery limit* (OBSL) facilities, which include storage (offsites) of raw materials intermediates and finished products, utilities, effluent treatment plant (ETP). Also, land is required for other facilities. We need to have a green curtain around the entire area not only for aesthetic beauty, but also for the plant to be eco-friendly. If the grassroots or Greenfield project is located in an industrially notified backward district or area, we need to provide housing also for the people working in the project. For this purpose, we need a plot of land not very far away from industrial area.

### 5.3.1 Main Plant Area

The process licensor indicates the area required for the main plant (battery limit, B/L). Generally, detailed engineering contractor does not change the overall plant layout given by the process licensor and, therefore, there is practically no change in the area given for B/L Plant.

### 5.3.2 Outside Battery Limit (OSBL) Facilities

The detailed engineering contractor in consultation with the project owner estimates the area required for all outside battery limit (OSBL) facilities described below.

#### 5.3.2.1 Storage Facility

By the word storage facility, we mean storage and handling of gas, liquid and solids as applicable. Raw materials, intermediates, finished products, by-products are required to be stored. The quantity that need to be stored is decided in consultation with the project owner. Logistics involved for raw materials supply source, finished products, by-products (co-products), marketplace, ease of availability and marketability are the major considerations deciding storage capacity. The storage of all the above ultimately requires Working Capital and, hence, the most optimum capacities are to be decided. The storage of solid materials is governed by their characteristics and, hence, special building facility may be required. For instance, hygroscopic materials like urea require humidity control in warehouse. Therefore, area requirement may change. The storage of liquid material can be in drums or in tanks (API type). The area required is governed by classification of liquids, into hazardous and non-or less-hazardous which is based on their flash point. The storage of hazardous liquids is governed by guidelines laid by the Factory Act and Petroleum Act. For example, the distance between the two storage tanks having flammable liquids, and the distance between tank and road is also governed by these regulations. If material is stored in drums, one should consider two-tier or three-tier system of storage. This would then decide area required for the storage. If the gas is being supplied by pipeline (such as natural gas, mainly methane, at say 20 bar pressure), there is no question of storage, but area required for gas-metering station may be considered.

#### 5.3.2.2 Utilities

The utilities used in a chemical plant are classified into basic and applied utilities. The basic utilities are water, fuel, power and refrigerants. The applied utilities are steam, cooling water, chilled water or brine.

Area required for the raw water storage and storage for 'fire water' (water used for firefighting operation) should be considered though these tanks that are generally underground tanks. No building is constructed above this. However, this area can be used for landscaping or at the most car/bicycle parking. Areas required for boiler house, instrument air supply plant, refrigeration unit, water treatment unit, inert gas generator, cooling tower are indicated by respective vendors in their GA (general arrangement) drawings. Also, one must account for area required for electrical substation, high tension (HT) and low tension (LT) rooms, and emergency power, diesel generator (DG) unit.

#### 5.3.2.3 Buildings

Buildings are required for the main plant as well as for auxiliary services and administration purposes. The plants manufacturing petrochemicals, commodity chemicals (such as soda ash, sulphuric acid) are open. The building area required within B/L plant is included in the estimate given by the process licensor. The buildings in this B/L area are generally buildings for say fermentation unit, compressor house, turbine house, control room and so on. On the other hand, for speciality products, such as dyes, pharmaceuticals pesticides, and so on, plants are housed inside buildings and are provided with exhausts and ventilators.

Buildings are classified into two main classes, namely, factory buildings and non-factory buildings. This segregation is for easy computation of depreciation. Estimate for various buildings is discussed in Section 5.4 (Building and Civil Works). Apart from that, we need to estimate area required for various buildings, as listed in Table 5.2.

#### 5.3.2.4 Effluent Treatment Plant (ETP)

The area required for ETP is indicated by the ETP process licensor who is supplying a turnkey plant. Otherwise, the detailed engineering contractor has to carry out estimate based on in-house generated know-how for effluent treatment. It is desirable to have a basic engineering package (BEP) for effluent treatment plant also.

Based on the above, we can estimate total area required for OBSL facilities.

As a rule of thumb the site development is carried out for area, which could be 50–75% higher than the above estimate (BL Plant Area + OSBL Plant Area). Within the plant, for easy movement of material and men, we need roads. In the absence of a plot plan, we may consider the road area is be 10% of the entire site developed.

After having considered roads, we can now take the sum of all areas to have the estimate of land required. As mentioned earlier, if expansion or forward/backward integration is desired, while applying for a plot one can take this also into consideration.

### 5.3.3 Estimate

Definitive estimate or actual price of land can be obtained by knowing land rate at the site. Depending upon the site data, the cost associated with site development can be estimated. In order to protect the plot from encroachments, boundary fencing is essential. At this stage, project owner has to decide whether he would have the chain link barbed wire or wall-type of fencing. The cost estimate could be easily prepared with the help of a plot plan. The protected area should have check posts and gates for controlled movement of materials. The number of gates could be estimated and hence the cost associated with it. After having the approximate layout of plant, the length and width of internal roads can be established. Civil engineering department can estimate the cost associated with roads considering load factor. If the plot

**Table 5.2** Estimate of Land Requirement

| | *Area, $m^2$* |
|---|---|
| 1. Plant | : |
| Battery Limit | : |
| 2. OSBL Facilities | : |
| Storage | : |
| Liquid storage (tanks) | : |
| Hazardous | : |
| Non-hazardous | : |
| Drumming area | : |
| Liquid storage | : |
| Solid storage building and silo | : |
| Gas metering station | : |
| Packaging and bagging unit | : |
| Utilities: | : |
| Water storage raw water storage and fire water storage | : |
| Water treatment plant | : |
| Boiler (Steam) | : |
| Co-generation | : |
| Instrument air | : |
| Refrigeration unit | : |
| Inert gas generator | : |
| Cooling tower | : |
| Electrical sub-station | : |
| Diesel power generating unit | : |
| 3. Buildings | : |
| Workshop | : |
| Warehouse | : |
| R&D building | : |
| Admin building | : |
| Gate and time office | : |
| Weigh bridge | : |
| Canteen | : |
| Workers centre | : |
| Fire Station | : |
| Excise office | : |
| Car park and cycle park | : |
| Truck parking and so on | : |
| 4. Effluent Treatment Plant | : |
| 5. Total Area (1 to 4) | : |
| 6. Site Development Area (Including landscaping) | : |
| 7. Roads within Factory | : |
| Total area required | : |
| Area for housing of plant personnel | : |

does not have easy access from nearby national/state highway cost associated with approach road can be estimated. A typical back-up sheet supporting land and site development cost is given in Table 5.3.

**Table 5.3** Estimate of Land and Site Development

| Item | Unit | | |
|---|---|---|---|
| 1. Cost of Land | | : | ₹ |
| Rate ₹/m$^2$ or ₹/hectare | | | |
| Area m$^2$/hectare | | | |
| Total | | | |
| 2. Cost of Leveling and Development | | : | |
| Rate ₹/m$^2$ | | | |
| Area | | | |
| Total | | | |
| 3. Cost of Fencing | | : | |
| Length | ₹/m | : | |
| Type of Fencing | | : | |
| Rate of Fencing | ₹/meter | : | |
| 4. Cost of Gates | | : | |
| Cost of gate | ₹/Gate | : | |
| Number of gates | | | |
| 5. Cost of Laying Road | ₹/km | : | |
| Approach roads connecting plot to main road, *m* internal roads, *m* | | : | |
| 6. Land for Colony, *m*$^2$ | | : | |
| 7. Expenditure towards Green Curtain (tree plantation) | | : | |
| 8. Total Land & Site Development | | : | |

As discussed in Chapter 3, following information about the plot will facilitate the estimate.

1. Location of plot, survey no.
2. Location place, Taluka, District, State.
3. Location from nearby Highway (State or National)
4. Plot contour map.
5. Plot Soil survey report, particularly at places of heavy loads.
6. Meteorological site data,

| | | |
|---|---|---|
| Temperature | : | Maximum, Minimum duration |
| Rainfall | : | Maximum, Intensity of rain fall |
| Humidity, Wind Velocity | : | Maximum whether hurricane or cyclone prone area |

7. Seismic- area classification.
8. Local discharge standards for gaseous, liquid and solid effluents.

## 5.4 BUILDING AND CIVIL WORKS

Building and civil works contribute between 5 and 15% to the project cost depending upon the type of project.

The buildings and other civil structures within the plant and in the immediate vicinity of the plant are often subjected to harsh environment (corrosive environment). For instance, a plant having unit processes such as sulphonation, halogenation, and so on, is subjected to corrosive environment. Many times not only acid-proof flooring is required but also the structural steel needs to be protected with the help of anti-corrosive paint. As a result, in general, the life expectancy of civil work in the main plant area is less than that located in the area away from the main plant. This implies different rates of depreciation for such buildings and civil work. Based purely on this concept, building and the civil works of the project are divided into two subsets, namely, factory buildings and non-factory buildings.

While giving know-how, the process licensor indicates whether plant is in an open area like any refinery (say Hindustan Petroleum Corporation Ltd.) or petrochemical complex, Complex at Vadodara or Nagothane) or is housed within buildings. Plants for speciality chemicals, dyes intermediates, pharmaceuticals, etc., are generally housed inside a factory building.

The plants built in an open area, have some buildings to house process compressors, turbine, boiler, etc., and a building is always required for control room.

A typical format for buildings and civil works is presented in Table 5.4.

Considerable amount of information needs to be generated by detailed engineering contractor to have a meaningful estimate of buildings and civil work.

Following information need to be obtained from the Process Licensor:

- Type of plant whether open air or within building
- Any special flooring is required or not
- Any special building with large equipment, e.g., compressor turbine, fermentor, etc., is there or not
- Area required for control room, analytical laboratory
- Any special environment control is required (temperature/humidity, etc).

The civil structures, being standards for compressor/turbine house, control room and laboratory, floor area is adequate for cost estimation.

The rest of the information on buildings and civil works for auxiliary services such as boiler-house, workshop, electrical sub-station, diesel power generating unit, administrative, buildings, R&D facilities, as well as warehouses, workshop yard facilities for storage of raw materials, by-products, intermediates and products need to be developed by detailed engineering contractor. All civil work associated with the above-mentioned units is clubbed under 'Factory Buildings'.

Considerable amount of civil work has to be done for roads from the plant site to nearby main road, culvert bridges within a plant, storm water drainage and also for the roads within the plot (i.e. battery limit plant as well as outside battery limit, OBSL). If effluent treatment plant consists of lagoons, equalisation ponds, one needs to carry out a good deal of land excavation work and lining of such tanks. Tanks required for storage of raw water, firewater and cooling tower basins involve considerable civil work.

If bore-wells are drilled for sustained water supply or to avoid soil liquefaction during earthquake due to higher levels of water table, one has to take into account civil work for these also.

For the smooth performance of the entire project, we need time office, dispatch office with weigh bridge, excise house, car park, cycle stand, truck terminal (for transportation of raw material and finished goods), worker's amenities including charge room, shower room, dispensary, fire tender house, railyard, etc. The civil work associated with these items is put together under the category of non-factory buildings. For pipe rack, cable racks, we need RCC and structural steel. A team of good civil engineers would be in a position to estimate cost with reasonable accuracy ± 10–15%. Process engineers and mechanical engineers should furnish details of weights of various equipments when they are fully loaded to civil engineers. For instance, $10 m^3$ tank for benzene and sulphuric acid, when full, will have totally different load for civil foundation because specific gravity for benzene is 0.8 while that for sulphuric acid 1.8. For civil foundation of rotating machinery, one has to take extra care. For instance, civil foundation for a steam turbine directly coupled to a compressor will be totally different than that for a day tank or a distillation column with kettle-type reboiler.

While accomplishing the above tasks, one must not forget the importance of aesthetic beauty of an entire project (without compromising its functionality). The expenditure incurred as fees to the architect should be included in non-factory buildings. If the project is big one, we need to have a model of the plant. The expenditure incurred on 'Plant building model' is also shown as non-factory item. If the project site is far away from an urban area, building of residential staff quarters becomes essential. The building cost associated with the township is considered to be a non-factory building cost.

Assumed charges (in ₹/Tonne) for estimation of cement, reinforced steel and structural steel form the basis of estimation and should be stated.

Table 5.4 exhibits the schedule of Buildings and Civil Works cost estimate. In this estimate also, there would be no foreign exchange component.

**Table 5.4** Buildings and Civil Works

| | |
|---|---|
| 1. *Factory Buildings* | ₹ |
| – Factory building for the main plant, and effluent treatment plant<br>– Factory buildings for auxiliary services steam, water, workshop, electrical power station<br>– Administrative buildings<br>– Research and Development Centre<br>– Warehouses, yard facilities for<br>• raw materials<br>• intermediates<br>• products and also for furnace oil/fuel oil/diesel oil | |
| Total Factory Buildings | ₹ |
| 2. *Non*-Factory Buildings* | |
| – Miscellaneous Non-factory buildings:<br>Canteen, gate house, time office, excise house, workers amenities, medical center, car park, cycle stand, etc.<br>– Quarters for essential staff<br>– RCC and other structural materials<br>– Garages<br>– Storm Water Drains<br>– Civil Engineering Work for effluent treatment plant – lagoons etc.<br>– Architects Fees<br>– Plant Model | |
| Total Non-factory Buildings | ₹ |

## 5.5 PLANT AND MACHINERY

Plant and Machinery is the most important component (element) of the project cost. Its contribution to the project cost could be in the range of 40–60% for majority of petrochemical projects. It would be less for the speciality products project (40–50%) due to higher costs of buildings and civil works. Being the single largest component of the estimate, Plant and Machinery cost estimate is covered under a separate chapter (Chapter 6).

## 5.6 KNOW-HOW AND ENGINEERING

The know-how and Engineering components of project cost consist of

- Know-how fees (Licensing Fees)
- Basic Engineering Fees
- Detailed Engineering Fees

### 5.6.1 Know-How Fees (License Fees)

The process licensor or technology supplier charges lump sum fees for giving know-how. Royalty payment to the process licensor is discouraged by and large.

It is to be noted that know-how can also be obtained eithar from Chemical Engineering Schools or in Research and Development Center (R&D) of the project owner. Seldom the process licensor would educate the project owner on know-why unless there is equity participation of the process licensor in the project.

If the process licensor is from abroad, the know-how fee is to be paid in foreign currency of his choice (generally, it is the currency of the country of origin or the global stable currency such as US $ or Euro). The statutory permissions from the concerned Government authorities and Reserve Bank of India (RBI) need to be obtained. For the process licensor from our own country, fee for this know-how is obviously paid in Indian currency.

The Know How now attracts GST (Service Accounting Code). This is to be paid by the project owner in Indian Rupees even when Know How is obtained from foreign Process Licensor. The lump sum payment is to be done during the project construction period as per agreed schedule. When the know-how is obtained from the foreign supplier, generally, basic engineering package is prepared by the process licensor. Thus, when the agreement is signed between the project owner and know-how supplier, a down payment is made which can be 20–30% of the that know-how fees. When basic engineering package is delivered, along with its fees, the balance 50–60% of the fees may be paid. The remaining 10–20% of know-how fees are paid after guarantee runs during plant commissioning are performed, to the satisfaction of the project owner. The above split is indicative and depends on both parties, namely, the know-how supplier and project owner.

### 5.6.2 Basic Engineering Package

The basic engineering package (BEP) is given as an integral part of know-how by the process licensor. For commodity chemicals such as urea, methanol, the process licensor provides BEP against some fees. If fees are paid in foreign currency, we need to pay tax in Rupees as in the case of know-how fees. In the case of special products such as perfumes, cosmetics, process licensor may not be in a position to supply BEP the way it is understood by project engineering organisations. Under such circumstances, the know-how supplier may engage services of Indian project engineering organisation, for preparing the Basic Engineering Package. Appendix 5.1 outlines contents of a typical Basic Engineering Package, to appreciate this term.

It should be noted that the know-how along the Basic Engineering Package, is given for the battery limit plant.

### 5.6.3 Detailed Engineering

Detailed engineering consists of engineering of an entire project for purchase of equipments, piping, instrumentation, electricals, and construction of a plant. At the end of detailed engineering, wherein a concept is translated into a plant having full-fledged facilities for the production of the desired product. Broadly speaking, detailed engineering is a conglomeration of technical and non-technical activities to make a project function.

Appendix 5.2 exhibits in broad terms the scope of various engineering disciplines while constructing the project. Depending upon the size of organisation, the engineering groups/division may be merged. For instance, small organisation may club mechanical and piping engineering together. However, the scope of work remains unaltered.

In cost-plus type of contract, the detailed engineering fees are mentioned as Rupees per man-hour and the total estimated man-hours are given resulting in the detailed engineering fees. The man-hour rate is the weighted average rate for each category of services or activities of all people including the heads of departments, design engineers, draftsmen, secretarial staff, organisational overheads and the most important 'profit'. The man-hours required, are obtained from various heads of department while senior management decides on man-hour rate. It is obvious that small organisations would have lower man-hour rates as compared to that by international project engineering contractors having ISO accreditation to their credit. Apart from detailed engineering activities outlined in Appendix 5.2, the detailed engineering contractor can offer services at a lump sum fees for overall project management, procurement of equipment and materials, inspection of various fabricated items at various levels of fabrication, expediting the same to adhere to project schedule, and finally construction of the plant. Once the plant is constructed, many times, the plant commissioning is also included in the scope of work. Thus the word 'detailed engineering' will include fees towards all the above activities as desired by the project owner. By and large, the detailed engineering is done by Indian project engineering company. Under special circumstances, permission may be obtained from the concerned authorities including the Reserve Bank of India to have detailed engineering contractor from a foreign country. For example, very big projects, such as power projects, where the entire funding is from the foreign promoter, the overall responsibility of project can be entrusted to foreign engineering contractor who inturn may appoint Indian sub-contractors. Many times, a common mistake is made to judge detailed engineering fees as some percentage of project cost. It should be noted that detailed engineering of distillation column system (column, reboiler, condenser, feed pre-heater) having material of construction, stainless steel 316 takes as much efforts as that made of carbon steel. However, the system price would be totally different. The former system could be 4 to 5 times costlier than that of carbon steel. The detailed engineering fees as per cent (%) of SS316 system would be far less than that of system made of carbon steel.

In addition to detailed engineering many times engineering services include procurement and construction services also. The contract then becomes EPC contract (Engineering, Procurement and Construction services).

The Know-How and Basic Engineering Package if resourced from foreign process licensor attract GST (Please refer to Service Accounting codes (SAC) of GST legal book). For a quick estimate one may consider it to be at the rate 18% in the absence of information. If know-how and Basic Engineering package is sourced from a foreign process licensor, GST has to be in Indian currency. The offer by Indian Engineering contractor (Detailed Engineering or EPC) includes GST.

**Table 5.5** Know-how and Engineering schedule

| | ₹ | *FEC* | ₹ *Total* |
|---|---|---|---|
| 1. Know–How or License fee | | | |
| GST | | | |
| 2. Basic Engineering Package | | | |
| GST | | | |
| 3. Detailed Engineering or EPC services | | | |

Specify Foreign currency say, 1 US Dollar \$ = X ₹, 1 Euro € = Y₹, 1 Japan Yen ¥, = Z ₹ as on xx month XXXX year.

For a turn-key contract all are considered as one lump activity and then GST is applied.

In the above schedule, while estimating rupees equivalent to foreign Exchange, the foreign currency should be clearly stated along with the prevailing currency exchange rate and the date. The identification of currency basket and foreign exchange rate would help in quick revision of the estimate for different time, should the need arise.

**Appendix 5.1** Contents of Basic Engineering Package

Following are the typical content headings of the Basic Engineering Package (BEP) given by the process licensor,

1. Design Basis
2. Process Description
3. Process Flow Diagram with Material and Energy Balance
4. Process Data Sheets
5. Preliminary P&IDs (Piping and Instrumentation Diagrams)
6. Utility Summary and for Larger Plant Utility Flow Diagram
7. Emissions (Gaseous, Liquid and Solid Effluents)
8. Instrumentation and Process Control: Philosophy and Overview
9. Instrument Process Data Sheets
10. Instrument Trip Schedule
11. Hazard Area Classification
12. Electrical Consumption Summary
13. Emergency Power Requirement
14. Piping Specification Index
15. Health and Safety Data
16. Building Specification

17. Equipment Layout (within battery limit area)
18. Quality Control
19. Plant Operating Manual

Please note that, in general, the detailed engineering contractor in consultation with the process licensor develops P&IDS.

## Appendix 5.2 The Scope of Work of Various Engineering Disciplines

The overall scope of various engineering disciplines during the detailed engineering is given below to appreciate and hence enable to estimate man-hours required for the detailed engineering.

### PROCESS ENGINEERING

Process engineers are essentially Chemical Engineers. The scope includes the following:

- Prepare a detailed techno-economic feasibility report for the project.
- Review of basic engineering package (BEP) received from the process licensor.
- Prepare basic engineering package (BEP) for outside battery limit facilities (OSBL) and effluent treatment plant.
- Prepare of piping and instrumentation diagrams (P&ID) in consultation with piping and instrumentation engineers.
- Assist in preparation of plot plan and equipment layout.
- Coordinate with other engineers during detailed engineering.
- Assist in seeking statutory clearances required for implanting the project.
- Provide assistance during project (process) commissioning.

### MECHANICAL ENGINEERING

This department generally comprises mechanical engineering graduates. Chemical Engineers with some experience can also be considered suitable for this job. The overview of scope of activities is given below:

- Prepare mechanical/fabrication specifications for all equipments such as heat exchangers, pumps, compressors, turbines, reactors, tanks, columns distillation/absorption, and so on, in such a way that process data sheet and mechanical specifications would be adequate enough for vendors to give realistic offers.
- Prepare specifications for systems such as steam generators (boiler), water treatment, cooling tower, turbines and compressors, refrigeration plant, air-conditioning, solid handling and so on.
- Review technical offers along with general arrangement (GA) drawing.

- Prepare load list in consultation with process engineers for all equipments, for civil engineers, to estimate and design foundation and structural supports, considering various rotating/mounting and vibrating equipment or machinery.
- Review technical bids by vendors for equipments along with the client and, if required, with process licensor, in some typical cases.
- Prepare and check fabrication drawings.
- Provide technical liaison within various engineering departments within the organisation and with client as well as vendor also.
- Prepare lube schedule and maintenance schedule for critical equipments or system, such as turbines, compressors, conveyors and so on.

## PIPING ENGINEERING

Piping engineering though often neglected, is a very important discipline in any continuous production unit. As such there is no professional degree for piping engineering, however, engineers with a post-graduate diploma/certificate course along with basic degree in chemical or mechanical engineering are the most compatible. The overall scope includes the following functions:

- Prepare a plot plan as well as equipment layout drawings in consultation with process, mechanical and civil engineers and seek approvals from the project owner as well as process licensor particularly from the safety point of view.
- Prepare/assist in layouts of tank farm, keeping in mind area classification based on hazards and seek statutory approvals.
- Prepare specifications for firefighting system with layouts of fire hydrants and sprinklers.
- Prepare/check general arrangement drawings of various systems such as refrigeration system, steam generators, inert gas generators, instrument air, and so on.
- Prepare insulation (hot or cold) specifications and painting specification indices of equipment, pipes, in consultation with process/mechanical engineers.
- Assist in developing P&I diagrams.
- Review piping specifications given by the licensor in Basic engineering package, with the aim to maximise indigenous components.
- Carry out stress analysis and provide support in case of various pipes running to and fro in the plant.
- Estimate the material take off for all piping material.
- Prepare specifications for piping material and assess offers given by various vendors.
- Prepare drawings for steam lines to seek approvals from the inspectorate of boilers.

- Prepare isometrics of piping layouts for pipes having diameter of, say, more than 150 to 200 mm.
- Interact with vendor for developing and fabricating plant model.

## CIVIL ENGINEERING

The engineers working in this department are civil engineers. The major scope encompasses the following:

- Develop a plot plan and equipment layout in consultation with other engineers, viz., process, mechanical, piping, electrical, etc.
- Prepare building layout in consultation with the architect, the owner, and other engineers.
- Prepare foundation drawing and carry out detailed design for building construction.
- Prepare enquiry documents for site development, civil and structural construction work.
- Prepare design drawings/specifications for various roads in the plant area and approach road, for strengthening of bridges on approach road (if required).
- Prepare the material take-off for structural steel, cement, etc.
- Review all offers for various civil works in the project.
- Have a liaison with the architect for general landscaping, and for staff colony, etc.
- Assist in preparing the plant model.

## ELECTRICAL ENGINEERING

Engineers working in this department are basically electrical engineers. In some exceptional cases, chemical engineers with total familiarity with electrical engineering aspects of a chemical plant may also be team members. Following activities would give overall scope of work of electrical engineers:

- Prepare single-line diagram with the help of BEP for major power-consuming units.
- Design power receiving and distribution system.
- Prepare zone-wise electrical load summary for the entire project, e.g. battery limit plant, utilities blocks, storage facility, effluent treatment plant, etc.
- Design high tension (HT) and low tension (LT) system.
- Prepare area classification (based on hazards) in consultation with process engineers.
- Carry out electrical system design with the help of area classification.
- In consultation with process engineers, process licensor and client, decide emergency power requirement and design system to generate and distribute the same.

- Prepare cable layout drawings identifying location of motors, push buttons for start-up or shut down, motor control cabinets.
- Prepare power and lighting layout drawings including cable trays, trenches, along with specifications of lighting fittings, etc., keeping in mind the area classification.
- Prepare specifications and review bids later on for HT&LT equipment, including transformer, switch gears, HT & LT motors, etc.
- Prepare material take-off for electrical items, such as cables, and for their installations.
- Design and install electrical safety systems such as earthing and lightening arrestors.
- Design public communication system.
- Prepare drawings and provide technical support to project manager to seek statutory approvals.
- Assist in plant commissioning.

### INSTRUMENTATION ENGINEERING

Engineers working in this department can be Instrumentation engineers, chemical engineers or electronics engineers. The main activities are centerd on process control by monitoring and controlling various process variables.

- Review of basic engineering package (BEP)
- Assist process engineers in developing P&I diagrams
- Prepare instrument schedule
- Design and specify control systems
- Prepare instrument, installation document to invite bids, review of the same
- Review vendors' bids for various instrument items and panels
- Prepare material take-off
- Assist in process commissioning.

## 5.7 EXPENSES ON FOREIGN TECHNICIANS AND TRAINING OF INDIAN TECHNICIANS ABROAD

During process commissioning of a project, we may require technical assistance of people from the process licensor. The licensor may include this as a part of know-how or may charge the project owner separately. In the second option, the project owner pays for air and surface travel, lodging and boarding in India. This expenditure is in rupees. In addition, the project owner has to pay in foreign currency at daily rate, known as per-diem rate, as per the guidelines of the Government. The foreign currency payment to the process licensor would attract tax to be paid in rupees. Thus knowing numbers of persons required for commissioning, we can estimate, with reasonable accuracy, this expenditure because air travel (to and fro), lodging and boarding expense, surface travel expenses are well known. The expenditure on people being trained abroad is also estimated in this way, and based on this foreign exchange is released in advance. Before signing the contract with know-how supplier, one can negotiate to include local lodging boarding, incidental expenses of training personnel, which would be looked after by the process licensor. There is no tax burden to project owner on this foreign currency expenditure. Tables 5.6 and 5.7 exhibit format of this schedule.

**Table 5.6** Expenses on Foreign Technicians in India for Commissioning

*Total Number of Persons* :
*Per Diem rate* : *US $/day persons*

| | *₹ FEC* | *₹* | *Total* |
|---|---|---|---|
| 1. Fees to the process licensor | | | |
| 2. GST | | | |
| 3. Air travel, lodging, boarding and other incidental expenses | | | |
| Total | | | |

**Table 5.7** Expenses on Training of Indian Technicians Abroad

*Total Number of Persons* =
*Per Diem rate* =

| | *₹ FEC* | *₹* | *Total* |
|---|---|---|---|
| 1. Expenses in foreign country | | | |
| 2. Air Travel (To & fro) | | | |
| Total | | | |

Exchange rate 1 US $ = *X* ₹.
1 Euro € = *Y* ₹.
1 Yen ¥ = *Z* ₹.
as on XX Month XXXX Year

## 5.8 MISCELLANEOUS FIXED ASSETS

Miscellaneous fixed assets (MFAs) account for various fixed assets, which have been not accounted in earlier components of the project cost. These assets, as we shall see, are equally important for smooth running of a project.

A clear-cut distinction is made between vehicles, computers and other assets of the project under consideration and this is mainly for computation of depreciation because depreciation rates are different for vehicles, computers and the other fixed assets. All company-owned vehicles such as cars, jeeps, ambulances, buses for transporting people if public transport system is not adequate, special tankers for transporting raw materials or finished goods or products and firefighting vehicles are included in 'Vehicles'.

The non-vehicle component includes furniture and fixtures for offices, R&D Centre, control room, security room, time office, canteen, change room, workers amenities, medical dispensary, etc. Also included are facsimile, telephone machines, telex machine, photocopiers, desktop computers or central computational facilities, laser printers, etc. Further, other items like water-coolers; aquaguards, air conditioners, firefighting equipment, plant model, etc., are included in miscellaneous fixed assets.

Computers and printers are counted separately due to different rate of depreciation.

Table 5.8 exhibits components of the Miscellaneous Fixed Assets schedule of the project cost.

**Table 5.8** Miscellaneous Fixed Assets

| | ₹ | *Total* |
|---|---|---|
| 1. Vehicles | | |
| Cars | | |
| Trucks | | |
| Buses | | |
| Firefighting vehicles | | |
| 2. Miscellaneous Assets | | |
| Others as described earlier | | |
| 3. Computers | | |
| Total | | |

The overall contribution of MFA to the project cost is in the range of 1–5%. This is not significant yet it is important. Hence during estimate too many man-hours need not be spent on this item.

Miscellaneous Fixed Assets, as one can appropriate normally, does not involve any foreign currency expenditure.

Please note that the foreign exchange component is generally not there unless special computers or firefighting tenders are imported.

## 5.9 CONTINGENCIES

Contingencies provision is made in the project cost to take care of under estimating of various estimates of project cost components. While preparing a detailed techno-economic feasibility report, it is not possible to have an accurate idea of various expenses. At this stage, since detailed engineering is not done, estimates of particularly, piping, electrical and instrumentation are likely to have more negative deviation from reality than those in case of plant and machinery items. The offers from various vendors are budgetary in nature. The in-house data may bring more uncertainty in estimate, as it may be obsolete and not specific. An excessive estimate may result in abandoning a project which otherwise was viable. If estimates are on reasonably higher side (than those realised at later stage) it does not matter. However, if resulting project cost estimate were to be far lower than that would have actually incurred (based on detailed engineering), the project owner has to generate additional funds and resources to meet the project cost escalation (which no owner would like to do). This is one of the factors responsible for project cost overruns. In order to take care of the above, contingencies provisions are made. Let us examine each component of project cost and try to identify components wherein contingencies provision can be made.

*Land and Site Development*

The land price is usually known in advance. However, the estimate of development of the site may need some contingencies.

*Building and Civil Work*

Despite the fact that rates of RCC, cement, structural steel are known with accuracy, the estimated quantity may deviate from the actual and, hence, contingencies provision should be made for building and civil works.

*Plant and Machinery*

This item of project cost needs contingencies provision because it involves several varied estimates, i.e. estimates of piping, electrical and instrumentation quantities, etc., which are done in the absence of detailed engineering and, therefore, are likely to have underestimates in some cases.

*Know-how and Engineering*

Though know-how fees are known in advance, the fees of basic engineering, and particularly, detailed engineering depends on deviations in scope of work. As a result contingencies are recommended here also.

*Expenses on Foreign Technicians and Training of Indian People Abroad*

It is desirable to have provision of contingencies because of the very nature of expenses.

*Miscellaneous Fixed Assets*

These are pure estimates many times on lump sum basis, out of blue except those for vehicles. As a result contingencies are recommended here also.

*Pre-operative Expenses*

These expenses are known with fair accuracy. There are some uncertainties regarding cost of the project office, establishment charges, legal expenses and cash outflow schedule during the construction period. The major contribution comes from the interest during the period of construction. Once cash inflows and outflows have been decided, interest can be accurately computed. Therefore, contingencies provision may not be a bad idea.

*Preliminary and Capital Issue Related Expenses*

Once financing pattern of the project is fixed, capital issue related expenses are known with fair accuracy and hence it is not recommended to have contingencies for the same.

*Margin Money*

Here consumptions of raw materials and utilities are well defined by the process licensor. The cost of production, selling price, credit to debtors, cash cost being reasonably well defined. The uncertainties associated with estimate of working capital (and hence margin money) are practically absent. Therefore, no contingencies provision is recommended for margin money. (Of course, one has to the consider particular case under study and then apply contingencies provision.)

Generally speaking, estimates for site development, building and civil work, plant and machinery, know-how and engineering, expenses on foreign technicians and Indians being trained abroad, and miscellaneous fixed assets pre-operative expenses are added together inclusive of Rupee equivalent to of foreign exchange components (FECs) and 10% of the above sum is deemed as the contingencies. By and large, it is in Indian Rupees. The project owner, after all, is required to satisfy financial institutions in case he is seeking term loan!

## 5.10 PRE-OPERATIVE EXPENSES

Pre-operative expenses are, in true sense, various expenses which have not been accounted so far but are actually incurred prior to smooth implementation and, hence, operation of a project under consideration. Table 5.9 exhibits elements of pre-operative expenses.

**Table 5.9** Elements of Pre-operative Expenses

| *Element* | *Cost (₹)* |
|---|---|
| Project office cost | |
| Establishment charges during the period of construction | |
| Feasibility report and market search report | |
| Insurance | |
| Mortgage and legal expenses | |
| Start-up expenses | |
| Financial expenses during the period of construction | |
| Total | |

Pre-operative expenses are distributed over entire project construction period. Let us discuss the meaning of various elements of pre-operative expenses.

### 5.10.1 Project Office Cost

The project office cost consists of cost associated in terms of salaries and wages, perquisites and overheads of all persons related to project implementation at the site. They include the project site manager, project site engineers, project accountants, supporting administrative and clerical staff, and the security personnel. Key persons are in the employment right from the first day while some supporting persons are employed as the project progresses. These persons are employed by the project owner and not by project implementation contractor. These people are absorbed suitably once project gets process commissioned. Their salaries and wages along with perquisites are considered here during the period of construction. The project office cost should also include their travelling and communication expenses. Office-stationary, etc., are included in overheads. Though the entire project cost will not be sensitive to project office cost, it is essential that realistic estimates are made taking into account the prevailing conditions.

**Table 5.10** Project Office Cost Estimate

| *Project Construction Period: × Months* | | | | |
|---|---|---|---|---|
| | *Number of People Employed* | *Salary* | *Perks* | *Total (₹)* |
| | Managers | | | |
| | Engineers | | | |
| | Account officers | | | |
| | Technical officers | | | |
| | Clerical staff | | | |
| | Security staff | | | |
| | Workers | | | |
| A | Total | | | |
| B | Project office overheads | | | |
| | Total project office cost (A + B) = | | | |

### 5.10.2 Establishment Charges During Period of Construction

Various personnel required for smooth running of a plant are recruited during the period of construction so that mechanical as well as process commissioning are carried out smoothly. All these persons need not be employed from the first day of project construction. For instance, people working in maintenance department are required only after rotating machinery (compressors, blowers, centrifuges, etc.) is delivered at site and is being erected and tested at site. The presence of maintenance personnel would enable them to understand machinery better and hence possibly this would result in better maintenance practice. The plant operators and quality control chemists are recruited just before the plant is getting ready for process commissioning.

Thus we see that as the project construction progresses, project owner would recruit more and more personnel. At the end of construction (and just before process commissioning) all persons required to run/operate the project would have been recruited. Salaries, perquisites and overhead expenses associated with them are then estimated realistically to arrive at establishment charges during the period of construction.

It should be noted that 'ideally', when plant starts production, the total number of people employed would be equal to (or more than) the sum of people under headings 'project office cost' and 'establishment charges' during the period of construction.

**Table 5.11** Establishment Charges During Period of Construction

| *Project Construction Period: × Months*<br>*Manpower Category* | *Employment Duration* | *Salary* | *Perks* | *Total (₹)* |
|---|---|---|---|---|
| Engineers | | | | |
| Maintenance Personnel | | | | |
| Chemists | | | | |
| Operators | | | | |
| Overheads | | | | |

### 5.10.3 Feasibility Report and Market Search Report

The project owner pays fees to detailed engineering contractor, for preparing detailed techno-economic feasibility report, also a called 'bankable document' to seek 'term loan' from financial institutions. All expenses towards feasibility report are included here. Market search report is prepared by competitive market search agency. Generally speaking, detailed engineering contractor does not prepare market search report, but incorporates salient findings about prevailing market and futuristic projections to make a comprehensive document. All expenses towards such market survey report are considered here.

### 5.10.4 Insurance

Typically, one can make provision of 0.5% (plant and machinery *plus* buildings cost) towards insurance premium or as per the recommendations of the insurance agency.

### 5.10.5 Mortgage and Legal Expenses

A provision should be made (lump sum amount) towards mortgage and legal expenses, in case the need arises as the project takes shape.

### 5.10.6 Start-up Expenses

Start-up expenses are those expenses likely to be incurred during process commissioning. The process licensor, based on his experience, indicates the time required to have guarantee runs of production. During this period one needs to make available raw materials and all utilities. In case of Petrochemical plants, from safety point of view, one needs to flush all process lines with an inert gas such as $N_2$. The expenditure towards $N_2$ during start-up could be substantial.

### 5.10.7 Financial Expenses During the Period of Construction

This last item of pre-operative expenses schedule is the most important item because its contribution to pre-operative expenses could be as high as 80%. Therefore, it is essential to understand how computations are made to arrive at financial expenses in the form of interest liability on the borrowed capital (term loan) during project construction period.

The entire project construction period is divided into small finite period, say, each of two months. Thus continuous construction activity has two months grids. For example, a project with a construction period of 30 months, can have 15 grids each of two months or 10 grids each of three months. Based on the past experience, cash outflow from the project in these discrete zones (grids) can be estimated, based on 'guessed' project cost. For example, land and site development expenditure can be incurred in first two to three months. Buildings and civil work can commence after site development is over or depending upon topography, can commence when site development is partly done. The activities towards detailed engineering start right from the first day with some down payment made to engineering contractor. The payment to him continues till the project is commissioned. The know-how fees are partly paid in advance, then after the receipt of basic engineering package and then partly (10–15%) after the plant or project is process commissioned and guarantees are fulfilled. While placing an order with the fabricator, an advance payment is made and thereafter in between payment may be required, say after inspection, this is followed by when equipment is dispatched and assembled at site. The schedule of payment to vendor depends upon the type of equipment and hence complexity of installation and mechanical commissioning. When capital issue is floated, we need money for preliminary and capital issue related expenditure. By and large public issue is floated towards the last quarter of project construction period. Margin money (25% of working capital) is required towards the end just before commissioning and so are the start-up expenses. Based on the above rationale, one can construct the entire project cost cash outflow statement with clear-cut indication of the money required in any grid. For the easy computation of interest, it is assumed that the entire expenditure in any grid is deemed to have occurred at the end of that period. For instance, the entire expenditure during the fourth, fifth and sixth month is deemed to incur at the end of sixth month. The error introduced due to this simplification does not change the project cost appreciably and it is well within acceptable limit.

Thus with the help of the rationale and procedure discussed, one can construct project cost cash requirement statement for a specific interval and hence over the entire project construction period. This is illustrated in Table 5.12.

The cash requirement is met through funds made available for the project. We shall deal separately on how to finance a project in Chapter 8. The cash requirement of any project is first met through the 'subsidy' (state or central) if available. Then promoter's contribution is taken to meet the cash requirement. 'Term loan' from financial institutions (ICICI, IDBI, etc.) is taken in instalments as per requirements to meet the projected expenditure. In case of a public limited project, shareholder's contribution is considered to meet the expenditure for the last few months of project construction period. Thus, we can have cash inflow statement, grid-wise, for financing the project under construction.

The term loan taken from the financial institution attracts interest charges (simple interest) as per interest rate fixed by the Reserve Bank of India. It is seen that entire term loan is not taken at once, but taken as per requirement over the construction period. As a result the interest liability would differ, from one interval to

**Table 5.12** Interest During Period of Construction

*Fund Flow Statement during construction period: 24 months, 2 months grid*

| *Project Cost Component (with contingencies)* | *1* | *2* | *3* | *4* | *5* | *6* | *7* | *8* | *9* | *10* | *11* | *12* |
|---|---|---|---|---|---|---|---|---|---|---|---|---|
| 1. Land and site development | ✓ | ✓ | | | | | | | | | | |
| 2. Building | ✓ | ✓ | ✓ | ✓ | ✓ | ✓ | ✓ | ✓ | ✓ | ✓ | | |
| 3. Plant and machinery | ✓ | ✓ | ✓ | ✓ | ✓ | ✓ | ✓ | ✓ | ✓ | ✓ | ✓ | |
| 4. Know-how | ✓ | ✓ | | | | | | | | | | ✓ |
| 5. Detailed egg | ✓ | ✓ | ✓ | ✓ | ✓ | ✓ | ✓ | ✓ | ✓ | ✓ | ✓ | ✓ |
| 6. Expenses of training of persons | | | | | | | ✓ | ✓ | ✓ | ✓ | | |
| 7. Miscellaneous fixed assets | | | | | | | | ✓ | ✓ | | ✓ | ✓ |
| 8. Pre-operative exp. | ✓ | ✓ | ✓ | ✓ | ✓ | ✓ | ✓ | ✓ | ✓ | ✓ | ✓ | ✓ |
| 9. Prelim & issue related exp. | | | | | | | | | | ✓ | ✓ | ✓ |
| 10. Margin money | | | | | | | | | | | | ✓ |
| TOTAL | X1 | X2 | X3 | X4 | X5 | X6 | X7 | X8 | X9 | X10 | X11 | X12 |
| Fund flow | | | | | | | | | | | | |
| Subsidy | | | | | | | | | | | | |
| Promoter's | ✓ | | | | | | | | | | | |
| Promoters' contribution | ✓ | ✓ | ✓ | | | | | | | | | |
| Term loan | | | | ✓ | ✓ | ✓ | ✓ | ✓ | ✓ | ✓ | | |
| Public issue | | | | | | | | | | | ✓ | ✓ |
| | Y1 | Y2 | Y3 | Y4 | Y5 | Y6 | Y7 | Y8 | Y9 | Y10 | Y11 | Y12 |

the other. For example, the term loan taken at the end of eighth month would attract interest for Sixteen months (if project construction period is twenty-four months). Similarly, term loan at the end of eighteenth month would attract interest of six months only; and so on. Thus, we can compute total interest liability on term loan, during the project construction period. This interest along with other components would make total pre-operative expenses. Once pre-operative expenses are known, the project cost can be estimated. Based on agreed debt: equity ratio, we can compute now term loan and repeat. The entire procedure to arrive at the project cost, through computation of interest during the period of construction, is bit of a trial and error procedure. The experienced manager would not take more than two-three trials to have the right estimate project post.

By having public issue earlier than term loan, we can substantially 'decrease' the interest burden during the period of construction. It means that the project cost can now be reduced. Therefore, one can reduce the 'Project Cost' by properly timing the public issue. All that matters is the confidence of shareholders in the organisation to deliver 'hefty' dividend. Established organisations can take the risk even for their Greenfield or Grassroots project by having public issue at an early date.

Thus, now it is possible to have estimate of pre-operative expenses by adding all components together.

The expenditure in grid No. 4 is *X*4 is met by term loan *Y*4 that attracts interest. The expenditure during sixth and eighth month of construction is deemed to have occurred at the end of the month. Therefore, it would attract interest for 16, i.e. (24–8) months at simple interest rate as agreed with financial institution. Table 5.13 depicts the same.

**Table 5.13** The Details of Interest Computed

| *Amount of Term Loan* | *Period of Interest (Months)* | *Interest* ₹ |
|---|---|---|
| Y4 | 16 | Z4 |
| Y5 | 14 | Z5 |
| Y6 | 12 | Z6 |
| Y7 | 10 | Z7 |
| Y8 | 8 | Z8 |
| Y9 | 6 | Z9 |
| Y10 | 4 | Z10 |
| Y11 | 2 | Z11 |
| Y12 | 0 | 0 |
| | | Σ |

## 5.11 PRELIMINARY AND CAPITAL ISSUE RELATED EXPENSES

Expenses incurred during the formation of a public limited company and other initial expenses are known as preliminary expenses.

In order to estimate public issue related expenses, we should know total quantum of public issue. The public issue related expenses are as follows:

- Brokerage and underwriting commission to banks managing public issue, which together can be 2–3% of the public issue.
- The other expenses to include are legal expenses towards the public issue, if any, printing of stationery and advertisement news media, television coverage, etc., These can be between 3 and 5% of the public issue.

Thus, we see that total preliminary and capital issue related expenses could be between 5 and 7% of public issue. Generally, 7% is adequate depending upon the accuracy of estimate.

The main question yet to be addressed is the quantum of the public issue. This would be discussed at length in Chapter 8.

The project cost is divided into two components, namely, term loan (debt) and equity depending on debt: equity ratio. From the equity portion a maximum of 49% can be public issue while 51% would be the contribution from promoters. Once we know the public issue, estimate of capital issue related expenses could be prepared.

Table 5.14 exhibits contents of this component of project cost. There would not be any foreign exchange expenditure unless issue is floated globally (like Euro-issue).

**Table 5.14** Preliminary and Capital Issue Related Expenses

| | ₹ *FEC* | ₹ | *Total* |
|---|---|---|---|
| 1. Preliminary expenses –1% of issue | – | ✓ | ✓ |
| 2. Brokerage underwriting commission % of issue | – | ✓ | ✓ |
| 3. Capital issue related expenses – % of public issue | – | ✓ | ✓ |
| Total | | | |

## 5.12 MARGIN MONEY (WORKING CAPITAL)

The margin money is the part of working capital, which is capitalised as a component of the project cost. Though it is possible to negotiate on the amount of margin money with the financial institution funding the project, it is desirable to estimate the same. This estimate inturn would facilitate negotiations. Therefore, we shall see how to estimate working capital and hence the margin money.

### 5.12.1 Working Capital

As the name suggests working capital is the capital required to make project work perform. When the project is commissioned and handed over to the production team to generate cash, the owner needs cash to meet expenses towards raw materials, utilities, packing material, salaries and wages of project personnel, maintenance spares, etc. Once products are manufactured, a substantial inventory is maintained to meet continuous demand of products. While some buyers might pay immediately, others might require credit for differed payments. The project owner is expected to run the entire show on money generated (cash inflow) by selling products. Thus we are in 'Catch 22 situation'. Unless you produce you cannot generate cash and unless you have cash with you to meet the expenditure at the beginning of production you cannot produce. In order to overcome this difficulty, project owner needs some money on hand to make the project function and, hence, the name Working capital.

For ongoing projects, working capital may also be required depending upon the financial health of the project. In that case working capital is defined as current assets *less* current liabilities (other than short-term bank borrowings). Current assets are those, which can be easily converted into cash (money).

Reserve Bank of India, in 1974, constituted a study group under the chairmanship of Mr P. Tandon to evolve some guidelines for banks to meet credit needs of entrepreneurs. This committee suggested some norms, popularly known as the Tandon Committee norms, for working capital. With liberalisation, it is now left to bankers and entrepreneurs to have their own arrangement for working capital.

The Tandon Committee recommended three approaches to compute working capital bank borrowings (RBI 1988).

1. The project owner needs to provide 25% from the owned funds and term loan the difference between total current assets and current liabilities excluding bank borrowings. This means banker would finance 75% of the working capital at agreed rates of interest and loan repayment schedule.

2. The project owner is expected to provide 25% of the total current assets, of term loan. A certain level of credit would be available for purchases and other current liabilities. The commercial bank would then provide the balance. The total liability would be less than 75% of current assets.
3. Same as in above (2) excluding core current assets from the total assets.

The first method being simpler for new proposed projects, we shall discuss the same here.

In the light of the above, it is desirable for engineers to know the meaning of current assets and current liabilities.

Current Assets Include the following elements:

- Raw materials available in stock for the main product as well as required for utilities such as fuel oil, thermic fluid, refrigerant, catalyst, and so on.
- Products and by-products in stock (at the cost of production).
- In-process stock, which comprises raw materials and chemicals within the process irrespective of nature of intermediate. For example, if it takes four days for naphtha to get reformed into aromatics and emerge as benzene, *p*-xylene and *o*-xylene as products in aromatics complex, the in-process stock would be four days consumption of naphtha, at a price of naphtha.
- Packing material has a considerable role in some consumer product industries. While petro-products are sold in tankers, drums, etc., pharmaceuticals, cosmetics and toiletries need very attractive packing. The stock of packing material in such an industry could be significant.
- Maintenance spare.
- Also included is cash and customer account (credit to customers who have not paid for goods and services received).

*Current Liabilities*

Current liabilities represent the short-term finance and include items like bank short-term loans, bank overdraft and trade accounts payable.

When the project is about to commence production in true sense, there are neither current liabilities nor current assets. It should be noted here that 'cash' under current assets means (in case of new projects) cash required to pay salaries of personnel and to support administrative expenses inclusive of salaries/wages for administrative people, sales expenditure and factory overheads.

### 5.12.2 Estimation of Working Capital Proposed Project

The Tandon Committee, after considerable amount of deliberations with industries has recommended norms for inventories and receivable (RBI 1988). The committee recommended norms for variety of industries such as cotton and synthetic textiles, man-made fibre, jute textiles, rubber products, fertilisers (N&P), pharmaceuticals, dyes and dyestuffs, basic industrial chemicals, vegetable and hydrogenated oils, paper industry and cement industry, and so on. Depending upon the industry, logistics between the raw material source and production site as well as that between they production site and market, the inventory period (recommended) would change. Over the last three decades (The Tandon Committee was constituted in 1974), surface transportation facilities (road, rail, and sea) have improved considerably. Port facilities, cargo-handling systems have been updated. As a result, it is obvious that some inventory norms can change radically. Therefore, to begin with we recommend following norms for petrochemicals in general. These are just guidelines and, therefore, be used with discretion.

All consumption figures for the proposed unit are worked out for 100% capacity utilisation, despite the fact that in the first year, capacity utilisation might have been considered to be 60–65% (see cost of production) for the feasibility report.

#### 5.12.2.1 Raw Materials

The storage of raw materials (stock of raw material) could be between one week to even four months depending upon the ease of availability and logistics involved. If the plant is located next to the raw material source inventory could be that of one week or even less. For example, a polybutene project based on isobutene ($iC_4$) from FCC Cracker located next to the refinery, $C_4$ stream would have an inventory of not more than even 3 days. On the other hand, an alpha-olefin sulphonate project based on imported alpha-olefin would require large inventory of the same (may be four months) depending upon minimum size of the consignment (ship-cargo). Thus the project owner/manager has to use his discretion and be realistic. The bankers would not permit 'flabby and profit making inventory' (rationale behind the Tandon Committee norms).

#### 5.12.2.2 Utilities

In utilities, raw materials required for generation of utilities are considered. For instance, if a power plant is constructed for captive consumption based on heavy residues of vacuum distillation unit (VDU) of refinery (gasification followed by a combined cycle) the inventory could be 15 days. In case steam is generated in a boiler, the fuel required, for instance, low sulphur heavy stock (LSHS), could be stored for 15 days or one month depending upon the ease of availability of LSHS at the production site.

When the power is purchased from the State Electricity Board, a provision for billing for one month could be made depending upon the project owner's agreement with the State Industrial Development Corporation and the State Electricity Board.

#### 5.12.2.3 Packaging Material

Packaging material is very important in pharmaceuticals, oils and fats industries, soap, toiletries and detergent industries, paints industry, etc. Depending upon the logistics of supply and need of packing materials, an inventory of 15 days to one month is adequate.

#### 5.12.2.4 Maintenance Spares

A provision is made for maintenance spare as 1% of plant and machinery item of project cost for one month. The majority of equipment is covered under the guarantee and warranty clause. The spares required are mainly for piping, electricals and instrumentation.

#### 5.12.2.5 Product Inventory

The logistics between the production site and marketplace decides the product inventory. For instance, for local consumer items, such as detergents, the inventory could be one month at the cost of production. On the other hand, in an export-oriented project, the project inventory could be as high as two months also. The working capital requirement for product inventory would be at the cost of production and not at the selling price.

#### 5.12.2.6 In-process Stock

One should have a good knowledge of the production process involving all unit processes and unit operations while raw materials are getting transformed into value-added products. It is difficult to ascertain values to various intermediates formed in the process. The residence time of the entire process material is considered and it is taken into consideration while computing in-process stock at the price of raw materials. A multi-stage process, like the manufacture of 'H' acid from crude naphthalene, would have a residence time, say, 7–10 days while a much simpler process of manufacture of formaldehyde (37–40% aqueous) from methanol can have a residence time of one day. It is obvious that multi-stage batch processes would have more residence time than continuous processes.

#### 5.12.2.7 Customer's Account (Credit to Debtors)

Customer's credit is deemed to be one month at the selling price of products for computation of working capital.

#### 5.12.2.8 Cash Cost

The cash is required to disburse salary and wages to all people involved in the project. Also, the cash is required to meet overheads, administrative expenses, sales expenses, etc. The working capital required is estimated for one month in this case.

Table 5.15 presents summary of working capital for a proposed project.

Depending upon resourcing of raw materials, catalyst, etc., the working capital and, hence, margin money would have foreign exchange component. The cost inclusive of freight and insurance (CIF) to the nearest cargo terminal (seaport) can be estimated in the absence of details from free on board (FOB) price as,

$$\text{CIF} = 1.1\ \text{FOB}$$

The Rupee equivalent to the CIF price in the foreign currency is obtained by multiplying if with the exchange rate. To this landed price then added the statutory duties and transportation cost to the production site.

Out of this working capital, as a rule of thumb, 25% is capitalised as margin money component of the project cost schedule. The balance 75% of working capital requirement is met through a short-term loan from commercial banks and financial institutions.

With liberalisation of economic policy and accelerated industrial growth, it is now left to bankers and the project owner to arrive at an estimate of reasonable and realistic working capital. While doing so the banker would ensure that no non-performing assets are generated. The above norms presented are merely guidelines for entrepreneur and should be used with discretion having the underline principle that flabby and profit-making inventories are discouraged by bankers.

From foregoing, the importance of working capital is now obvious. Many a times, failure to realistically account for working capital leads to unwanted project cost overruns.

**Table 5.15** Estimate of Working Capital (For the proposed project)

| *No.* | *Item* | *Inventory Months* | ₹ | *FEC* | *Total* |
|---|---|---|---|---|---|
| 1 | Raw materials | | | | |
| | 1.1 | | ✔ | | |
| | ⋮ | | | | |
| | 1.4 Imported raw materials | | | ✔ | |
| 2. | Utilities | | | | |
| | 2.1 | | | × | |
| | ⋮ | | | × | |
| | ⋮ | | | × | |
| 3. | Packing materials | | ✔ | | |
| 4. | Maintenance spares | | ✔ | | |
| 5. | Product inventory at cost of production | | ✔ | | |
| 6. | In-process stock | | | | |
| 7. | Customer's account | | | | |
| 8. | Cash cost | | | | |
| | Working Capital | | | | |

### 5.12.3 Working Capital for Ongoing Product

For ongoing project working capital is commonly referred as net working capital and is given by:

Working Capital or Net Working Capital

$$= \text{Current assests} - \text{Current liabilities} \qquad (5.12.1)$$

## 5.13 THE PROJECT COST SCHEDULE

A schedule of the project cost is now prepared after having carried out the estimate of various components of 'Project Cost', as exhibited in Table 5.16. The estimate of each component should have a back-up estimate (Detailed estimate). For example, land and site development estimate should have all details listed in Table 5.2 under land and site development.

A spreadsheet concept is used for tabulation. It is more helpful in assessing the project. Indian Rupees and Rupee equivalent to foreign exchange component are clearly stated. It is desirable to have a currency basket table. Depending upon the vendors from abroad, the process licensor, we may have to import some items in plant and machinery (even raw materials) from the vendors originating from different countries. For example, the process licensor may be from USA requiring know-how fees and fees for basic engineering package in US Dollars; the supplier for turbine (co-generation unit) may be from Germany requiring payment of equipment in Euro, while some other equipment may be imported from Japan demanding payment in Japanese Yen. Thus, we need to identify the currency requirement, and the exchange rate should be explicitly stated, for example, is equivalent to X ₹ in the prevailing month of the prevailing calendar year. The currency basket table would assist us in great deal when the project is implemented and foreign exchange rates are fluctuating. This would also help us in updating the estimates at a later date.

**Table 5.16** Project Cost Components (Greenfield Project)

| *Sr. No.* | *Component* | ₹ | ₹ *FEC* | *Total* | *Comments* |
|---|---|---|---|---|---|
| 1. | Land and site development | | | | |
| 2. | Building and civil works<br>Factory building<br>Non-factory building | | | | |
| 3. | Plant and machinery | | | | |
| 4. | Know-how and engineering | | | | |
| 5. | Expenses on foreign Technicians and training of Indians abroad | | | | |
| 6. | Miscellaneous fixed assets | | | | |
| 7. | Pre-operative expenses | | | | |
| 8. | Contingencies | | | | |
| 9. | Preliminary and capital issue Related expenses. | | | | |
| 10. | Margin money | ↓ | ↓ | ↓ | |
| | Total | → | → | | |

## REFERENCES

*Application for Financial Assistance:* The booklet by ICICI Mumbai.

*Report of the Study Group to Frame Guidelines for Follow-up of Bank Credits*, The Reserve Bank of India (1988).

*Manual of Industrial Project Analysis in Developing Countries.* IDBI (1980).

***Project Cost Overruns could be fatal.***

# 6 Plant and Machinery

## 6.1 INTRODUCTION

The plant and machinery item of the entire project cost schedule is very important because its contribution to the cost of project is the highest. For example, in case of petrochemical projects the plant and machinery component could be in the range of 40–60% of the project cost. As seen earlier in Chapter 4, the accuracy of an estimate of the project cost is enhanced if we have a reasonably good estimate of the plant and machinery. Therefore, it is desirable to understand various components of the plant and machinery and methods of their cost estimate. In view of its importance it is desirable to devote a separate chapter to the same.

A chemical plant consists of a variety of *equipments* (reactors, heat exchangers, towers for separation, rotating equipment such as pumps, blowers, compressors, turbines, and so on); interconnecting *piping* (pipes, valves, bends, elbows, flanges, etc); *instrumentations* (temperature, pressure and flow mass or volume indicators, controllers, PLC system, DCS systems, etc.) and *electricals* (motor drives, motor control cabinets, power receiving station, emergency power generation and distribution, cable and cable trays etc.). In any plant, since these components make the highest contribution to the cost, selection and sizing of equipments are, therefore, very important.

When an equipment is purchased, by and large, the vendor offers 'ex-works' price. Packing, forwarding and transportation costs are either at actual or at fixed percentage of the equipment cost. The statutory duties such as sales tax, excise, (VAT), octroi and project import duty, as appropriate, are paid at actual. In general, vendors of equipment, piping, electricals and instrumentation supply provide offers as 'ex-works' and are hence transported to the site from the place of fabrication or the warehouse, as the case may be. This involves packaging, forwarding and transportation cost. Further, installation costs are generally ignored but they form a fair amount of capital expenditure. Therefore, installation costs associated with equipment, piping, instrumentation and electricals need to be accounted. In order to conserve energy and to have safe operations in a plant, equipments and piping need to be insulated. For example, steam lines have hot insulation, brine lines have cold insulation, furnaces or fired heaters have multiple layers of different hot insulation, cryogenic storage tanks are protected from heat by cold insulation, and so on. Therefore, one has to include the cost of insulation. Equipment, storage tanks, process pipes, utility lines are painted to protect from external corrosion as per the norms (utility lines have colour codes) and, therefore, painting cost is estimated. Besides, all materials at the site need to be financially secured against the natural calamities, accidents during transportation to the site, storage and installation by way of insurance and, hence, premium is paid. Thus, we see that apart from purchased cost of equipment, piping, electrical and instrumentation, one incurs the above extra expenditure till all equipments and components are installed and hence the plant is made functional. Though this extra expenditure never exceeds equipment, piping, electrical and instrumentation price put together, but being an expenditure, the project owner has to account for the same. Many times estimation engineer ignores these small but important expenditures. As a cumulative result, in reality, the cost overruns become inevitable.

The elements of Plant and Machinery Schedule are listed in Table 6.1.

We shall see now how to carry out estimates of 'Plant and Machinery' items one by one. In order to carry out estimate at various levels, we need some technical inputs. Depending upon the accuracy of estimate (type of estimate) the details of inputs required will change.

**Table 6.1** Plant and Machinery Cost

| | *Indigenous (₹)* | *Foreign Component (₹)* | *Total (₹)* |
|---|---|---|---|
| *Main Plant (B/L)* | | | |
| Equipment | | | |
| Piping | | | |
| Instrumentation | | | |
| Electricals | | | |
| *OSBL Facilities* | | | |
| **A** Sub-total | | | |
| Spares | | | |
| **B** Sub-total | | | |
| Packing & forwarding | | | |
| Transportation to site | | | |
| Installation | | | |
| Painting & Insulation | | | |
| Insurance | | | |
| Goods and Services Tax (GST) | | | |
| GST on imported items | | | |
| **Grand Total** | | | |

The entire plant of a Greenfield (Grassroots) project can be divided into following broad zones namely,

Battery limit plant (B/L) wherein main production activity is carried out, and outside battery limit (OSBL) Facilities which include (i) utilities generation, e.g. boilers, cooling towers, air-conditioning/refrigeration unit, inert gas generator. Instrument air, etc., (ii) storage facilities for raw materials, finished goods, intermediates, etc., and (iii) effluent treatment plant (ETP).

For implementing a project, we need definitive/detailed estimate to prepare a detailed techno-economic feasibility report (a bankable document) and for other purposes, we can have budgetary or order of magnitude estimate. It is obvious that equipments constitute a major part of the estimate and, hence, we shall concentrate on the equipment first. To comprehend the entire estimate exercise, we shall see how a definitive or budgetary estimate be prepared for equipment, piping, electricals, and instrumentation. Once we have this with us, based on the experience one can estimate insulation, painting, packing and forwarding transportation, insurance and installation as a percentage of all the above including spares.

GST (Goods and Services Tax) has now replaced local Sales tax and Excise duty, octroi etc. GST on Plant & Machinery item of the project cost schedule and GST on project import are well laid down. In the absence of detailed information for preliminary estimate GST on indigenous plant and machinery items may be considered at 28% and GST on project import at 18%. For some specific spares, such as turbine shaft, one can have Harmonized System Nomenclature (HSN) code and then have specific GST rate. Therefore one can easily estimate effect of GST.

The entire estimation exercise has to be on a sound basis and reasoning so that outcome would be more realistic and meaningful.

## 6.2 THE BASIS

The basic engineering package (BEP) or more complete front-end engineering package is the document, which forms basis of the detailed engineering. The BEP is given by the process (technology) licensor. Based on this document project engineering company carries out detailed engineering and project management activities leading to plant construction followed by commissioning. Generally speaking, the basic engineering package is obtained from the process licensor only after signing an agreement and after making a part of payment for know-how and engineering. This is done only after obtaining clearances, if required, from the statutory bodies and arrangements for project financing are done. The detailed techno-economic feasibility report is required for the above purpose. This means that we shall have limited information from the process licensor to prepare a techno-economic feasibility report. Therefore, in order to prepare a detailed techno-economic feasibility report for Financial Institutions and the concerned Govternment departments, we need to have the following information (which may be obtained after executing a memorandum of understanding (MOU) between the process licensor and project owner and sometimes even the detailed engineering contractor).

- A brief description of the process with preliminary process flow diagrams (PFDs) with overall material and energy balance.
- A list of equipment, with 'Four line specifications'.
- Plant layout of at least major equipment.
- Utility requirements along with utility specifications.
- A list of drives/types along with power requirement (HT/LT, emergency drives).
- Piping material take-off for B/L plant of similar or nearby capacity, if available.
- Quantities and specifications of all emissions, namely, gaseous, solid and liquid from the plant to aid design of effluent treatment facilities.

- Instrumentation philosophy along with identification of digital distributed control system (DCS), programmable logic controllers (PLC) and, if possible, software and hardware cost estimation.
- Special requirements within Battery Limit Plant from SHE management point of view.

For a complex plant such as ammonia and urea via coal gasification, a detailed engineering contractor is required to develop utility flow diagrams of steam, cooling water, and also single line diagram for electrical power distribution. The detailed engineering contractor also develops an entire plot plan identifying the plant blocks such as main plant, utilities, storage and tank-farm, all buildings, gates, and so on. This should be preferably to the scale to assist in estimating piping requirement for carrying fluid material to and fro from the main plant to the storage area and utilities from utility generation units to the main plant.

Since equipments constitute a major component of plant and machinery, we shall focus our attention on methodologies to carry out cost estimation of equipments. We have two types of estimate of interest to us, namely, detailed or definitive estimate and budgetary estimate. The order of magnitude estimate is carried out for the entire plant and not commonly for equipment.

## 6.3 EQUIPMENT COST ESTIMATE

Here we shall see how estimation of cost of equipment is done at various desired types of estimates.

### 6.3.1 Detailed/Definitive Cost Estimate

Detailed or definitive cost estimate can be obtained from fabricators of equipment only after providing them the process data sheet from basic engineering package. More detailed mechanical fabrication inputs are required wherever equipment is non-standard.

A typical specification of a reactor is given here to have a detailed estimate from the manufacturer.

| | |
|---|---|
| Equipment No. | R 1001 |
| Brief Description | Hydrogenation reactor |
| Capacity | $2m^3$ |
| Height/Dia., Ratio | 1.2:1 |
| Material of Construction | SS316 |
| Design Temperature | 125°C |
| Design Pressure | 30 bar |
| Cooling/Heating | Limpet coil (carbon steel) |
| Chilled Water/Steam at | 5 bar |
| Agitator | Gas inducing type, double mechanical seal, shaft supported on bottom, 5 HP drive. |
| Reactor baffles | 4 |
| Reactor top and bottom | Torispherical dished ends welded joint |

Along with the above data sheet an engineering sketch of equipment should be given indicating nozzle size and orientation. This information would enable equipment fabricator to give definitive offer without mechanical design and fabrication drawing.

This is also applicable to imported equipment. Once price (free-on-board, FOB) in foreign currency is known, we can have insurance and freight charges from the shipping agent or air cargo agent to get cost inclusive of insurance and freight (CIF) price at the port, near to project site.

In some cases, the basic engineering package might not be available. In such a situation one has to have budgetary cost estimate.

### 6.3.2 Budgetary and Preliminary Cost Estimate (Indigenous)

The two powerful tools used in the budgetary cost estimate are similarity principle and parametric cost estimation.

#### *6.3.2.1 Similarity Principle*

We need not have detailed specification of equipment but can have a brief specification of the same for budgetary or preliminary cost estimate. Brief specification of equipment is also known as 'Four-Line' specification. A typical 'Four-Line' specification of the reactor is given below:

| | |
|---|---|
| Equipment No. | R 1001 (Hydrogenator) |
| Capacity | 2 $m^3$ |
| Material | SS 316 |
| Design temperature | 125 C |
| Design pressure | 30 bar |
| Cooling/heating | Limpet coil |
| Agitator | Gas inducing type, 5 HP drive. |

The above 'Four-line' specification (though it is a six-line specification, engineers use the term for brief specification) is adequate for any competent vendor to give budgetary offer (quotation).

Project engineering organisations have their own databank like that of various manufacturers. The 'databank' is a powerful tool in the hands of cost-estimating engineer. Therefore, it is not always necessary to invite offers from manufacturers. The cost estimation engineer encounters two issues:

1. How to estimate price of equipment from similar piece of equipment having design pressure, design temperature, nearly the same but having identical material of construction?
2. How to update price to the present scenario from the past data?

Please note that the design pressure and the design temperature of the equipments under considerations can be nearly the same but material of construction might not be identical. For instance, it is possible to estimate the price of a reactor having design pressure 15 bar and temperature 120°C made of SS 316 L from the reactor having design pressures 19 bar and temperature 150°C made of SS 316. The reactor made of SS 316 L might be approximately 10% costlier than that made of SS 316. If we know the ratio of the material and fabrication cost for SS 316L to carbon steel we can estimate the price of the reactor under consideration from the price of carbon steel reactor of nearby capacity and pressure ratings. Typically, this ratio is say, 5: thereby making stainless steel equipment much costlier than that of carbon steel.

#### 6.3.2.2 Parametric Cost Estimation

There always exists a relationship between equipment price (cost to the owner), its characteristic parameters (independent variables) and time. We shall deal with the time factor separately. The relationship with parameters might be based on sound theoretical basis, semi-empirical basis or total empirical basis by data correlation with parameters. The parameter is an independent variable resulting in price. For example, in a heat exchanger, the parameter could be heat transfer area for a given type of heat exchanger (1-1 shell and tube heat exchanger, plate heat exchanger, and so on).

The various price-parameter equations could be broadly classified as;

$$P = a_0 + a_1 X \qquad \text{(Linear expression)} \qquad (6.1)$$

$$P = a\,(X)^n \qquad \text{(Power law expression)} \qquad (6.2)$$

$$P = a_0 + a_1 X + a_2 X^2 + a_3 X^3 + a_4 X^4 + \ldots + a_n X^n \qquad \text{(Polynomial expression)} \qquad (6.3)$$

In all the above expressions $X$ is the independent parameter.

Kharbanda & Stallworthy (1988), and Couper (2003) have given a comprehensive descriptions of parametric estimation.

There could be more than one parameter also. Further, it could be in any form of expression. For example, the price (in US \$) of a refrigeration unit is given by (Vatavuk, 1995):

$$P = a \exp (b - cT + d \ln R) \tag{6.4}$$

where, $T$ = condensing temperature and $R$ = tons of refrigeration, and $a$, $b$, $c$ and $d$ are the constants.

Whatever expression is used it must fit the data statistically well.

Being easy to handle the power law model is the most popular model among estimation engineers.

Price, $$P = a_0 \,(\text{parameter } X)^n \tag{6.5}$$

Thus we have,

$$\{P_a/P_b\} = \{X_a/X_b\}^n \tag{6.6}$$

where, $P_a$ and $P_b$ are prices (cost to the project owner) of equipment with parameters $X_a$ and $X_b$ and $n$ is dimensionless number and is based on the recent-past experience resulting in a good correlation.

For example, for a heat exchanger the parameter, $X$ is area of heat transfer. Therefore, price of a new heat exchanger having similar specification can be estimated from that of the old exchanger available as

$$\frac{\text{Price of a new exchanger}}{\text{Price of an old exchanger}} = \left[\frac{\text{Heat transfer area of a new exchanger}}{\text{Heat transfer area of an old exchanger}}\right]^n \tag{6.7}$$

Table 6.2 exhibits parameter(s) used in cost capacity relation for some equipment for illustration purpose.

**Table 6.2** Parameters used in Cost Capacity Correlation for Some Important Equipment.

| *Equipment* | *Parameter* |
|---|---|
| Blower | volumetric flow rate, $Nm^3/hr$ |
| Centrifuge | power, kW |
| Compressor | capacity, compression ratio, $Nm^3/hr$, $(P_2/P_1)$ |
| Drum dryer | area, $m^2$ |
| Fan | volumetric flow rate, $m^3/hr$ |
| Furnace | heat load, Mkcal/hr, or MW |
| Heat exchanger | area, $m^2$ |
| Packed tower | height/diameter ratio, L/D ratio, packing type |
| Reactor | volume, $m^3$ |
| Refrigeration unit | capacity, Ton or kW |

For various equipments, the data available, in public domain, for Indian conditions are rather inadequate to update any meaningful estimate. Nonetheless, considerable information on constants $a_0$ and $n$ is available from the published literature in USA. Though prices in dollars will not be appropriate in India, the validity of these equations as far as constant $n$ is concerned would not, in our opinion, make much difference in estimate.

Peters and Timmerhaus (1991) mentioned that the value of $n = 0.6$ popularly known as 'six-tenth rule' though it varies from 0.2 to 1.0 and at times greater than 1.0 also, is good enough for cost estimate in the absence of data.

Recently, Remer and Chai (1990 b) analysed data for variety of equipment with varying sizes for conditions prevailing in USA. Their recommendations for $n$ values are given in Table 6.3.

**Table 6.3** The Values of Exponent '*n*' in Eq. 6.5

| *Eqipment* | *n* |
|---|---|
| General equipment | 0.68 |
| Heat exchangers | 0.68 |
| Fluid handling | 0.63 |
| Vessels, storage tank towers | 0.63 |

(Adopted from Remer and Chai (1990 b))

It is seen that $n = 0.68$ would be more appropriate than $n = 0.6$.

For gaseous and particulate air pollution control, equipment costs could now be escalated with the help of VATAVUK air pollution control cost indices (VAPCCI) (Vatavuk 1995) for conditions in USA.

From the foregoing it is clear how we can estimate cost of equipment by scaling up or down. To aid estimation engineer a series of articles, which have been published in *Process Engineering*, England (UK) since February 1995 presenting cost capacity relationship for a variety of equipment, may be referred. Couper (2003) has presented an excellent account of Equipment cost-capacity algorithms which should be guidelines for compilation of cost capacity data for Indian conditions as well.

#### 6.3.2.3 Estimation By Considering 'Time factor'

All prices (costs) change with time. This change in most cases pushes the prices upwards. For that reason all estimates are time-defined. It is, therefore, necessary to identify reference time when we report estimate. Thus an estimate could be 'as of now' and the date is mentioned or it can be defined for time period such as first quarter 2004 (January–March) for which it is valid.

By inflation we mean increase in price reflected in our cost of living. On the other hand by escalation we mean increase in the price of equipment or any other item. By and large, it is observed that cost of living increases with time – meaning thereby inflation is always positive and in the limit it is zero. Seldom we come across negative inflation. This is not true in case of escalation. Demand and supply scenario and business compulsion may result in negative escalation. In a growing economy, inflation and escalation go hand in hand and in a positive way. Let us, therefore, quickly overview factors responsible for inflation.

#### 6.3.2.4 Some Important Factors Influencing Inflation

*Geo-political considerations:* These are complex issues affecting economy in general. Political crises in a country supplying major energy source to the other country may trigger inflation in the receiving country.

*Natural calamities:* Earthquakes, floods, droughts, etc., need massive financial assistance resulting in resource scarcity for other developmental work. This may trigger inflationary trend.

*Policies of the Government (state as well as central):* The upward revision in the interest rate to make industry more efficient may backfire triggering inflation.

The globalisation of business now means industry has to have commitments towards Total Quality Management (TQM) and Safety Health and Environment (SHE) management. Accreditation to ISO standards may result in higher prices of equipments.

The policy of the Government towards labour such as pension funds, welfare funds, bonus, leave travel allowance, and so on, can result in inflationary trend.

The Government collects revenue by way of GST from the project. Any changes in these would result in change in the price of an equipment. Due to rationalisation of duty structure the prices have resulted in reduction.

*Formation of cartel:* The formation of cartel by two or three fabricators of equipment, for example, glass-lined equipment, may result in upward swing in the price.

*Technology Innovation:* Innovation in technology would always result in reduction in the cost of manufacturing. If the entrepreneur would like to pass on this benefit to customers, the price of the product will reduce eventually.

*Competition*

Globalisation results in competition, which in turn may bring down prices due to innovative and efficient manufacturing practices.

All the above factors, except technology innovation, will push price upwards while the innovations in technology will bring down prices. Whatever may be the reasons for escalation of costs (price) they obviously change raw material costs.

On the other hand, escalation in price can be negative also. For example, the manufacturer of glass-lined equipment can reduce the prices under compulsion if there are not many orders, and at the same time he may be keen on running his fabrication shop as well.

We shall address here how to estimate price of equipment (cost to the project owner) based on the data available in the recent past (say 5 years). It is a well-known fact that prices of equipment change as time progresses. The standard raw materials for fabrication of equipment used in a chemical Industry are carbon steel, stainless steel and non-metals like rubber, fibre reinforced plastics, etc. Their prices change due to market forces like demand/ supply or external forces like import duties, taxes, transportation and or internal forces like cost of production, and so on. The labour cost is not only related to salary and wages but also to productivity. These costs are governed by the national economics; inflationary trends being its main component. The fabricated equipment price consists of two components, namely, material (hardware) cost and labour cost. The labour cost often includes weighted labour cost comprising engineering man-hours, draftsman man-hours, workers man-hours, factory and administrative overheads and profit of the owner.

In India, in the absence of well-documented index for a chemical plant and machinery equipment, the recommendation of Kharbanda (1977) should hold true. The chemical plant equipment index is the wholesale price index for machinery and transport equipment. A rule of thumb could be that the escalation rate for equipment would be twice that of overall rate of inflation reported by the Government.

$$\frac{\text{Price in 2004 (First quarter)}}{\text{Price in 2002 (First Quarter)}} = \frac{\text{Index in 2004 (First quarter)}}{\text{Index in 2002 (First quarter)}} \quad (6.8)$$

$$\text{Price in 2004} = \text{Price in 2002 } (1 + e_{2002\text{-}03})(1 + e_{2003\text{-}04}) \quad (6.9)$$

where $e$ = escalation rate expressed in fraction.

### 6.3.3 Imported Equipment

For imported equipment, the easiest way is to have a budgetary fax quote (or email quote). However, if we have the equipment price in the past in foreign currency, we can use equipment cost index of the country of origin. For the equipment of the US origin, we can effectively use chemical engineering CE) plant cost index known as 'CE plant cost index' to update the price of equipment. These indices are published every month in the journal '*Chemical Engineering*' published by McGraw-Hill (USA). Matley (1982) explained the rationale behind the revised CE plant cost index. The CE plant cost index would be discussed separately. In England (UK), *Process Engineering* journal publishes index for equipment to update estimate over a period, Once equipment price is known as free on board, (FOB) we can estimate with the help of insurance and freight rate, the landed equipment price in foreign currency at the port (say, JNPT Mumbai). As a rule of thumb, in the absence of detailed information, one can consider the cost of equipment inclusive of insurance and freight (CIF) to be 10% more than that of FOB price.

Thus we have,

$$\text{CIF price} = 1.1 \text{ FOB price} \quad (6.10)$$

Once CIF price is known rupee conversion at the prevailing exchange rate can yield price (Rupee price Equivalent to foreign exchange). Import duty (project import duty) as applicable to the project is added to Rupee equivalent price to arrive at the total cost of equipment to the project owner at the landing port.

While preparing the equipment cost estimate it is desirable that one should have 'currency basket' by identifying equipment along with the country of origin giving FOB and CIF prices in their respective foreign currency. The estimation engineer is then required to state explicitly the exchange rate being considered. The leading national newspapers do present exchange rates of important foreign currency.

From the above, it is now clear how one can estimate equipment prices, both from indigenous source and imported source, taking into account the cost capacity relationship and time value of money (inflation/escalation).

## 6.4 PIPING, INSTRUMENTATION AND ELECTRICALS, COST ESTIMATE

In 'plant and machinery', equipment cost is more important than anything else. We shall now see how best we can estimate cost associated with piping, instrumentation and electricals. Before that, it would be more appropriate here to understand the meaning of piping, instrumentation and electricals.

*Piping:* Piping includes all interconnecting pipes, fittings, elbows, bends, and various types of valves, gaskets, etc., within as well as outside battery limit plant area.

*Instrumentation:* Instrumentation includes all measuring and controlling devices and probes for temperature, pressure and flow indicators and controllers, online analytical tools, digital distributed control system (DCS); programmable logic control (PLC) system, and also remote control or long distance control MODEM system, etc., in the entire plant.

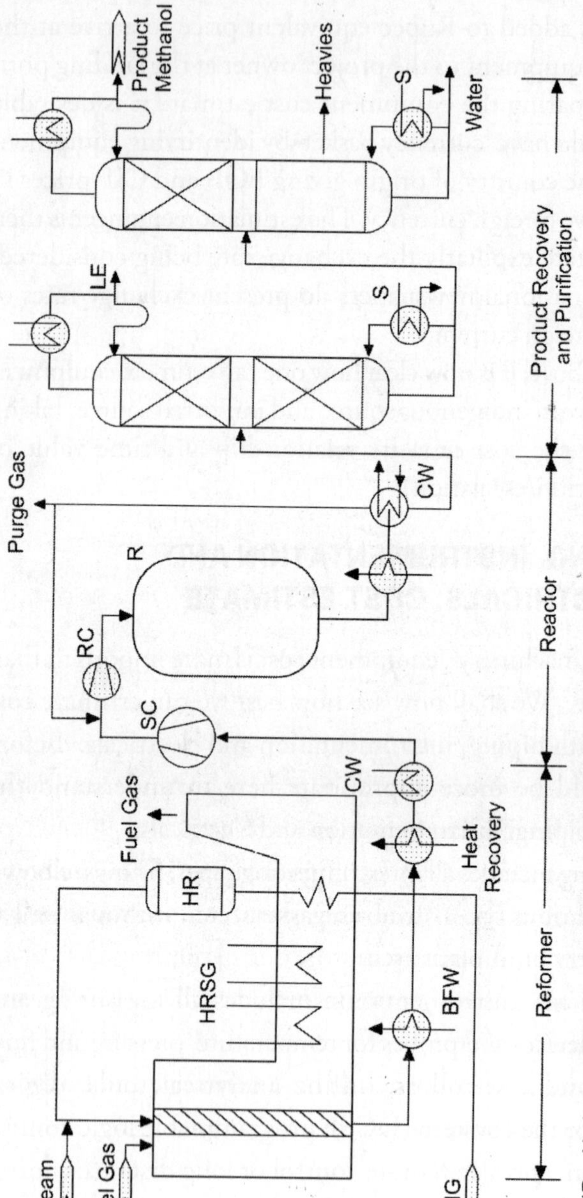


HR: Hydrogen Sulphide Removal
RC: Recirculating Compressor
S: Steam
HRSG: Heat Recovery Steam Super Heated
R: Reactor
CW: Cooling Water
SC : Syngas Compressor
LE: Light Ends

**Fig 6.1** Natural Gas to Methanol: Simplified Process Diagram

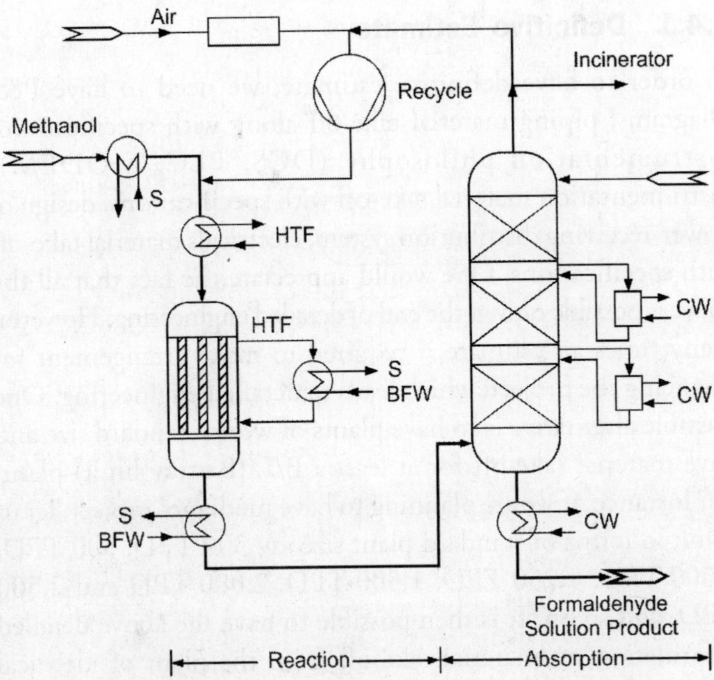


**Fig 6.2** Methanol to Formaldehyde: Simplified Process Diagram (HTF: Heat Transfer Fluid, BEF: Boiler Feed Water, CW: Cooling Water S: Steam)

*Electricals:* Electricals to include power receiving substation, controls and distribution of the same the in entire plant, all types of drives (Low Tension LT & High Tension HT), emergency power generation and distribution system, uninterrupted power supply to central computers, motor control centres, start-off and put-off switches, cables, various starters, switches, plant lighting, lightening arrestors, etc.

We shall see now how one can have definitive and budgetary estimates for the above items.

### 6.4.1 Definitive Estimate

In order to have definitive estimate, we need to have P&I Diagrams, piping material take-off along with specifications, instrumentation philosophy (DCS, PLC, MODEM), instrumentation material take-off with specifications, design of power-receiving distribution system, electricals material take-off with specifications. One would appreciate the fact that all the above is possible only at the end of detailed engineering. However, many times an estimate is required to make arrangement for financing the project, which leads to detailed engineering. One possible alternative is to have plants of world standard size and have material take-off for at least a B/L (Battery limit) plant. For instance, if we are planning to have methanol project, let us think in terms of standard plant size say 300 TPD, 500 TPD, 1,000 TPD, 1,250 TPD, 1,500 TPD, 2,000 TPD and 2,500 TPD, and so on. It is then possible to have the above detailed information on material take off from the plant of identical capacity built elsewhere. The standardisation of plant capacity not only gives us realistic capital outlay in a short time but owner of the project can now advantageously negotiate fees for basic engineering package and at times for Know-how also. Once detailed material take-off (MTO) is known, the definitive cost estimate can be easily prepared.

### 6.4.2 Budgetary or Order of Magnitude Estimate

Generally speaking, budgetary estimates 'of piping, instrumentation and electricals are taken as some per cent of equipment cost. Familiarity of estimation engineers with a plant under consideration, his knowledge of complexity of the plant based on process flow diagrams (PFDs) would help in having a more realistic estimate. Since these estimates are going to be additive to the equipment cost estimate, the final estimate of plant and machinery may not have much deviation from reality (additive property of estimate).

Typically, one may have the following break-up of estimate as per cent of total equipment cost.

Piping - 15–30%
Instrumentation - 20–40%
Electricals - 15–30%

The upper or lower limits need to be judiciously used based on our knowledge of process complexity through process description (and PFDs).

In order to illustrate the above, let us consider two projects:

– Manufacture of methanol from natural gas
– Manufacture of formaldehyde from methanol

The simplified process diagrams for the above are presented in Figs 6.1 and 6.2. A brief description of the processes (step-wise) is given below:

*Methanol from Natural gas: The sequence of steps in the manufacturing process as follows:*

1. Natural Gas (NG) is process are as follows: first compressed to reformer pressure, if required.
2. NG is desulphurised by adsorption of low levels of $H_2S$ on ZnO bed at temperature around 350°C.
3. The desulphurised NG is then steam reformed to produce syn-gas at around 900°C and 25–30 bar pressure.
4. The hot syn-gas is cooled and compressed to the reactor pressure.
5. Considerably amount of energy is recovered from reformed gas (syn-gas) and flue gas in a reformer producing superheated steam at high pressure.
6. The syn-gas compressor and recycled gas compressor are coupled to steam turbine.
7. The reaction is carried out typically, at 250°C and 70 bar pressure.

8. The reactor exit stream is condensed to recover crude methanol and the balance is recycled.
9. The crude methanol is then fractionated in series of columns to yield the product of desired specification. The energy required for distillation is provided by hot reformed gas and steam. In some processes heat pump concept is used to conserve the energy.

*Formaldehyde from methanol:* The steps involved in manufacturing of formaldehyde from methanol are as follows:

1. Methanol is vaporised and mixed with air as well the as the recycled gas.
2. The conversion of methanol to formaldehyde occurs near atmospheric pressure and the temperature used is around 300°C over a molybdenum oxide and iron oxide catalyst.
3. The product gas containing formaldehyde is absorbed in water to produce around 40% formaldehyde solution, which is sold as such or purified to meet the specifications. The absorber has inter-stage coolers (plate heat exchanger).
4. Part of the product gas is recycled.
5. The steam is produced at, say, 20 bar.

From the above, it is evident that manufacture of methanol is much more complex than its conversion to formaldehyde (product). Larger quantities of piping is required in methanol plant to withstand higher temperature and pressure than that in formaldehyde plant. The distributed control system in methanol would be much more complex than that used in formaldehyde plant. (Fig. 6.2.). Further, electricals would be more in methanol plant than that would be in formaldehyde plant. It is thus seen that contribution of piping, instrumentation and electricals as percentage of equipment would be far different in methanol plant as compared to formaldehyde plant.

## 6.5 OSBL FACILITIES COST ESTIMATES

Outside battery limit facilities, known as OSBL facilities, consist of systems generating utilities, auxiliary support to utilities generation, storage of raw materials, finished products, intermediates and effluent treatment plant.

### 6.5.1 Utilities

There are two types of utilities, namely, basic utilities and applied utilities. The fuel (liquid, gas and solid), water, power, refrigerant and air are the basic utilities. On the other hand, steam, brine, inert gas ($N_2$) and heat transfer fluid are the examples of applied utilities. The estimation engineer is required to estimate facilities needed to store raw water, fire-water (water required for fire-fighting), liquid fuel tanks, solid fuel such as coal-handling system, ash-handling system and gas-metering station, power receiving station, emergency power generator (DG set) etc. By and large applied utilities are bought out modular plants, steam boiler, cooling tower, thermic fluid heater, brine plant are some examples of such modular units of applied utilities. Auxiliary systems for utilities generation are ash-handling system, cooling tower and boiler blown units, boiler feed water treatment unit, process water treatment unit are also modular bought out items. Their price includes equipment, piping, instrumentation and electricals for such a module.

All such modular plants need utilities at their battery limit. For instance, the vendor of a high-pressure boiler would need electric power say at 440V, treated water and the fuel to his specifications. The vendor would give steam at rated capacity and pressure. The flue gas composition would be made available along with the quantity so that flue gas stack can be sized and purchased.

The estimation engineer has to estimate the peak and normal demands of all utilities, particularly power. Based on the detailed layout, he has to estimate piping, electricals and instrumentation required to generate the specific utility and the same for distributing to the main plant. If the utility module were considered, the vendor would include within his battery limit all piping, electricals and instrumentation associated with the same.

### 6.5.2 The Effluent Treatment Plant (ETP)

In order to estimate price of an effluent treatment plant (ETP), one needs to know quantity and quality of effluent and discharge standards prevailing at the production site. The process licensor gives quality and quantity of effluent generated. The process licensor might provide effluent treatment procedure for special pollutants. Specialised vendors offer effluent treatment plant (ETP) as a turnkey plant. In such a case, what we have discussed for utilities above is applicable here also. In such a situation, location of the ETP in a plot plan should be indicated. This would make it then possible to estimate piping requirement for effluents originating from the plant and going to the ETP site. Similarly, from ETP battery limit, one can estimate piping requirement for taking treated effluent to discharge point. If the technology for effluent treatment is developed in-house, it is always desirable to have a basic engineering package developed not only to facilitate cost estimation, but also construction and operation of the effluent treatment plant. The ETP plant can also be used for water recovery from boiler blow down and cooling tower blow down.

### 6.5.3 Storage Facilities

The storage facilities include storage of raw materials, products, co-products, by-products and fuels in the form of liquid, solid, semi-solid fluids. When gas (natural gas) is used, we have gas-metering station.

The storage of hazardous material is designed as per prevailing safety regulations and the factory act. Some storage tanks are site fabricated. Many times storage tanks are mounted with breather vent lines, which in turn are connected to the flare. Storage under inert gas necessitates inert gas lines from inert gas generation plant. A sprinkler system is desired while storing chemicals having low flash-point such as naphtha.

The storage of some fuels demands extra care. For example, storage facility for low sulphur heavy stock (LSHS) necessitates heating provision not only for tanks but also for transfer line. The set-point temperature of LSHS may vary from 65 to even 80°C depending upon source of supply. By and large electric heating system is used but steam heating can also be used depending upon local economics.

The storage facility for cryogenic gases such as ethylene, propylene, liquefied natural gas (LNG), and so on, needs cryogenic containers operated under auto-refrigeration at atmospheric pressure. The civil foundation has to be carefully designed to avoid ice formation due to moisture in the soil. Experienced engineer should carry out the cost estimate of such a facility otherwise estimate can be totally erroneous.

The storage of solids at times needs not only low temperature but also humidity control. The storage of solids in bags (50 or 100 kg capacity) needs specially designed warehouse to facilitate forklift movement or stacking bags.

It is thus seen that OSBL facility is required to be estimated thoughtfully. The contribution of piping might be more than that by instrumentation and electricals as percentage of equipment.

## 6.6 MISCELLANEOUS ITEMS OF THE PLANT AND MACHINERY SCHEDULE

After having seen how to estimate main components of plant and machinery schedule, let us see how to estimate the other miscellaneous items. Many times cost overruns are attributed to failure on the part of estimate engineer to look into these components.

### 6.6.1 Spares

It is always desirable that the essential spares remain with the project owner right from the beginning. One can list the same and make provision for the same based on the experience of the owner, detailed engineering contractor and process licensor. Otherwise, provision should be made on ad hoc basis. Typically, for indigenous items, spares could be 3–4% of the entire equipment, piping, electrical and instrumentation. For imported items, spares could be 10% of the foreign exchange component.

### 6.6.2 Packing and Forwarding

The vendors often quote prices ex-works. Provision for packing and forwarding for all the above in case of indigenous item is made as 2% of indigenous item.

### 6.6.3 Transportation to Site

Transportation of equipment and other material to the plant site often gets ignored, which should not be the case.

Generally, vendor gives offer for ex-works and hence the project owner has to make arrangements for transporting equipment from works to the plant site. For imported items, they need to be transported from the port of landing to the plant or project site. For heavy and odd equipment, it is always desirable to have a quotation from heavy machinery transport contractor. In the absence of a detailed information, one may consider transportation charges to be 1–2% of all items listed in B of Table 6.1.

### 6.6.4 Installation

After having plant and machinery items at site, one needs to install the same. Skilled persons people with appropriate skills are engaged to carry out installation. One may have to use cranes, and other devices. At any level of estimate this factor is difficult to estimate and one needs to rely heavily on the experience of the past. Nonetheless, following guidelines may take away total uncertainty. For equipment and OSBL facilities, installation can vary between 10 and 15% of the cost of equipment and OSBL facilities. Installation of carbon steel reactor would be more or less identical to that of stainless steel 316 (SS 316) reactor, however, the latter being costlier than carbon steel, the instillation cost as percentage of equipment cost would be lower in the case of reactor fabricated out of SS 316 as compared to that in case of carbon steel reactor.

Piping installation cost could be in the range of 10–20% of the piping cost and it includes piping-supporting structure also.

For electricals, installation can be in the range of 15–25% of electricals while for instrumentation, it could be 20–30% of instrumentation.

### 6.6.5 Painting and Insulation

Majority of equipment, piping, similarly tank farm needs additional painting to withstand plant environment. Structural steel members, platforms, etc., may need anti-corrosion paint coating depending upon the plant working environment.

Similarly, utility pipes for cooling water, instrument air or other gases need to be painted as per Indian Standards. In order to avoid or minimise tank farm vent losses, we may have to paint tanks in silver white reflecting paint.

From plant safety point of view, hot surfaces need insulation. Depending upon the energy conservation philosophy, we need to insulate hot utility lines with hot insulation and cold lines with cold insulation.

Considering its total contribution, it is not desirable at any stage of estimate to have this estimate based on area required for painting and insulation. As a rule of thumb, insulation and painting is deemed to be 2–3% of total of indigenous and foreign exchange component in 'B'.

### 6.6.6 Insurance

In fact, 1% of all the fixed assets should be considered to be insurance during transport, storage and installation for indigenous and foreign items.

### 6.6.7 Goods and Services Tax (GST)

Recently, from July 2017, GST (Goods and Services Tax) has replaced site related excise duty and sales tax, octroi etc. For the majority of plant and machinery schedule, GST is 28% as lumped value. There are some items like turbines, boilers etc attracting GST at 18 %. While preparing detailed techno economic feasibility report (bankable document) one should consider the appropriate value of GST for equipment, piping, electrical, instrumentation etc. The higher figure of GST 28% will give conservative estimate and is adequate for the first estimate.

At present crude oil and fuels derived from it are not covered by GST and earlier Excise and Sales tax remain in force. The values of these are decided by Central and State Government from time to time. In future they may be covered by GST.

If goods are manufactured in one state say Maharashtra State and also sold in Maharashtra State we have state SGST and centre CGST both are equally divided in total GST. For example reactors, exchangers etc. attract total GST 28%. Then SGST would be 14% and CGST 14%. In case of estimate of Plant and Machinery items one value of total GST is adequate. When the goods are sold in the other state, we have interstate GST as IGST which central Govt. will collect. For individual GST rate one needs to follow Harmonized System Nomenclature (HSN) code. For services such as Know How, Basic Engineering, Detailed Engineering and EPC (Engineering Procurement and Construction) contract one has to follow Service Accounting Codes (SAC) to have estimate of GST. In order to have right GST cost figures one should refer to appropriate and latest GST document as GST rates might undergo revision from time to time.

### 6.6.8 Octroi

For the ease of movement of cargo the Octroi is abolished. This would not only save precious fuel but also reduce delivery time from factory warehouse or the factory to market (warehouse). The direct manifestation of Octroi waiver is reduction in transit time and hence reduction in inventory of raw materials and finished goods.

### 6.6.9 Project Import Duty

For a quick estimate (preliminary estimate) the project import duty under GST regime may be considered at 18%. For specific spare say, turbine shaft one has to use HSN code and get the import duty rate. In addition to this, provision should be made for cost associated with clearance of consignment and custom ware house charges if any.

All the above items put together result in the estimate of 'Plant and Machinery' cost (Table 6.1).

## 6.7 ORDER OF MAGNITUDE (QUICK) ESTIMATE

Many times, we are interested in the order of magnitude or quick estimate of the project cost to assess at a very early stage of economic viability of the project to decide whether it is 'worthwhile'.

The project owner might be looking for cost estimate of the process being developed in his research centre to ascertain the economic viability of the process. By carrying out the sensitivity analysis of the process under investigation the route can be modified by eliminating the most expensive step. Gerrard (2000) documented the cost estimating methods available for this purpose. They are based on the following:

- identifying main process steps and estimating their costs,
- a simple flow sheet identifying main equipments,
- design temperature and design pressure for the main equipment, and
- material of construction (MOC)

We then have,

$$\text{Cost} = f(\,Q, T, P \text{ and } M) \tag{6.11}$$

where $Q$ = capacity, $T$ = temperature, $P$ = pressure and $M$ = material of construction. The function $f$ is complex in nature.

In India, unfortunately like in plant equipment, enough published data is not available by means of which the cost can be estimated by the above expression. For conditions prevailing in United Kingdom (England), Gerrard (2000) presented various methods such as those by Wilson, Taylor, Timms, and Bridgewater. There exists a good scope of work to have such comprehensive correlations available in public domain in India.

A possibility of having some information on the cost of a plant from a project engineering company always exists. Such information or data could be from two sources, namely,

1. Plant of different capacity but, built in India in recent past (say, 2-4 years ago).
2. Plant of different capacity built abroad (say USA, UK, Germany and Japan, etc) in the recent past.

Let us see under each of the above sources how we can obtain the desired order of magnitude estimate.

### 6.7.1 Plant of Different Capacity Built in India, in Recent Past

In this situation, we have two tasks, namely, update the cost of the plant from the 'recent' past data and from the above, estimate the cost for the plant of a given capacity under considerations. There are two main considerations involved, the first is directly based on capacity while the second is based on sales turnover.

#### 6.7.1.1 Cost Capacity Relation

*Cost update:* Updating the cost data from past to present can be done with reasonable accuracy using chemical plant cost index which is readily available in the developed countries. Such indices are regularly published in developed countries, for example, USA and UK. For instance, CE plant cost index is published monthly in *Chemical Engineering* (published by McGraw-Hill) and UK plant cost index is published in *Process Engineering* (Published by Miller Freeman PLC, UK). In India, such indices are not easily available in open published literature. Therefore, one has to rely on wholesale price index for machinery and transport equipment or annual rate of inflation (to be precise, on escalation).

In the absence of such reliable data, one can use even general annual rate of inflation. The resulting inaccuracy gets absorbed due to nature of the estimate.

Thus, Cost of a plant in 2004 end = (Cost of a plant in 2002-end) $\times (1 + e_{(2002\text{-}03)}) \times (1 + e_{(2003\text{-}04)})$ (6.12)

where $e$ = fractional escalation in that period.

*Cost scale-up:* Having considered cost updating, let us now consider scale-up or scale-down for the plant under consideration. The power law model can be used here also as in the case of equipment

$$\text{Cost} = \alpha\,(\text{capacity})^n \qquad (6.13)$$

Therefore, we have,

$$\frac{\text{(Cost of plant A)}}{\text{(Cost of plant B)}} = \left[\frac{\text{(Capacity of plant A)}}{\text{(Capacity of plant B)}}\right]^n \tag{6.14}$$

The value of $n$ will depend upon the chemical being manufactured. It is presumed that for both plants the technology is identical. The plant consists of equipment, piping, electricals and instrumentations. One has to consider transportation, installation, insulation, painting duties, etc., for various equipments. Therefore, the value of $n$ can be deemed as lumped value for all these items. As a rule of thumb, $n$ varies from 0.7 to 0.9. For some exceptional case, $n$ can be as low as 0.5. In India, we do not have such reliable data published. However, if desired one can rely upon the latest data being published in series of articles published in *Process Engineering* (UK publication) issues of 1997. As a first approximation, we can use the exponent, $n$, published by Remer and Chai (1990 a) for a large number of plants with different sizes and using different feedstock. It is important to note that they have recommended $n = 0.7$. Please note that these data are old. However, for Indian conditions we recommend $n = 0.75$. During the span of last few decades technological changes have reduced the plant costs. Further, the emphasis has also changed as in the case of sulphuric acid plants. These plants are now looked upon as vital source of power in developing countries, rather than source of sulphuric acid alone. Please note that $n$ value has to be different from that in the equipment, and the old classical 6/10th rule ($n = 0.6$) is no longer valid for plants also as seen for equipment earlier. In order to get the feel of the issue, we present values of $n$ for some important chemicals as published by Remer and Chai (1990a) in Table 6.4. The analysis of error in estimate caused due to $n = 0.75$ for various other values of $n$ and for various capacity ratios (Eq. 6.14) is presented in Table 6.5.

**Table 6.4** Cost Capacity Relationship for Some Commodity Chemicals [Cost = $\alpha$ (Capacity)$^n$]

| *Plant* | *Process* | *n* |
|---|---|---|
| Ammonia | Steam reforming of methane | 0.72 |
| Benzene | Toluene $H_2$ (Detol) | 0.73 |
| Butadiene | Butylenes | 1.02 |
| Chlorine-caustic | | 0.69 |
| Coking | Delayed | 0.73 |
| Cracking | Fluid catalytic cracking | 0.70 |
| Ethylene | Naphtha | 0.85 |
| Ethylene dichloride | | 0.71 |
| Ethylene glycol | Ethylene oxide | 0.59 |
| Fischer Tropsch | | 0.77 |
| Formaldehyde | Methanol | 0.66 |
| Glycerin synthetic | | 0.67 |
| Methanol | Gas based | 0.71 |
| Methanol | Coal based | 0.79 |
| Nitric acid | | 0.60 |
| Oxo alcohols | Hydroformylation | 0.74 |
| Phenol | Cumene | 0.72 |
| Phthalic anhydride | *o*-xylene | 0.72 |
| Styrene | Benzene ethylene | 0.67 |
| Sulphuric acid | Contact | 0.70 |

*Source:* The above data adopted from Remer and Chai (1990a).

**Table 6.5** Relative Error in Estimates [Cost = $\alpha$(capacity)$^n$]*

| *Exponent in Reality* | *Capacity Increase Multiplier*** | | | | | |
|---|---|---|---|---|---|---|
| *'n'* | $\psi$ *= 1.5* | *2.0* | *2.5* | *3.0* | *4.0* | *5.0* |
| | | | *% Error* | | | |
| 0.50 | – 9.6 | – 15.9 | – 20.5 | – 24.0 | – 29.3 | – 33.1 |
| 0.60 | – 5.9 | – 9.9 | – 12.8 | – 15.2 | – 18.8 | – 21.4 |
| 0.70 | – 2.0 | – 3.4 | – 4.5 | – 5.3 | – 6.7 | – 7.7 |
| 0.75 | 0.0 | 0.0 | 0.0 | 0.0 | 0.0 | 0.0 |
| 0.80 | 2.1 | 3.5 | 4.7 | 5.7 | 7.2 | 8.4 |
| 0.90 | 6.4 | 10.9 | 14.7 | 17.9 | 23.1 | 27.3 |

*If $n$ = 0.75, the table exhibits percentage error caused while using different value of $n$ at a given capacity.

**$y = (C/C_o)$; where $C$ = capacity for estimate, and $C_o$ = original or base capacity.

For the purpose of estimate, the data should be from near past and not far past. One has to ascertain that over the period considered for estimation the federal Government policies were uniform. Sudden currency devaluation, drastic changes in duties, tax structures, geo-political considerations or natural calamities may result in the escalation of cost. Thus we can estimate cost of chemical plant based on the cost of the same plant but of different capacity built in recent past, say, 5 years back.

#### 6.7.1.2 Turnover Ratio

Similar to cost capacity relationship, one may use turnover ratio concept.

$$\text{Turnover Ratio} = \text{Sales}/(\text{Cost of project}) \qquad (6.15)$$

The fixed variables affecting the turnover ratio are the operating conditions such as temperature and pressure. The other parameters are the material of construction, prevailing duties in India and the rate of inflation. It should be noted that the selling price and the cost of equipment might not escalate in the same proportion. There is no comprehensive published information available on the turnover ratio of even variety of commodity chemicals in Indian conditions. However, it might be possible to generate the same by analysing the annual reports of various projects or companies.

### 6.7.2 Plant of Different Capacity Built Abroad in Recent Past

At a preliminary screening level, battery limit (B/L) plant cost may be known to us for a plant built in, say, USA, but of different capacity. Such information is often published in professional journals such as *Hydrocarbon Processing* (Gulf Publication, USA). We shall, now, see how such cost data can be advantageously used to estimate (order of magnitude estimate) the project cost in India. In such situation we have following three tasks to accomplish:

1. Escalate price of chemical plant in the country of origin from the past data to present day of estimate.
2. With the help of location index, convert the plant cost to India,
3. Use cost capacity relationship to have the cost estimate of the plant under consideration in India.

#### 6.7.2.1 Cost of Chemical Plant from the Past Data with the Help of Cost Indices

In developed countries like USA, UK, Germany, etc., estimate of plant cost from that in recent past can be easily done with the help of CE Plant cost indices published monthly and yearly also. Peters and Timmerhaus (1991), Kharbanda (1977), Gerrard (2000) and Couper (2003) have presented details of various cost indices used in estimation.

The cost index (CI) for a chemical plant is generally a composite index (lumped index) of various main components of project cost such as building and civil works, plant and machinery, know-how and engineering. Therefore we can have cost index (CI) as

CI = $a$ (Building and Civil Works) + $b$(Plant and Machinery) + $c$ (Know-how and Engineering).

$$\text{Where } a + b + c = 1 \tag{6.16}$$

Further the Plant and Machinery could be divided as

CI = $p$ (Equipment) + $q$ (Piping) + $r$ (Electricals) + $s$ (Instrumentations) + $t$ (Erection) + $u$ (Insulation)

$$\text{Where } p + q + r + s + t + u = 1. \tag{6.17}$$

Depending upon the method of cost estimation, every country has its own data bank and based on the above rationale a cost index is constructed. By and large the perception of chemical plant being same everywhere, the details deviate to a smaller extent. As a result of this, cost index of one country cannot be used in totality in any other country. It is always desirable to use the cost data from the recent past.

In our context, Chemical Engineering Plant Cost Index (USA) and Nelson-Farrar Refinery Construction Cost Index are adequate and, therefore, we shall overview the same here.

*The CE Plant cost index* (USA) is published regularly (monthly and yearly basis) in *Chemical Engineering* (McGraw-Hill publication). Arnold & Chilton (1963) and Matley (1982) presented the details of CE plant cost index. The CE Plant cost index was then revised in 2001 (Vatavuk 2002). The major difference between the old CE Plant index (1982) and the revised (2001) is in the weight factor for skilled as well as unskilled labour workforce. This was revised from 32 to 45%. The percentage weight factors for four major parts of the CE Plant cost index can be listed in Table 6.6.

**Table 6.6** Weight Factors for CE Plant Cost Index

| *Component* | *% Weight Factor* | |
|---|---|---|
| | *(1982)* | *(2001)* |
| 1. Plant equipment machinery and support | 61 | 50.7 |
| 2. Building materials and labour | 07 | 04.6 |
| 3. Construction Contract Labour | 22 | 29.0 |
| 4. Engineering and Supervision | 10 | 15.7 |
| *In Plant equipment machinery, we have* | | |
| 1. Fabricated equipment | 37 | 33.8 |
| 2. Process machinery | 14 | 12.8 |
| 3. Piping | 20 | 19.0 |
| 4. Pumps and compressors | 7 | 6.4 |
| 5. Process control equipment | 7 | 10.5 |
| 6. Electrical equipment and materials | 5 | 7.0 |
| 7. Insulation, painting and structural support | 10 | 10.5 |

Like CE Plant cost index in USA, such Plant Cost Indices are also regularly being published in *Process Engineering* for Australia, Austria, Belgium, Canada, Denmark, France, Germany, Italy, Japan, the Netherlands, Spain, Sweden, USA and UK (England). All these indices (published by *Process Engineering*) are calculated to the base of 1990 = 100 (averaged). In Plant cost index weighting of various factors can be listed as below (Cran 1973).

| | |
|---|---|
| Mechanical Engineering | 37 |
| Electrical Engineering | 08 |
| Civil Engineering | 10 |
| Site Engineering | 19 |
| Overheads | 26 |

We can use CE Plant cost index as follows:

$$\frac{\text{(Plant cost in year 'A')}}{\text{(Plant cost in year 'B')}} = \frac{\text{CE Plant cost index in year 'A'}}{\text{CE Plant cost index in year 'B'}} \quad (6.18)$$

This would enable us to update plant cost based on recent past data in the country of origin.

*Nelson–Ferrar Refinery Construction Index* is mainly used for estimating the cost of a refinery being planned. The index is very old with the base value 100 for the year 1946 for the US conditions. The contribution of various components is listed below (Peters and Timmerhaus, 1991).

Iron and Steel = 20
Skilled Labour = 30
Common Labour = 30
Building Material = 8
Equipments (miscll.) = 12 (All figures are in %)

Ferrar (1985, 1999) has presented more insight into Nelson-Ferrar cost index.

All the above cost indices would undergo revision from time to time and, therefore, it is desirable to keep oneself updated. As a thumb-rule we recommend that cost estimation from indices in developed countries be limited to past 5 years. The rationale behind is that during that period the actual change in the prices of equipment is not drastic due to factors beyond control and the productivity related factor is more or less constant so that the estimate is within the desired accuracy level.

*Illustration*

The B/L plant cost in the year 1999 for a product *X* having capacity 20,000 TPA was 16 million US$. How much it would cost in August 2003?

The plant cost in August 2003

$$= \frac{\text{The Plant cost in 1999} \times \text{CE Plant cost index August 2003}}{\text{CE Plant cost index 1999}}$$

= 16.0 million US$ × (402.4)/(390.6)

= 16.5 million US$

(We do not have information during which month of 1999 the plant cost was reported. Therefore, the CE plant cost index for average 1999 is considered in the above example.)

The illustration shows how one can update the plant cost with the help of cost indices. Our task is to convert that to Indian condition, which is done with the help of Location Index.

#### 6.7.2.2 Location Index

In order to convert plant cost from the other country to Indian condition we use location Index. By definition we have,

$$\text{Location Index (LI)} = \frac{\text{(Price at location 'A')}}{\text{(Price at location 'B')}} \qquad (6.19)$$

India being vast, the labour related cost do differ within the country and, therefore, it is possible to have different location index (LI) within India. However, for all practical purposes, while converting plant cost from, say, USA, UK, Germany, France, Italy, Japan to India, we neglect internal variation in LI. In order to convert plant cost from any other country to Indian conditions, we have to use location index. This index relates the cost of two plants based on similar technology (strictly speaking, identical technology) beyond that given by currency exchange rate. This is due to the variation in material and labour (skilled and unskilled) cost in the country of origin. The regulations by the Government might incur additional expenditure. Considering fluid economic scenario globally, no attempt has been made lately to arrive at a Location Index based on analytical reasoning. Ideally speaking, in a free economy all over the world plant cost should remain the same. The data given in published literature state the battery limit plant cost inclusive of equipment, civil work, engineering and supervision.

Let us see how Location Index would help us in estimating the project cost for Indian conditions from the data available from USA. As seen earlier with the detailed breakdown of the plant cost, as per CE Plant cost index, we can say that the plant hardware cost is, say, 55% (inclusive of plant machinery and structural steel, cement for building and civil works) and 45% as labour cost. Here the "labour" includes skilled and unskilled labour. In the absence of reliable data for Indian conditions, we can assume 60% contribution is from material and 40% from labour. Thus in reality we have,

$$\text{Plant cost} = 0.60 \text{ material cost} + 0.40 \text{ labour cost} \quad (6.20)$$

The basic material prices in India are higher than those in USA, say by 40% (considering statutory duties in India such as project import duty, excise duty etc). The labour component consists of not only salary and wages but also productivity. Though salaries and wages are low in India, our productivity is also on lower side due to so many factors. As a result the labour cost is considered to be 80% of that in USA. Therefore, we have,

Relative plant cost = 0.6 (1.4 material cost) + 0.4 (0.8 labour cost)

Location index = 1.16

that is approximately = 1.2 (6.21)

The relative cost is the location index.

If we consider 50% contribution of both the factors, the location index would be 1.1. Further, if material is made available at international price, and the fabrication shop is medium scale (where overheads and salaries of people are on lower side) the location index can be even less than unity. In such a situation, it is desirable to fabricate a plant in India and export the skid-mounted modular plants. If the plant involves very high-pressure, high-temperature reactions and majority of equipment needs to be x-rayed the labour component could be different. So would be the case if the material of construction involves exotic material of construction. In other words, knowledge of process plays important role in deciding the location index. For instance, the location index for methanol to formaldehyde plant would be far different from that for methanol to acetic acid plant.

The above approximation is a good one because after all we are interested in order of magnitude estimate. Thus we have the plant cost in India that is given by:

$$\text{Plant cost in India} = \text{Location index} \times \text{Price in US\$} \times \text{Exchange rate} \qquad (6.22)$$

With the increase in automation and better working conditions, productivity of Indians is expected to improve, thereby bringing down labour component.

Following the above rationale, we can arrive at the Location Index with respect to any other country. Kharbanda and Stallworthy (1988) have presented a detailed comprehensive account of Location Index. It is important that one should have knowledge of material of construction of the plant. For exotic material of construction, the Location Index is likely to change. In India ratio of price of SS plate to CS boiler quality plate is around 4.0, which may not be the same in the country of origin. Grauman and Willey (1998), Burns and Kumar (1996) listed comparative data of different materials of construction in USA. Relative costs of heat exchangers and vessels for exotic material of construction given by Burns and Kumar (1996) are presented in Table 6.7.

**Table 6.7** Relative Cost of Equipments in Exotic Material of Construction

| *Base Material : SS 316 Material of Construction* | *Price : Unity ( 1) Relative Cost* | |
|---|---|---|
| | *Heat Exchangers* | *Vessels* |
| SS 316 | 1.0 | 1.0 |
| Hastelloy B2 | 3.6 | 4.5 |
| Hastelloy C276 | 3.5 | 4.3 |
| Titanium Grade 2 | 2.2 | 2.8 |
| Grade 7(Pd) | 3.0 | 3.7 |
| Tantalum | 8.0 | 10.0 |
| Zirconium | 3.0 | 3.8 |

*Source:* Adopted from Burns and Kumar (1996).

The above ratios are indicative and based on prices and productivity in USA. While converting cost data to Indian conditions where higher prices are prevailing for exotic material of construction, one can have higher Location Index. The plant cost estimate now includes "Plant and Machinery and Building & Civil works" (components of the project cost) and engineering and supervision, which may be 60 to 70% of the project cost, as we understand. Therefore, now one can easily estimate the project cost. Please note that the Location Index is subjective. However, it should serve our purpose of order of magnitude estimate for very preliminary screening of projects. After having estimated the plant cost in India, the estimate for the capacity under consideration would then through cost capacity correlation (Eq. 6.14).

Thus, with the help of plant cost index, location index and cost capacity relationship, we are in a position to have an order of magnitude estimate of plant under consideration with the help of data available from foreign country.

*Illustration*

It is desired to have a quick estimate of the project cost for the product in the above illustration with capacity 50,000 TPA.

The B/L plant cost in August 2003 was estimated to be 16.5 million US$

The equipment weight factor from CE Plant cost = 0.507

The 'plant and machinery' component of the B/L plant

= (Equip weight factor) × (Location index) × (Price in US$ ) × (Exchange rate)

= (0.507) × (1.2) ($16.5 \times 10^6$US$) × (45 ₹/US$)

= ₹ 45.17 Crore

= approx. ₹ 46 Crore.

We shall assume OSBL Facility to cost 15% of the B/L Plant cost

Therefore, the total plant and machinery component of a Greenfield project is

= 46 + 0.15 × 46

= 46 + 6.9 = ₹ 52.9 Crore, for the capacity 20,000 TPA

In order to estimate for new capacity of 50,000 TPA we can use Eq. 6.14 and assume the exponent $n = 0.75$.

Therefore,

$$(\text{Plant and Machinery})_{50,000} = (\text{Plant and Machinery})_{20,000} \times (50,000/20,000)^{0.75}$$

= 105.17, approx = ₹ 105.2 Crore

Further, we make assumption that the contribution of the 'Plant and Machinery' in the project cost is 50 %. With this assumption, the project cost for the proposed Greenfield project is ₹ 210.4 Crore (= 2 × 105. 2) approximately ₹ 211 Crore.

The above procedure illustrates how to arrive at the quick order of magnitude estimate from the information available for different capacity and in a different country.

## 6.8 COMPUTER-AIDED COST ESTIMATE

There are commercial softwares available in the market to carry out cost estimation. The user is cautioned to confirm their suitability for Indian conditions because their database might be from USA or Europe. As economics is the function of time and place, the user of such softwares has to bear this in mind. It is always desirable to handcheck some sample estimates to confirm validity and applicability of the computerised estimation. The black box approach is discouraged in estimation.

From the above discussions it is clear now how to estimate cost of 'Plant and Machinery' component of project cost under various scenarios. In Table 6.1, we have presented summary of all components of "Plant and Machinery" items to facilitate assessment of the feasibility report by financial institutions and also revision at the later date. It is always desirable to tabulate foreign currency basket with currency rates at that specific time. This would aid estimation at later dates should foreign exchange rates undergo some changes.

## REFERENCES

Arnold T. H. and Chilton C.H., *New Index Shows Plant Cost Trends, Chem. Engg* 70 (4) 143 (1963).

Burns R.H. and Kumar P., *Conquer Corrosion in Harsh Environments with Tantalum, Chem. Engg. Progress* 92(3) 32 (1996).

Couper J.R., *Process Engineering Economics*, Marcel Dekker Inc., New York, USA (2003).

Cran F., *Process Engineering Indices Help Estate the Cost of New Plant, Process Engg* 18 (Hair Jan. 1973).

Dysert L., *Sharpen Your Capital Cost-Estimation Skills, Chem. Engg.* 108.(10)70(2001).

Ferrar G.L., *How Nelson Cost Indexes Are Compiled*, Oil and Gas Jl 145 (Dec 30,1985).

Ferrar G.L., *How Nelson-Ferrar Indexes of Chemical Costs Have Changed,* Oil and Gas Jl 68 (July 5, 1999).

Gerrard A.M., *Guide to Capital Cost Estimating,* 4th Edn, Institution of Chemical Engineers, UK (2000).

Guthrie K., *Capital Cost and Operating Costs for 54 Chemical Processes, Chem. Engg* 77 (13) 140 (1970).

Grauman J.S. and Willey B., *Shedding New Lights on Titanium in CPI Construction, Chem. Engg* 105 (8) 106 (1998).

Kharbanda O.P., *Process Plant & Equipment Cost Estimation,* Sevak Publications, Mumbai (1977).

Kharbanda O.P. and Stallworthy E.A., *Capital Cost Estimating for the Process Industries,* Butterworth and Co Ltd, London (1988).

Matley J., *CE Plant Cost Index Revised, Chem. Engg* 89 (8)153 (1982).

Peters M.S. and Timmerhaus K. D., *Plant Design and Economics for Chemical Engineers* 4th Edn. McGraw - Hill Inc. (1991).

Remer D.S. and Chai L.H., *Estimate Costs of Scaled-up Process Plants, Chem. Engg* 97 (4) 139 (1990 a).

——— *Design Cost Factors for Scaling up Engineering Equipment,* Chem. Engg Progr. 86 (8) 77 (1990b).

Vatavuk W.M., *Updating the CE Plant Cost Index, Chem. Engg* 109 (1) 62 (2002).

——— *Air Pollution Control Escalate Equipment Costs, Chem. Engg* 102 (12) 88 (1995).

***Sensitivity Analysis is a Sensible Way in Estimation.***

7

# Cost of Production

## 7.1 INTRODUCTION

In the chemical project economics, cost of production plays a key role. It represents operating expenses, which are of recurring in nature. They have significant impact on the selling price and ultimately profitability. In its simple form, purely on economic considerations, the dependence of selling price on the cost of production is given by:

Selling price = $\beta$ (Project cost) + Gross cost of production (7.1)

Where Gross cost of production = Cost of production + Administrative expenses at administrative site if located separately. (7.2)

$\beta$ represents the return on investment (project cost and other investment related costs such as interest etc.).

Operating expenses are incurred after the plant is commissioned and the production begins. These expenses, though incurred regularly and repetitively, are divided into direct and indirect costs. The direct costs have a direct bearing or relation to the quantity of finished saleable product produced. Raw materials, utilities, catalyst, packing material and effluent treatment chemicals are the examples of direct costs. Indirect costs are salaries, administrative costs, factory overheads, selling expenses, etc., and they have no direct relation to quantities of product produced.

The project may be a multi-product plant or a multi-location unit. The manufacture of alkanolamines, namely, mono-, di- and tri-ethanolamines, is an example of a multi-product plant.

By just changing the operating conditions the product mix can be varried using the same feedstock, namely, ammonia and ethylene oxide. A refinery producing a variety of products and a pharmaceutical unit producing different products on campaign basis are also examples of multi-product plants. In each and every case allocation of costs depends on company accounting policy. The costs incurred require a well-defined approach. The costs could be apportioned on the basis of their direct costs or quantities of common raw materials consumed, or on the basis of number of days or hours the plant was operated or their selling prices.

The entire project, many times, is divided into two sites, namely, the site of manufacturing and the site from which overall management of purchase of raw materials, sales liaison with various agencies, corporate planning, etc., is done. For instance, many manufacturing sites in Thane-Belapur Industrial belt (near Mumbai in Maharashtra State) have administrative offices (in the above sense) in south Mumbai. In order to comprehend the operating expenditure, we shall separate it as the cost of production at the manufacturing site and administrative expenses at administrative site. Both together are called gross cost of production as seen in expression 7.2. The gross cost of production in the feasibility report presents the operating expenditure.

For an ongoing project, except depreciation and financial expenses (interest), all operating expenses are clubbed together under the cost of production. For instance, professional fee paid to the consultant for the advice, say, on recovery of the catalyst, is included in the cost of production in that particular financial year. However, when the detailed techno-economic feasibility report is prepared, we find it rather impossible to envisage such a non-standard routine expenditure. Therefore, to assist estimation engineer, we present here the main components of the 'cost of production' schedule and procedure to estimate the same.

## 7.2 ELEMENTS OF COST OF PRODUCTION

As seen earlier the entire Greenfield project is divided into two parts, namely, the battery limit plant (B/L) wherein the main manufacturing activities are taking place and outside battery limit (OSBL) plant facilities consists of utilities, storage, effluent treatment plant, and others. Therefore, we shall see how to account financially all elements of cost of production for both.

Following are the main components of the cost of production schedule appearing in the detailed techno-economic feasibility report (Table 7.2)

### 7.2.1 Raw Materials, Chemicals and Catalyst

The details of raw materials, auxiliary chemicals and catalyst required for the project under consideration, are given by the process licensor- know-how supplier, in the basic engineering package (BEP). These are presented in terms of tonnes of material consumed per tonne of product or kilogram of catalyst consumed per tonne of product formed. The entire specifications of raw materials, auxiliary chemicals and catalyst are given in terms of material specification sheet.

In some processes, particularly catalytic, the raw materials consumption can vary from time to time. By and large, we get consumption figures for the start of the run (start-up), middle of the run and end of the run (just before changing the catalyst). While making a bankable document for term loan, if one has access, the consumption figures at the end of the run may be considered as a conservative approach.

The price of raw materials consists of the money we spend to buy them and deliver the same at the manufacturing site (plant). The three components of any raw material cost, therefore, consist of the basic price, the statutory duties as when applicable (such as excise, sales tax, (eventually VAT) and import duty) and the transportation charges. A separate back-up schedule is prepared to support the cost of production schedule. In case of imported raw materials, the quotations (offers) are for FOB (Free on Board) prices. One has to consider transportation to the nearest port and insurance during transit to have CIF (cost inclusive of freight) price. In the absence of detailed information, one can have

$$\text{CIF price} = 1.1 \text{ FOB price} \tag{7.3}$$

The CIF price is converted into Rupees by the prevailing exchange rate. The import duty is then added to have what is known as the *landed price*. Further transportation charges to the plant site from the port are considered. The CIF price has to be paid in foreign currency while import duty has to be paid in Indian Rupees. Like project cost component, here also one has to have a currency basket identifying all foreign currency along with their exchange rate.

For an export-oriented project, all statutory duties, namely, import duty, excise and sales tax may be totally waived by authorities.

The contribution of raw material to the cost of production is generally in the range of 50–70%. This component is, therefore, the most important component in the cost of production schedule. Utmost care should be exercised to estimate the same.

### 7.2.2 Utilities

Utilities required in a chemical plant are grouped as basic utilities and applied utilities. While water (raw), power, fuel and refrigerant are considered as basic utilities, we consider steam, cooling water, chilled water or brine as applied utilities. Let us illustrate this with the help of an example of steam as an applied utility. In order to generate steam, we pump treated water into a boiler wherein energy required for producing steam is supplied by burning fuel with an excess air. We need power to pump water and fuel (assuming liquid fuel such as LSHS, fuel oil, and so on). Also, power is required for air blower. We thus see that the applied utility steam can now be converted into basic utilities, namely, water, power and fuel. Often the process licensor indicates utilities required as steam, cooling water and chilled water. Like raw materials, we have all data regarding consumptions and specifications of utilities from the process licensor. Here, the data may be implicit. In many modern plants, co-generation as energy conservation (ENCON) means is adopted as a built-in concept. For example, in methanol and ammonia plants superheated steam is produced at a pressure around 100 bars. It is then expanded through a turbine. The syn-gas compressor and recycle compressor are directly coupled to a steam turbine through a governor. Instead of having energy recovery with the help of a turbine and a barometric condenser, steam can be extracted at desired pressure and flow rate to meet heat (energy) requirement in a plant by condensation of this extracted steam. Such turbines are known as *extraction turbines*. Depending upon the pressure rating of the steam generated, the treatment method for water to the boiler and heat recovery steam generator (HRSG) will vary and hence the chemicals consumed. In such a situation, consumption of water treatment chemicals and ion-exchange resins would add to the cost of utilities.

For the rotating drives, such as compressor and turbine, we need lubricating oil. The consumption of lube oil has to be accounted for.

These applied utilities need to be converted into basic utilities. Once basic utilities are known, all equipment, piping, instrumentation and electricals can be estimated under OSBL component of the Plant and Machinery Schedule (Chapter 6). Many times the vendor gives the entire system as a module. In such a situation, the price of a bought-out unit is considered. Otherwise by using primary utilities and equipment cost one can generate the cost of an applied utility. This approach of derived cost of an applied utility might facilitate preliminary feasibility study. However, for preparing a detailed techno-economic feasibility study, one should have basic utilities and fixed cost associated with them as the OSBL facility.

Water requirement and its specifications at various levels of demand need to be carefully worked out for the entire project including housing colony, if any. Water required for drinking purpose, steam generation, process, cooling tower is treated separately having consumptions of various chemicals such as biocides, flocculants and coagulants, dispersants, and so on. Even the sea water used for cooling purpose as in the case of coastal refineries, needs special treatment programme. In addition to this, all sea water coolers will have exotic material of construction thereby adding to plant and machinery cost. Though treatment chemicals are in parts per million (ppm) levels, due to very high (say 20,000 $m^3$ per hour), water circulation rates their contribution to utilities consumption expressed in terms of money, can run into few lakhs.

If power is not available due to power cuts or scheduling, one may need to have captive power plant. Fuel used for such a plant would add to utilities consumption.

Similarly, one has to consider the need for refrigeration system where not only electrical consumption is important but also consumption of refrigerant could be important. With the state-of-the-art technology in modern days, the consumption of refrigerant could be minimum. When heat transfer fluids, other than steam, are used one has to account for their consumption too and, hence, addition to utilities cost. In consultation with project engineering company (who would be involved in detailed engineering and project construction), one has to develop the utilities consumptions (peak and average) and specifications for the entire project.

If power and water are available at concessional rates (based on the industrial policy of the State Government) at a particular project site, it should be explicitly stated.

### *The Other OSBL Facilities*

The off-site facilities such as storage tanks, at times may require utilities such as inert gas say, nitrogen ($N_2$) for blanketing purpose. We, therefore, need to have a plant to manufacture $N_2$.The requirement of nitrogen is met either by air liquefaction followed by cryogenic distillation or by adsorption process. Occasionally used process of inert gas generation uses combustion of hydrocarbon such as LPG, NG and NGL. Here also utilities are required.

Storage of hygroscopic materials need humidity controller.

If low sulphur heavy stock (LSHS) is used as a fuel electric power or steam may be required to heat the storage tank to keep the temperature above the pour point (60–80°C) The transfer line is also electrically heated or jacketed for steam.

The flare stack may also need fuel to keep the flame sustained. The detailed engineering contractor estimates these utilities.

The information we get from the process licensor is for the battery limit plant. In addition to the above, one must account for all raw materials, chemicals required for effluent treatment plant (ETP). For instance, the effluent treatment plant such as wet air oxidation may require a catalyst; if Fenton chemistry is used to detoxify (partially) the waste, one requires ferrous sulphate ($FeSO_4$) and hydrogen peroxide ($H_2O_2$) and sulphuric acid to adjust the pH and then caustic soda to precipitate iron as hydroxide. This will then add to raw material consumption. The effluent treatment plant also requires utilities such as electric power for surface aerators, mixers, clarifiers, compressors for air, pumps, and so on.

The effluent treatment plant is not only for the process effluent but also for treating boiler and cooling tower blow-downs. Recovery of water from such blow-downs by membrane unit makes sense in a large petrochemical complex. This would then add to capital as well as operating cost (cost of production). There are tertiary treatment plants for recycling water from ETP.

Apart from the above, power is required in administrative buildings and other buildings for illumination purpose. Treated water is required for drinking purpose in the plant and administration buildings, in the canteen and water is also required for facilities (toilet and bath).

The costs of all chemicals used in treating basic utilities, i.e. ion exchange resins, membranes, treatment chemicals for membranes, heat transfer fluids, transformer oils, lubricating oils and refrigerants are added to the basic utilities cost. Thus utilities cost consists of the cost associated with the basic utilities and treatment chemicals including resins and membrane.

Thus one has to consider all the raw materials and utilities required not only for battery limit (B/L) plant but also for off-sites, including effluent treatment plant.

By and large, in petrochemical complex, raw materials and utilities together can contribute between 60 and 85% towards the cost of production. The exception is caustic-chlorine industry where utility in the form of power, dominates over the raw material.

### 7.2.3 Packaging

The next important factor in the cost of production is the cost associated with packing material. The cost packaging could be high for consumer products such as toiletries, cosmetics, beverages, pharmaceutical, products and paints. On the other hand, for bulk chemicals (commodity chemicals), the cost of packing could be very low. While perfumes are sold in 25 to 100 ml bottles with spray device, bulk chemicals, such as methanol is sold in 2001 drums and road tankers. Some chemicals, such as *o*-xylene, benzene, toluene, are also sold straightway in road tankers having capacity of 10 – 20 cubic meter.

Thus packing cost would depend on end-use of product and hence generalisation could be risky. It needs to be estimated depending upon the product under consideration.

### 7.2.4 Salary and Wages

The contribution of salary and wages can vary between 5 and 10% in the cost of production for petrochemical projects and about 15% in pharmaceuticals and fine chemicals project due to highly skilled work personnel. Salaries and wages of all people working at production site along with their perquisites are considered. The number of people working in a totally automatic plant could be less than those working in multi-stage batch process plants. While estimating the number of employees in the plant, a rule of thumb can be applied such as total people employed at site should not be less than sum of people employed in the project office and those employed during the period of construction. As a back-up towards estimate, we need to identify people of all categories, such as works manager, manager, chief engineers, production managers, maintenance engineer with the entire team right up to helpers, production supervisors, senior operators, junior operators, helpers, people in stores, supporting personnel in human resource development department, security personnel, and so on, working in the plant along with their salaries and perquisites.

### 7.2.5 Factory Overheads

Factory overheads include all expenses associated with operating a plant, which have not been accounted so far. Repairs and maintenance charges (consumable stores), insurance, miscellaneous expenses, such as communication expenses, office, stationary, writing materials, and so on, are included in factory overheads. Repairs and maintenance charges can be computed as listed in

Table 7.1. It must be remembered that cost of spares in the *plant and machinery* item is not the cost of maintenance.

**Table 7.1** Repairs and Maintenance Estimate

| *Year* | *% of Bldg and Civil Works* | *% Plant and Machinery* |
|---|---|---|
| 1 | 1 | 0.5 |
| 2 | 1 | 1.0 |
| 3 | 1 | 1.5 |
| 4 | 1 | 2.0 |
| 5 | 1 | 2.5 |
| . | . | . |
| . | . | . |
| . | . | . |
| 10 | 1 | 2.5 |

If the plant is handling corrosive chemicals, consumables for repairs and maintenance could be on the higher side say 1.5 to 2% as against 1% shown above.

For a preliminary estimate, in the absence of detailed information from the process licensor, one can obtain consumption figures from *Petrochemical Handbook and Gas Processing Handbook,* published in *Hydrocarbon Processing* (Gulf Publishing Co., Houston, Texas) and other professional magazines.

In the cost of production, the contribution of raw materials is in the range of 50–70%. Utilities contribute 10–15% to the cost of production. Thus raw material and utilities together contribute about 60–85% towards the cost of production. As seen from the above, the cost of production is least sensitive to the cost of packaging, salaries and wages, and factory overheads. Thus estimation of raw material and utilities is very important. It is obvious that if operating cost of the project has to be brought down, by lowering the cost of production, the technology needs to be upgraded continuously thereby, lowering raw materials and utilities consumptions, adopt standardised production practices

(ISO Standards) and have in-house Research & Development programme to upgrade the existing technology. The R&D expenditure as % of the total sales turnover is far less in our country than that in the developed countries. As a result, our costs of production are always higher due to somewhat inefficient technology. Many times, the management concentrates on keeping salaries and wages under control as a tool towards reducing the cost of production. The contribution of this factor towards the cost of production being of the order of 10%, one cannot achieve substantial reduction in the cost by not offering a reasonable salary package. On the other hand, the demoralised workforce can reduce production rate particularly in batch processing involving various unit operations and unit processes.

## 7.3 GROSS COST OF PRODUCTION

The elements of cost of production discussed above essentially deal with the cost incurred (would be incurred) at the production site. As mentioned earlier, there is a distinct possibility of having a general administration at different sites. The cost incurred at this site should also be taken into consideration as listed below.

### 7.3.1 Administrative Expenses

The number of people at admin site are listed along with their salaries and perquisites. The administrative overheads include office communication charges, office stationary in all forms, insurance and other miscellaneous operating expenses related to the smooth functioning of the office.

### 7.3.2 Sales Expenses

The number of people in the sales division is counted in case they are not accounted earlier and the salary of all such people with perquisites is considered. Selling expenses do include all promotional expenses such as advertisements on television, documentary in cinema house, advertisement in professional magazines, bulletins, and so on.

Having estimated expenses at admin site, one can now compute gross cost of production.

Gross cost of production = Cost of production + Administrative expenses + Sales expenses. (7.4)

As a rule of thumb the administrative expenses (often known as *admin expenses*) do not exceed 15% of the cost of production at the production site. In future, with vastly improved communication systems, this scenario would change.

## 7.4 NORMATIVE COST OF PRODUCTION

When the question of subsidy by the Central Government arises, as in the case of fertilisers, the computation of the cost of production differs slightly from that discussed above. The cost of production is now known as *'normative cost of production'* which is equivalent to gross cost of production (i.e. cost of production + administrative expenses + sales expenses). While computing selling price of the product, 'retention price' is calculated by taking into account post-tax returns as spelled out by the finance ministry from time to time. (There are fixed post-tax returns on equity and one cannot take arbitrary figure). With liberalisation of economy and decontrol of administered pricing, the concept of normative cost of production shall be vanishing from the scenario in future.

## 7.5 MONITOR THIS WAY

Having understood the elements of the cost of production, it is now easier to monitor the cost in day to day functioning of the plant. There are two components in cost of production. One is the actual consumption of materials and the other is the cost of these materials. The cost of raw materials can be minimised by resourcing them globally or by entering long-term contract with the supplier. The production team can only monitor consumptions. Log-sheets are maintained on routine basis in plants having continuous as well as batch processes. This record would give us an idea on consumption of raw materials and utilities on daily basis or per batch as the case may be. These figures could be compared with those given by the process licensor via the basic engineering package. The corrective actions are then taken to keep the actual consumption in line with the given norms or, if possible even lower (Consumption) through upgradation.

There is nothing one can do about controlling salaries and wages. The management negotiates with respective unions to decide annual increments and perquisites. The reduction in the salary bill could be achieved through voluntary retirement schemes (VRS) or via compulsory retirement scheme (CRS).

Having log-sheets dealing with maintenance of equipments, one can monitor the consumption of consumable stores. If a particular make of valves and fittings are found to be lasting for shorter duration than expected, one can change the vendor. It should be remembered that there is no substitute for quality and quality is always costlier.

## 7.6 THE SCHEDULE

For project evaluation purpose only, we consider lifespan of any project to be ten years even though the project continues to operate profitably thereafter. The capacity utilisation of a newly conceived project varies from year to year. The project may not achieve 100% capacity utilisation due to so many factors beyond the control of the project owner. The various factors such as raw material supplier may not honour his commitments due to some problems in his plants, there could be some equipment failure or system failure resulting in unscheduled stoppage of the plant, the sales team may not be in a position to penetrate the market to the anticipated extent, dumping of finished products by neighbouring countries into market, are responsible for lower capacity utilisation of the project. Considering all these, we have the lowest capacity utilisation in the first year and capacity utilisation progressively increases. For feasibility studies, by and large, we consider maximum capacity utilisation to be 95% and this is towards the end of project lifespan. To begin with we have 60–65% capacity utilisation in the first year followed by 65–70% in the second year, and so on. A typical schedule for the cost of production is presented below in Table 7.2.

**Table 7.2** Cost of Production Schedule Design capacity: X TPA of product

| *Year* | *1* | *2* | *3* | *---* | *10* | *Comments* |
|---|---|---|---|---|---|---|
| % Capacity utilisation | 60 | 65 | 70 | --- | 95 | |
| Actual capacity | | | | | | |
| Raw materials, chemicals and catalysts | | | | | | Details in Appendix 7.1 |
| Utilities | | | | | | |
| Packaging | | | | | | |
| Salary and wages | | | | | | |
| Factory Overheads | | | | | | |
| Total cost of production | | | | | | |
| Admin expenses | | | | | | |
| Sales expenses | | | | | | |
| Gross cost of production | | | | | | |

While preparing the detailed techno-economic feasibility report, pertinent details of estimates are provided as supporting or back-up document and are indicated in comments column as given in

Appendix 7.1. For major raw materials or catalyst, it is desirable to have at least a budgetary offer and commitment to supply the raw material. For example, if polybutene project is planned based on the $C_4$ stream from FCC cracker of a refinery, it is desirable to have a firm commitment to supply the $C_4$ stream by way of letter from the refinery. In case of utilities, it is also desirable to have a letter from the respective state industrial development corporation, indicating rate of water, and electricity with commitment to supply the same.

It is always desirable to have rates of raw material and utilities in terms of basic rate and the duties. This would ease out efforts in revision of the estimate by knowing duties prevailing at the time of the revision. Appendix 7.1 typically presents such details.

**Appendix 7.1**

**Raw Material Component**

| Raw Material | X | Y | Z |
|---|---|---|---|
| Base rate ₹/T | | | |
| Excise | | | |
| Sales (VAT) | | | |
| Import duty | | | |
| Transportation | | | |
| Total ₹/T | A | B | C |

Raw material consumption expressed as T/T of product.

| *Raw material* | *Consumption (T)* | *Rate (₹/T)* | *Component (₹)* |
|---|---|---|---|
| X | P | A | (P) (A) |
| Y | Q | B | (Q) (B) |
| Z | R | C | (R) (C) |

Similar detailed back-up should be given for all elements of the cost of production.

## SUGGESTED READINGS

*Application for Financial Assistance*, The Industrial Credit and Investment Corporation of India.

*Explanatory Notes for Filling up the Application Form for Financial Assistance from All-India financial Institutions*, The Industrial Credit and Investment Corporation of India.

*They are available at corporate offices of ICICI. & IDBI.*

***Technology Upgradation is a Pre-requisite to Minimise the cost of Production.***

# 8

# Project Financing

## 8.1 INTRODUCTION

The question of financing a project needs to be addressed differently after understanding which project needs financing: is it a Greenfield project or add-on project or is it a part of an ongoing project? We shall address these issues to understand principles or concept behind financing or funding. Since all along we have concentrated on the proposed project, we shall first overview 'know-why' of financing a proposed Greenfield project and then address pertinent issues of add-on project and ongoing project.

## 8.2 GREENFIELD PROJECT

It is essential that all arrangements to finance the project be made prior to commencement of project construction activities. While financing a project, we need capital to support (i) the cost associated with fixed assets (the project cost), and (ii) requirements of working capital to make project function, or operate.

In this chapter, we shall see various options available for financing a project (in private sector). A project is considered to be a public sector undertaking (PSU) when the government owns 51% of equity or more in it. We shall overview project financing and try to understand 'why' rather than 'how' formalities of obtaining term loan. The objective here is to introduce basic concepts rather than to go into details of how to raise funds in the market to meet the needs.

The project promoter/owner or entrepreneur can exercise option of financing the entire project through his own source or reserves of the organisation he owns, if the project is small. As project capital outlay becomes larger and larger, he may borrow capital from his friends and may make them the joint owners through shares. The contribution of others may not be sufficient and at the same time owner would not like their contribution exceeding this, because he may lose control of the project. If these sources cannot meet the project cost, the promoter has the other option left to him and that is to borrow the capital from financial institutions (such as The Industrial Credit and Investment Corporation of India (ICICI), The Industrial Development Bank Of India (IDBI), World Bank, etc.) and commercial banks at predetermined interest rate.

Earlier the State Governments used to offer capital subsidy to attract project to their respective state particularly in the industrially notified backward districts to have a sustainable development of all regions. The capital subsidy is a sort of gift given by the government. Therefore, we have

$$\text{Project cost} = (\textit{Subsidy}) + \text{Owner's capital} + \text{Borrowed capital} \qquad (8.1)$$

Though *the capital subsidy is discouraged*, we shall see the rationale behind the same. The owners' or shareholders' capital is called *Equity*. The borrowed capital can be partly met by debentures, deposits and long-term loan from financial institutions. We shall not consider debenture and deposit issues, but we shall assume that all borrowed capital is obtained from the financial institutions in the form of term loan.

*Subsidy*

Immediately after independence, the industrial growth in India was centred around metro cities. This led to tremendous pressure on civic amenities (Mumbai being a classic example of this). Also, it led to uneven development of states and within states, to various districts. In order to have more or less even dispersal of industries throughout the country, the central as well as state governments identified 'industrially backward' districts or regions within the respective states. The concept of capital subsidy was introduced to attract entrepreneurs or business community to such places. Not only capital benefit but also incentives and assistance to reduce operating cost were offered and are still in practice. These benefits include exemption on sales tax, to some extent excise duty, exemption on project import duty, electricity at a concessional rate, exemption on corporate tax and so on. Co-generation plants and effluent treatment plants are funded at reduced interest rates. These are also given the benefit of 100% depreciation while computing profit for the corporate tax purpose.

While financing a project, we have to take into consideration site-specific capital subsidy. Therefore, we have to arrange for funding of the project cost *less* capital subsidy. Our economic and industrial policies are undergoing transition due to economic liberalisation. As a result of this, the carrot of capital subsidy may be slowly withdrawn. While selecting the site for proposed project, one should consider this aspect.

### 8.2.1 Owners' Capital (Equity)

The owners' capital is frequently referred as equity. Project promoter(s), project promoting organisation(s), and public who together contribute to equity capital of a project are real owners of a project under implementation. The lender(s) of borrowed capital are not the owners because the borrowed capital is serviced by way of interest and it is expected to be paid back (returned) as per agreed loan repayment schedule. The question, we have to address now is that who could be the equity holder. The project promoter(s) may find it impossible to finance entire equity through his own sources. He, therefore, may invite people to be joint owners by way of raising public issue. A risk, however, always exists that if someone buys all shares from market his holding may exceed the contribution of the promoter. In such an eventuality, the promoter would lose the hold, on the project, which he would not like to do. In other words project 'take-over' is a distinct possibility. Therefore, it is desirable that promoter's contribution is more than 50% in equity, say, 51% and shareholders' contribution 49%. Foreign institutional investors are now permitted to invest as per guidelines issued by the Reserve Bank of India.

The next question, is who could be the promoter(s). The entrepreneur is, of course, the main promoter. It may happen that he may not have enough financial resources available with him. In which case, the state industrial development corporation, on behalf of the state government may join hands with him and act as a joint promoter. The technology, which is not easily available, may become available if the process licensor also joins as a promoter. In such a situation, we have the process licensor or his associate organisation joining the entrepreneur as co-promoter. In some situations even the existing organisation can be a promoter. Thus, we can summarise this in the following way:

**Equity**

Promoters (51%)

- Entrepreneur
- The Organisation
- Foreign Collaborator (process/technology licensor)
- State Industrial Development Corporation
- Unit Trust of India
- Life Insurance Corpotation of India Ltd and so on.

General public 49%

Please note that all promoters listed above need not contribute together in each and every project as promoter. However, entrepreneur or the owner must contribute himself because others would not believe in credibility of the project (despite the fact it is financially sound on paper) if there is no financial stake by the promoter.

There always exists a minimum contribution from the entrepreneur. If he is a technocrat, then the contribution can be less. The details would change from state to state and from time to time and would depend upon the availability of funds. It is, therefore, recommended that such details be obtained from the state industrial development corporation. Various advantages associated with the participation of a technology or process licensor, as a promoter, have been outlined earlier in Chapter 2. By and large, the board of directors would consist of nominees of all the promoters in proportion of their contribution.

After having promoters' contribution in the equity, the remaining equity financing is done by issuing shares (also known as stock) to public in the case of public Limited company. The company is listed on stock exchange (Bombay Stock Exchange, BSE or National Stock Exchange (NSE)). The first sale of shares (stock) is known as initial public offer (IPO). Generally, the issue is managed by a Bank who acts as a manager to the issue (says for example, State Bank of India, Bank of Baroda and so on) and for which it receives fees. That is why we have in project cost component, the item "Preliminary and capital issue related expenses". In the case of share or public issue, the project owner does not provide any assurance to pay back money invested and dividend thereupon in case of failure of business (Bankruptcy). The share holders take entire risk. The share holder can earn dividend on his investment. If business is good the dividend can be substantially higher than the interest on fixed deposit in nationalized bank (zero risk investment). The dividend is on the face value of share. The share holder can earn more money by selling his shares in the appreciated market. If company is doing good business share prices go up and during bad period of the business share prices go down. The share market indices, namely

Sensex and Nifty, are barometers of the market trend. Sensex is the abbreviation of Bombay Sensitive Index. It is the bench mark (April 1979=100) index of the Bombay Stock Exchange. Similarly, Nifty is the bench mark index of National Stock Exchange. The detailed discussion of Sensex and Nifty and their utilization in predicting market trend of shares (stock) of a particular company is excluded from the scope of this book.

### 8.2.2 Borrowed Capital (Debt)

The borrowed capital financing also known as debt financing has mainly two components,

- Loan in the form of secured loan by issuing bonds or debentures. The loan can be unsecured loan also.
- Loan from Financial Institutions, national or international (International Monetary Fund, IMF, World Bank) or Banks. When it is payable within a fixed period it is known as term loan.

Debenture is nothing but a bond. In this case the return of the capital (loan amount) with the interest thereupon on maturity is secured against assets of the company. Moreover the rate of interest is fixed. In this sense it differs from equity financing by shares wherein there is neither security of money invested nor about the dividend. The large established corporate houses, the Government for construction of mega infrastructure projects raise the capital via bonds (debentures). For construction of Konkan Railway bonds were issued. Such bonds with the Govt, are well secured. The same is true for well established big corporate houses.

The bonds (debentures) can be converted at later date to share capital. Such bonds are known as convertible bonds. Thus we have two types of debenture namely, convertible and non convertible debentures. The project owner pays lower interest rate on the convertible bond than that applicable to non convertible debentures. In the financial statement interest paid on debentures is financial expenses (interest paid on term loan, working capital and that on debentures).

The loans in the form of debentures and deposits can be obtained from public. However, it is generally not a large amount. Many times for a new project it might not have been even planned at least at the level of feasibility study. For a mega project there can be funding through equipment supplier in the form of supplier credit.

The term loan is obtained from financial institutions such as The Industrial Development Bank of India (IDBI), The Industrial Credit and Investment Corporation of India (ICICI), The World Bank, International Monetary Fund (IMF) and commercial banks. The foreign exchange for imported components of project cost can be arranged through the Indian banks having overseas operation, for instance, State Bank of India, Bank of Baroda, etc. In case the process licensor is participating as owner in the project, he may arrange soft loan from his country of origin. The same is also possible if he is just a process licensor. A part of term loan, particularly, foreign exchange component 'forex' can be arranged through a trade pact between our country and the country of origin of process licensor or any other country. For instance, process licensor may originate from England (UK), but if a vendor from Japan is supplying imported equipment it is possible to have a 'soft' loan from a bank in Japan as well. The borrowed capital attracts interest. The project owner has to take necessary clearances from the Reserve Bank of India to borrow and to pay the interest in foreign currency.

The term loan is repaid as per the agreed repayment schedule between the financial institution and the project owner. The main requirement for obtaining term loan from financial institutions is a detailed techno-economic feasibility report prepared by well-known project engineering organisation having a proven track record. This report is also called a *bankable document.* We shall overview, towards the end, the feasibility report in Chapter 14.

After having understood the meaning of subsidy and owner's capital, let us see whether there are any norms or guidelines on how much one can borrow in terms of term loan from the financial institutions.

*Debt : Equity Ratio, Norms (Guidelines)*

Before we present norms or general guidelines, let us understand the rationale behind Debt : Equity (D:E) ratio for projects of different sizes. For smaller projects, or say for add-on battery limit project, it is possible to fund the same entirely, or to a large extent, from reserves or owner's capital. Therefore, Debt : Equity ratio can be on lower side. As the size of the project increases, financial institutions may provide higher loan depending upon the proven track record of the entrepreneur or promoter(s). For mega projects of national interest, such as refinery and petrochemical complex or refinery and power-generation project, a very high Debt : Equity ratio is possible. At present, the D:E ratio is also negotiable and depending upon the credit ratings the term loan is arranged. The following guidelines (Table 8.1) are generally followed and would be useful to understand the extent of term loan (these are not having any legal binding).

**Table 8.1** Guidelines for D:E ratio

| *Project Cost (₹ in Crores)* | *D : E, Ratio* |
|---|---|
| Up to 100 | 1 : 1 to 1.5 : 1 |
| 100-500 | 1.5 : 1 to 2 : 1 |
| 500-1000 | 2 : 1 to 3 : 1 |
| 1000 onwards | 3 : 1 |
| 10,000 onwards | 4 : 1 |

Higher Debt : Equity Ratio means that the financial institute is taking more risks, which is possible in the case of business house having proven track record of successful execution and operation of projects. The Lower Debt : Equity Ratio means that the promoters are taking more risk. The financial institutions while agreeing on Debt:Equity ratio, do carry out risk analysis of the project. The credit ratings will decide the ratio. In fact when public issue is declared, the risk rating is given so that shareholders know a *priori*, the risk they are taking.

The borrowing can be based on *floating* or *fixed* interest rates. However, we exclude the details of the same from this book. In the text to follow we shall consider fixed interest. There also exists a possibility of convertible bonds being offered by the financial institutions as borrowing, which on performance of the project might be converted into equity (shareholder). This conversion details are also beyond the scope of this book and therefore excluded.

Thus, in summary we can present the project financing in the following manner:

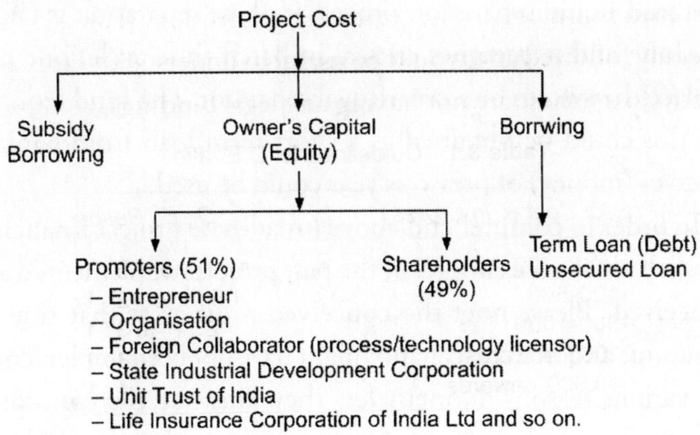

## 8.3 ADD-ON PROJECT

As discussed in Chapter 1, by add-on project we mean the project could be a battery limit, forward or backward integration or an expansion project. The financing of such projects could be on similar lines, as discussed above for Greenfield projects. It is also possible that a battery limit project could be totally funded from the reserves of the organisation. For example, a project to produce maleic anhydride by scrubbing off gases from the existing phthalic anhydride plant is a battery limit project. This project could be entirely financed from the reserves.

If the project owner is planning to double the capacity of existing 600 TPD ammonia plant to meet the demand of phosphatic fertilisers (NPK), he might secure term loan from the financial institutions say, ICICI and the equity could be entirely contributed out of funds from the existing business.

## 8.4 ONGOING BUSINESS

An ongoing business (project), at times, needs funds to overcome unforeseen problems related to equipment failures. For example, in liquid-liquid separation process if phase separation is taking too long and it becomes critical in batch time cycle, one may replace the system by a centrifugal separator. The fund required for this could be obtained as a short-term loan from bank or reserves (money) of previous year could be used.

In order to comprehend above broad-base project financing, we shall see some examples of the past projects implemented and conceived. Please note the conceived projects at that time of economic and market scenario might have not been implemented for various reasons. Nonetheless they illustrate the concept of project financing.

## 8.5 ILLUSTRATIONS

Following illustration of the actual and conceived projects would give a fair idea of the above concept. These project might have under gone some changes over a period of implementation or may change during the course of implementation and some might have not been implemented. Nonetheless they illustrate the project financing concept.

### 8.5.1 M/s UB Petroproducts Ltd,

| | |
|---|---|
| Project: | The manufacture of 7,000 TPA Propylene glycol 8,000 TPA Polyether polyols (12,000 TPA propylene oxide for captive consumption) |
| Scenario: | Around 1989 |
| **Project Cost:** | ₹ 71 Crores |
| **Project Financing:** | |
| Debt : Equity | = 1.84 : 1 |
| Term loan (₹) | = 46 Crore |
| Equity (₹) | = 25 Crore |
| **Equity Provision** | |
| Project Promoters | |
| UB Ltd and Associates: | 24.8% |
| Tamil Nadu Industrial Development Corporation (TIDCO): | 26.0% |
| Montedip (Italy) Enimont Group: | 10.0% |
| Total Promoters' contribution: | 60.8% |
| Public issue | 39.2% |

*Source:* Chemical Business July 5 - 19, 1989, p.p 101, and the press release for public issue

*Comments*

The project was promoted by an organisation along with the State, Tamil Nadu Industrial Development Corporation (TIDCO). There is participation of an organisation belonging to the process licensor as a promoter. The total promoter's equity is 60.8% (*more than 51%*) and public issue is 39.2% (*less than 49%*).

### 8.5.2 M/s Narmada Chematur Petrochemicals Ltd

| | | |
|---|---|---|
| Project: | The manufacture of 20,000 TPA Aniline 10,000 TPA Toluene diisocyanate (TDI) | |
| Scenario: | 1997 | |
| **Project Cost:** | 308.19 ₹ Crore | (Feasibility time) |

**Project Financing:**

| | | |
|---|---|---|
| Debt : Equity | = | 1.5 :1 |
| Term Loan | = | 184.91 |
| Equity | = | 123.28 |
| Total | = | 308.19 |

| **Term Loan Provision:** | | **₹(Crore)** |
|---|---|---|
| Foreign Currency | = | 94.91 |
| Indian Component | | |
| ICICI | = | 20.00 |
| IDBI | = | 50.00 |
| IFCI | = | 20.00 |
| Total term loan | = | 184.91 |

**Equity Provision**

| | | |
|---|---|---|
| Promoters | | |
| Gujarat Narmada Valley Fertilisers Company Ltd. (GNFC) | = | 68.55 |
| Chematur Engineering AB (CEAB) | = | 6.00 |
| IBI Chematur, Bombay (Mumbai) | = | 1.50 |
| Total contribution by promoters (61.6% of equity) | = | 76.05 |
| Public issue (38.4% equity) | = | 47.23 |
| Total Equity | = | 123.28 |

(*Source:* Sood, V.K., Dave M.K. and Patel, R.P., "Implementation of Aniline and TDI Project-NCPL, *Chem. Indu. News,* 957 September 1998.-Sood V.K. Private communication)

The above figures are at feasibility level only.

*Comments*

The project cost is ₹ 308.19 Crore. The Debt : Equity ratio could have been 2:1 as per our norms or guidelines. However, promoters decided to have Lower Debt : Equity Ratio of 1.5:1. This may be due to their confidence in mobilising higher equity. Not only the foreign process licensor is joining hands with GNFC, but also its Indian associate company is participating in promoting the company. The contribution of foreign company and its Indian associate is around 10% of total promoter's contribution. Please note that the local state industrial development corporation, GIDC in this case, is not participating. The term loan is obtained from three leading financial institutions instead of preferably one. The foreign currency (forex) requirement is met through State Bank of India (SBI) and Bank of Baroda (BOB).

### 8.5.3 Hindustan Organic Chemicals Ltd (HOCL)

Following is the scenario when project announcement was made through media.

| | |
|---|---|
| Project: | The manufacture of 20,000 TPA Methyldiisocyanate (MDI) |
| Scenario: | 1997 (Feasibility) |
| **Project Cost:** | ₹ 386.73 Crore |
| **Project Financing:** | |
| Debt : Equity | = 1.5:1 |
| Term Loan | = 232.04 |
| Equity | = 154.69 |
| Total | = 386.73 |

**Provision for Equity**

| | | |
|---|---|---|
| Promoters | | |
| Hindustan Organic Chemicals Ltd | = | 47.33 |
| Chematur AB (Foreign) | = | 31.56 |
| Total promoters' contribution | = | 78.89 |
| (Indian promoter 60% and process licensor 40%) Public issue | = | 75.8 |
| (Prometers' 51% and public issue 49%) | | |

*Source: Chem. Weekly*, P. 74, 15, April, 1997.

*Comments*

In this project also Debt : Equity ratio used is 1.5 : 1. It means promoters are confident of managing equity. The process licensor is also a joint promoter and has agreed to have 40% shares in promoters' contribution. The same process licensor has however, contributed less (~ 10%) in the project of GNFC. In the equity, promoter's contribution is 51% and shareholders' contribution is 49%.

### 8.5.4 Guru Gobind Singh Refinery, Bhatinda Punjab

This grassroots refinery (9 MMTPA) is a very good example of public private partnership.
The owner is Hindustan Mittal Energy Limited (HMEL) – a joint venture refinery promoted by Hindustan Petroleum Corporation Ltd (HPCL) and Mittal Energy Limited (MEL).

| | | |
|---|---|---|
| **Project cost** | (₹) 21,500 Crore | |
| **Term Loan** (debt) | (₹) 13,500 Crore | |
| **Equity** | (₹) 8,000 Crore | (D:E = 1.6875 :1) |

In equity: entirely by promoters

| | |
|---|---|
| HPCL | 49% |
| MEL | 49% |
| Financial Institutions | 02% |

Promoters were advised to bring down stakes to 30% each via IPO (Initial Public Offer).

### 8.5.5 Reliance Sibur Elastomers Pvt Ltd;

This is an example of international collaboration with equity participation.
May be this could be example of the state of the art technology made available by the process licensor via equity participation.

| | |
|---|---|
| **Project:** | 100,000 TPA Butyl rubber |
| **Project Cost:** | $ 450 Million (approx. ₹ 2400 Crore) |
| **Project Promoters:** | Reliance Industries Ltd (India) 74.9% |
| SIBUR (Russia's leading petrochemical company) | **25.1%** |

*Source: Chemical.Industry Digest, pp* 16, August, 2012.

## 8.6 WORKING CAPITAL

We need finance or money to constant a plant (Project). We also need money for operating the plant till the product is sold and the price is realised. The earning from sales is recycled but a time gap between the operating expenses and sales realisation remains. To bridge this gap we need working capital. This can be reduced in practice by minimisation of inventory of raw material and product and speedy recovery of sales price from customers (credit to customer is bare minimum).

We have seen earlier in Chapter 5, how to estimate working capital requirement for the smooth operation of the project. As an approximation, 25% of total working capital required is allowed to capitalise in the project cost as margin money. The balance 75% is obtained as a loan from banks as short-term loan. This loan is in the form of a running account like bank overdraft or cash credit and the project owner has to pay interest on this working capital borrowing, and the loan is required to be paid back.

Thus we have now a broader idea about how projects can be funded. The details of loan application, supporting documents required, etc., are beyond the scope of this book.

## 8.7 VENTURE CAPITAL

Venture capital is another source of financing an innovative project concept. An innovator or a project initiator may have a novel product or a technic but may not have enough funds to start his business. He then looks for a seed investment and a supporting partner to realize his concept. A Venture Fund is his best option.

Venture Capitalists are private bankers or funding institutes who finance projects involving new products, or novel technologies or successful products in new market territories. A Venture Capitalist takes a calculated risk and provides an equity funding along with the owner and also arranges institutes (financial institutes or banks) to fund the rest of the project cost (capital) as term loan (debt). Venture Capitalists per se, involve themselves in the project operation. Hence the projects in which the Venture Capitalists invest are normally not very large capital value projects. In fact they are small to medium projects which the state governments also want to encourage.

Venture Capitalists invest in good marketable ideas which are likely to have good success chances. They do take a risk but unlike lending institutes, private equity Venture Capitalists play an important role as "board members" and consultants. To ensure success of the invested business and recovery of their investment with attractive returns Venture Capitalists sometimes participate in the operations of the project and also help the entrepreneurs to go to the right people to advice and employ. In other words, venture capitalist goes out of way to see venture succeeds because of his financial stakes in the business.

Venture Capitalists' business requires sufficient returns on capital they are going to put in equity, to attract other equity and debt (term loan) funds. This has to be much more than the interest earned on term loans. This approach is justified because their investment involves larger risks. Venture Capitalists target for 30-40% return on their investment. Some investments give only 10% returns but on an average 20-25% is achieved by established Venture Capitalists.

Venture Capitalists buy stakes in entrepreneurs' business, nurture it for a short period of time and then exit with unloading the equity to another investment banker. A share value rise or Price/Equity ratio (P/E ratio) of 20-30 is not uncommon after 5 years. A growth of sales of an order of 10-20 times is a normal expectation of a Venture Capitalist. That is the time Venture Capitalists exit the company. Venture Capitalists generally look for exit in 3-5 years. Sometimes it extends to 7 years but a stay beyond that is not acceptable.

Venture Capitalists do not generally invest at concept level or research level. Most projects are tried at small scale, market seeding results are obtained and have a potential to grow very big. Thus venture capitalists take calculated risk. The tech-entrepreneur then finds a facilitating partner in a Venture capitalist.

## SUGGESTED READING

*Application for Financial Assistance*, The Industrial Credit and Investment Corporation of India.

*Explanatory Notes for Filling up the Application form for Financial Assistance from All-India Financial Institutions*, The Industrial Credit and Investment Corporation of India.

***Business Loan Triggers Performance.***

# 9 Interest

## 9.1 INTRODUCTION

The concept of interest is very interesting for engineers dealing with project economics. We shall adopt here the managerial view of 'interest' rather than the social economist's view. Dewitt (1996) has presented an excellent account of theories of interest. In this chapter, we however, exclude the interaction between interest, inflation and escalation from our scope of work. For instance, the government may increase the interest rate and force the industry to become more competitive. This idea may backfire also. In order to give boost to the domestic industry the government may as well reduce the interest rate.

The project engineer is often faced with:

- How to service debt or term loan obtained for the project construction and its implication on the profitability?
- How to purchase an asset on instalment basis?
- How to decide between various alternatives available?
- How to make provision for continuous replacement of equipment after very short service life?

In all the above situations, we are confronted with one common issue and that is money. The question in our mind would be how much it is going to cost if I borrow money or if I purchase a system on instalment, and so on.

## 9.2 BASICS REVISITED

Interest is defined as the compensation, in the form of money that one has to pay on borrowed capital at an agreed time interval. In other words, moneylender would try to get a compensation higher than that of prevailing inflation. The government while fixing the rate of interest takes into account the inflation. The relationship is complex in nature. For instance, one may fix higher interest rate on institutional borrowings to curb or contain inflation by forcing them borrow less and become more efficient. In a pragmatic sense interest means interest rate, which is compensation per unit time. The interest rate is generally expressed as $X$% per annum rate meaning thereby on ₹ 100 principal one has to pay ₹ $X$ per year as the interest. The borrower has to repay the principal back to the moneylender in previously agreed timeframe such as in monthly, quarterly, half-yearly or yearly instalments. It is a bad practice not to repay the borrowed capital from financial institutions or banks and then convert it into non-performing assets. Such malpractices become a drag on the sustainable development of the nation.

There are following three main components of interest:

1. True compensation rate that a moneylender would like to realise.
2. Charge that a moneylender would like to levy on the borrower, which may be in the form of surcharge for manhours spent by his staff on management of issue of loan.
3. Cost of inconvenience caused to the moneylender if the loan is returned earlier. In this particular case, money made available to the moneylender may not be effectively utilised. The other inconvenience to the moneylender arises from the failure of loan repayment. As a result of this, the moneylender tries to add some cost to the true interest rate.

One would now appreciate that sound financial institutions develop expertise and competency to avoid problems associated with inconvenience. Their funding to business is expected to be on a very sound basis. These financial institutions generally entertain business houses, having proven track record. They evaluate financial viability of projects before sanctioning the loan. The loan given by them is known as *term loan* and it is for a longer duration. Financing working capital for business houses is not common with financial institutions. The interest rates of financial institutions are governed by the government norms through Reserve Bank of India. On the other hand, banks, which offer loans for working capital do have to incorporate costs of inconvenience because the loan duration is short. The disbursement is against items of value or current assets. The interest rate for working capital would be higher than that for term loan because the funds for a bank are from the depositors in the form of fixed deposit receipts on which the bank has to pay interest. Therefore, working capital attracts higher rates of interest than those offered to depositors.

When individual puts his money in the the fixed deposit in banks for long term, he expects higher rates of interest because during the long term, he would have missed other opportunities to have higher returns on the capital.

Thus there are different perceptions of interest to different people.

### 9.2.1 Types of Interest

From managerial point of view, we are concerned with two types of interest, namely, simple interest and compound interest.

*Simple Interest*

The interest is charged only on borrowed capital (loan) and not on the interest accumulated. This is expressed as % interest rate, i.e. $X$% interest rate means on the loan amount of ₹ 100 the interest is ₹ $X$ per year. The time concept is important.

The future worth, F, of the present principal P is:

$$F = P(1 + in) \tag{9.1}$$

where, $n$ = number of years

$i$ = fractional interest rate

*Compound Interest*

In compound interest, the interest is charged on interest and principal. This concept is very useful when we consider future worth $F$, of the present principal P.

$$F = P(1 + i)^n \tag{9.2-a}$$

where, $n$ = number of years

$i$ = fractional interest rate

In other words, the present worth $P$ of future profit, $F$, would be

$$P = F/(1 + i)^n \tag{9.2-b}$$

where $F$ is the profit in $n$th year. The expression (9.2) forms the basis of discounted profit flow (DPF) technique of project evaluation discussed in the Chapter 12.

One should bear in mind that in the DPF technique $i$ is not merely the interest rate but it is hurdle rate of return.

### 9.2.2 Nominal and Effective Interest Rates

The concept of nominal and effective interest is important to engineering economics. Interest is frequently payable more often than once a year. The interest rate 10% payable per annum can be deemed as 0.83% payable monthly, 2.5% payable quarterly or 5% payable half-yearly.

For many loan transactions, interest is computed and charged more often than once in year. It means that there is interest on interest during that period. Many finance companies/banks offering personal loans, often compute interest monthly. Let us consider a loan with an interest rate of 24% but the loan is charged at 2% monthly. Assume that the loan amount is ₹ 100. The amount owed at the end of 12 months (1 year) would be 126.82 (= 100 × $(1.02)^{12}$). If the same amount, ₹ 100, is borrowed at 24% interest rate compounded annually the amount owed would be 100(1+0.24) = 124. This is less by 2.82. The monthly compounding then can be deemed as yearly compounding at the interest rate 26.82%. In other words, effective interest rate is 26.82%. Thus a borrower will prefer to pay 24% per annum the rate of interest while the lender will prefer 2% per month.

We can now generalise the above as let interest be compounded $m$ times at the rate $(i/m)$ per compounding period,

The nominal interest rate, $i = m\,(i/m)$ (9.3)

The effective interest rate, $i_{eff} = (1 + i/m)^m - 1$ (9.4)

When term loan is obtained from financial institutions, payment of interest is done on half-yearly basis (interest might be compounded quarterly). The exact terms are the result of negotiation between the borrower (project owner) and the lender (financial institutions).

## 9.3 LOAN REPAYMENT

As seen earlier, the borrowed capital needs to be serviced by way of interest. The debentures and other unsecured loans attract interest. Not only borrowed capital should be serviced but equity participants must also get return on equity. For shareholders, return on equity can de deemed as 'interest' paid by the project. This return on equity is called *dividend*. The difference is that dividend is left to discretion of the board of directors of an organisation depending upon health of the business in that particular year. Therefore, it slightly differs from the term 'interest' and hence called dividend.

Let us now see various options available for repayment of loan with interest.

**OPTION I**

The principal ($P$) is paid at the end of the borrowing term and simple interest is charged every year (Simple Interest).

**OPTION 2**

The principal ($P$) is paid in equal instalments and simple interest is paid thereupon.

**OPTION 3**

The moratorium period is two years and the loan is paid in eight years with equal instalments.

**OPTION 4**

The principal ($P$) and interest are paid together in equal amounts (Loan on instalment).

**OPTION 5**

Interest is paid along with the principal ($P$) at the end of borrowing term (Compound Interest).

In addition, we can use half-yearly or quarterly repayment schedule with or without interest being compounded in the form of effective interest rate.

These options are illustrated in Table 9.1

**Table 9.1** Comparison of Loan Repayment Options Basis

Loan = 100 units
Rate of Interest = 12%

**Option 1**

| *Year* | *Principal* | *Interest* | *Loan Repayment (with Interest)* | *Principal Left* |
|---|---|---|---|---|
| *(a)* | *(b)* | *(c)* | *(d)* | *(e)* |
| 0 | 100 | – | – | – |
| 1 | 100 | 12 | 12 | 100 |
| 2 | 100 | 12 | 12 | 100 |

| | | | | |
|---|---|---|---|---|
| 3 | 100 | 12 | 12 | 100 |
| 4 | 100 | 12 | 12 | 100 |
| 5 | 100 | 12 | 12 | 100 |
| 6 | 100 | 12 | 12 | 100 |
| 7 | 100 | 12 | 12 | 100 |
| 8 | 100 | 12 | 12 | 100 |
| 9 | 100 | 12 | 12 | 100 |
| 10 | 100 | 12 | 112 | 0 |

Total payment = 100.0 + 120.0 = 220.0

**Option 2**

| *(a)* | *(b)* | *(c)* | *(d)* | *(e)* |
|---|---|---|---|---|
| 0 | 100 | – | – | – |
| 1 | 100 | 12 .0 | 10 + 12 = 22.0 | 90 |
| 2 | 90 | 10.8 | 20.8 | 80 |
| 3 | 80 | 9.6 | 19.6 | 70 |
| 4 | 70 | 8.4 | 18.4 | 60 |
| 5 | 60 | 7.2 | 17.2 | 50 |
| 6 | 50 | 6.0 | 16.0 | 40 |
| 7 | 40 | 4.8 | 14.8 | 30 |
| 8 | 30 | 3.6 | 13.6 | 20 |
| 9 | 20 | 2.4 | 12.4 | 10 |
| 10 | 10 | 1.2 | 11.2 | 00 |

Total payment = 166.0

**Option 3**

| *(a)* | *(b)* | *(c)* | *(d)* | *(e)* |
|---|---|---|---|---|
| 0 | 100.0 | – | – | – |
| 1 | 100.0 | 12.0 | 12 | 100.0 |
| 2 | 100.0 | 12.0 | 23.1 | 88.9 |
| 3 | 88.9 | 10.7 | 21.8 | 77.8 |
| 4 | 77.8 | 9.3 | 20.4 | 66.7 |
| 5 | 66.7 | 8.0 | 19.1 | 55.6 |
| 6 | 55.6 | 6.7 | 17.8 | 44.5 |
| 7 | 44.5 | 5.3 | 16.4 | 33.4 |
| 8 | 33.4 | 4.0 | 15.1 | 22.3 |
| 9 | 22.3 | 2.7 | 13.8 | 11.2 |
| 10 | 11.2 | 1.3 | 12.5 | — |

Total payment = 172.0

**Option 4**

| (a) | (b) | (c) | (d) | (e) |
|---|---|---|---|---|
| 0 | 100.00 | – | – | – |
| 1 | 100.00 | 12.0 | 17.70 | 94.30 |
| 2 | 94.30 | 11.32 | 17.70 | 87.92 |
| 3 | 87.92 | 10.55 | 17.70 | 80.77 |
| 4 | 80.77 | 9.69 | 17.70 | 72.76 |
| 5 | 72.76 | 8.73 | 17.70 | 63.79 |
| 6 | 63.79 | 7.66 | 17.70 | 53.75 |
| 7 | 53.75 | 6.45 | 17.70 | 42.50 |
| 8 | 42.50 | 5.10 | 17.70 | 29.90 |
| 9 | 29.90 | 3.59 | 17.70 | 15.79 |
| 10 | 15.79 | 1.89 | 17.68 | 0.00 |

Total payment = 176.98; say, 177
(The instalment in year no. 10 is slightly less due to rounding off).

**Option 5**

| (a) | (b) | (c) | (d) | (e) |
|---|---|---|---|---|
| 0 | 100.00 | – | – | – |
| 1 | 100.00 | 12.00 | 0 | 112.00 |
| 2 | 112.00 | 13.44 | 0 | 125.44 |
| 3 | 125.44 | 15.05 | 0 | 140.49 |
| 4 | 140.49 | 16.86 | 0 | 157.35 |
| 5 | 157.35 | 18.88 | 0 | 176.23 |
| 6 | 176.23 | 21.15 | 0 | 197.38 |
| 7 | 197.38 | 23.69 | 0 | 221.07 |
| 8 | 221.07 | 26.53 | 0 | 247.60 |
| 9 | 247.60 | 29.71 | 0 | 277.31 |
| 10 | 277.31 | 33.28 | 310.59 | 000.00 |

Total payment = 310.59

We, thus see that payments in all the above cases do differ in magnitude but they are equivalent. All future payments or series of payments that would repay the present loan, with interest are deemed to be equivalent. This concept of equivalence is also important in project management. When money (100 units) is obtained as loan, it can be serviced for ten years in say, by any one of the options from the above. At the end of ten years (loan term) the borrower has returned all money (principal and interest) and the lender has received the principal (100 units) with compensation.

### 9.3.1 Term Loan Repayment

The term loan obtained has to be serviced through interest paid to the financial institutions. The loan repayment is as per the agreed schedule. The interest is not charged on the part of term loan that is repaid. The financial institutions do appreciate various difficulties an entrepreneur has to face during early period of the project. The capacity utilisation may be 60–65% and the cash inflow to project may not be adequate to start loan repayment. Therefore, generally a grace period is given to the project owner, during which he need not payback part of the term loan he has taken. This period is known as *moratorium period*. However, the project owner has to pay interest on the term loan. Generally, this period is two years from the date of commencement of production for large projects. This period is negotiable during the loan procurement process. If the health of the business house is good, one need not avail this facility of moratorium period. It should be noted that the project owner would not start repaying the capital but he has to pay full amount of interest during the moratorium period. After the moratorium period is over, loan repayment is usually done in half-yearly equal instalments. Thus if the project life is ten years and moratorium period is two years, the entire loan can be repaid in eight years with sixteen equal half-yearly instalments.

Let us see how the interest schedule is prepared by taking into consideration the loan repayment schedule. Table 9.2 exhibits one such schedule for the term loan of ₹ 160 lakh and interest rate 12%. The interest is paid every six months but is compounded, let us say, every three months.

The effective interest rate at the end of six months would, therefore, be

$$I_{eff} = (1 + 0.03)^2 - 1 = 6.09\%$$

**Table 9.2** Loan Repayment and Interest Schedule

Term loan = ₹ 160 lakh
Interest rate = 12%
Moratorium period = 2 years

The first instalment of ₹ 10 lakh is paid at the end of two years along with interest.

₹ in lakh

| *Year* | *Amount Loan* | *Interest* | *Amount Loan* | *interest* | *Total Interest* |
|---|---|---|---|---|---|
| 1 | 160 | 9.744 | 160 | 9.744 | 19.488 |
| 2 | 160 | 9.744 | 160 | 9.744 | 19.488 |
| 3 | 150 | 9.135 | 140 | 8.526 | 17.661 |
| 4 | 130 | 7.917 | 120 | 7.308 | 15.225 |
| 5 | 110 | 6.699 | 100 | 6.090 | 12.789 |
| 6 | 90 | 5.481 | 80 | 4.872 | 10.353 |
| 7 | 70 | 4.263 | 60 | 3.654 | 7.917 |
| 8 | 50 | 3.045 | 40 | 2.436 | 5.481 |
| 9 | 30 | 1.827 | 20 | 1.218 | 3.045 |
| 10 | 10 | 0.609 | – | – | 0.609 |
| Total interest (₹) | | | | | 112.056 |

The first instalment can be paid immediately at the end of the moratorium period of 2 years. Then during the first-half of the third year the interest would be levied on the principal amount *less* the term loan instalment paid at the end of second year. In such a situation the total interest accrued during the 10-year life of a project with a moratorium period 2 years would be:

$$\text{Total interest} = 11.50\,(T)\,(i) \tag{9.5}$$

Where, $T$ = Term loan

$i$ = fractional interest at the end of six months.

For the example given in Table 9.2, Total interest

$$\begin{aligned}\text{(Eq. (9.5))} &= 11.50\,(T)\,(i)\\ &= (11.50) \times (160) \times 0.0609\\ &= ₹\ 112.056.\ \text{lakh}\end{aligned}$$

On the other hand, if the first loan repayment instalment is paid at the end of 2½ years, the total interest would be

$$\text{Total interest} = 12.50\,(T)\,(i) \qquad (9.6)$$

For the example given, in Table 9.2, the total interest burden would be ₹ 121.8 lakhs (Eq. 9.6).

The above formulae will help in quick estimate of the total interest burden.

It is not necessary to have loan repayment over the entire life of the project. The loan can be repaid earlier also as per the agreed schedule with the funding agency.

### 9.3.2 Working Capital Borrowings

Apart from the term loan, project owner needs working capital to start with. The borrowing from bank is, generally, 75% of the total working capital requirement. This is short-term borrowing and hence attracts higher interest rate, generally speaking 25–30% higher rate of interest than that is applicable to term loan from the financial institutions. The working capital is paid back as soon as sufficient reserves are generated by the project. For a good project, the working capital is repaid during the first year or second year, i.e. during the moratorium period for the term loan.

The sum of interest on term loan and interest on working capital is known as *financial expenses* for that particular year. The computation of financial expenses is important to calculate the operating profit when the estimate of working results of a project is prepared (projected, as in Chapter 11.

## 9.4 PERIODIC PAYMENTS: INSTALMENTS

At times, due to cash flow problems, we are forced to buy some systems or assets on hire basis. For instance, if the project owner is exporting materials through the port (JNPT) near Mumbai, he may as well have a warehouse in nearby area say Panvel or Uran. Due to cash flow problems, he might opt for hiring the facility rather than purchasing the same. Some initial payment, as a token of commitment, is required to be paid, as 'down payment' to the owner of the facility and the balance amount need to be paid in instalments as negotiated.

Let us see how the owner of the warehouse looks at this deal as an opportunity of making money. If he gets the entire money by selling the property he would have invested the same somewhere else and would have earned interest on it. By offering rental deal, he is going to earn the same interest through instalments.

The payment made at the end of first instalment date is now available to the facility owner for investment somewhere at the market interest rate. The future worth of this instalment $L$ would be

$$F_1 = L(1 + i)^{n-1} \tag{9.7}$$

where $n$ = number of period during which interest is charged.

The second instalment would have future worth as

$$F_2 = L(1 + i)^{n-2} \tag{9.8}$$

The last instalment $L$ does not fetch any benefit.

Suppose the market price of the facility/equipment after the down payment is $P$, the owner would have invested this money somewhere else and would have realised benefit $F$

$$F = P(1 + i)^n \tag{9.9}$$

It follows that the vendor would now try to realise $F$ via instalment $L$ over period $n$.

Therefore,

$$F = L(1+ i)^{n-1} + L(1 + i)^{n-2} + ... + L \tag{9.10}$$

Multiply Eq. (9.10) by $(1 + i)$ and subtract Eq. (9.10) from the resulting expression to get

$$F = L\{(1 + i)^n - 1\}/(i) \tag{9.11}$$

From Eq. (9.11) we have instalment, $L$

$$L = (F)(i)/\{(1 + i)^n - 1\} \tag{9.12}$$

The relationship between the present market price $P$ and instalment $L$, can then be realised through Eqs. (9.9) and (9.12) as

$$L = P(1 + i)^n(i)/\{(1 + i)^n - 1\} \quad (9.13)$$

The application of the above analysis is illustrated.

$L$ is also known as equated periodical instatment. If the period is in months, $L$ is equated monthly instalment (EMI).

*Illustration*

It is desired to have a chemical warehouse to store chemicals received, valued at ₹ 15 lakh. If down payment of ₹ 2 lakh is made at the time of signing the deal, what would be the monthly instalment, if the payment is to be completed in three years? The owner has valued his money at 1.5% per month.

The value of asset is ₹: 15 lakh

The down payment is ₹: 2 lakh

The money to be paid equivalent to the market rate now over 36 months is ₹: 13 lakh.

If the landlord had the entire money with him for over 36 months, he would have realised,

$$F = 13\,(1 + 0.015)^{36} = ₹\,22.22 \text{ lakh.}$$

The landlord would like to recover this money from a buyer by fixing an instalment, $L$, with the help of Eq. (9.13).

$$L = \frac{13(1+0.015)^{36} \times 0.015}{((1+0.015)^{36} - 1))}$$

$$= ₹\,0.46998 \text{ lakh}$$

Say, the instalment would be = ₹ 47,000 month

## 9.5 ANNUALISED COST

### 9.5.1 Selection From Various Alternatives

Many times a process engineer is confronted with a problem of selecting a system or a piece of equipment from among multiple choices. For instance, for drying ammonium sulphate produced from gypsum, one can have either a rotary dryer system or a fluidised bed dryer system. The ultimate choice would then be governed by economic and other considerations as outlined below. The system would have a fixed cost component as the sum of purchased equipment cost (at the site), installation cost, piping, electrical and instrumentation cost. In addition, there will be an operating cost. Here, we use the interest concept to compute part of the annualised cost in the form of interest on the fixed component. The entire system is assumed to have purchased from term loan (even if it were from equity, return on equity can be deemed as similar to interest). The cost of this capital would be the interest accrued at the end of the year. Since the capital repayment would be from the general reserve pool arising out of project profit, we do not consider here a loan repayment. The maintenance cost of both the systems could be either estimated or be obtained from vendors.

The operating costs, such as utilities consumption and manpower requirement, are also estimated from the data supplied by vendors. The annualised cost would be then computed by adding all the above cost factors as illustrated below.

Annualised cost:

System cost $= X$

Interest at the rate $i$ for one year $= Xi/100$

Operating cost:

Consumption of utilities $= U$

Repairs and maintenance $= R$

Manpower $= M$

The Annualised cost $= (Xi/100) + U + R + M$ (9.14)

Depreciation being notional, cost is not considered here.

Apart from the above quantification of cost, the other viability factors that need to be considered here are: space (plot area) required for systems, guarantee/warrantee offered by vendor, and the last but most important is the proven track record.

Similar reasoning can be applied to purchase of a piece of equipment. For instance, in the process of manufacture of formaldehyde solution, we have a choice of inter-coolers on absorption of formaldehyde vapours in water to produce 37–40% solution. The absorption is exothermic in nature. It is possible to use a packed absorption tower with inter-stage coolers. The coolers could be either shell and tube heat exchanger or plate heat exchanger. Here the cost of piping, electrical and instrumentation would remain more or less the same. Therefore, we can consider under fixed cost component, only cost of heat exchanger delivered at the site and its installation. The remaiming methodology remaining the same, we can now estimate the annualised cost of both heat exchangers. With the help of viability parameters discussed above, one can arrive at the decision whether to purchase a shell and tube heat exchanger or a plate heat exchanger.

Thus annualised cost consideration along with viability parameters would enable us to select a system from various options available.

## 9.6 CAPITALISED COST

Many times, a process engineer is in a dilemma over selecting equipment from different materials of construction thereby, having a wide variation in the cost of equipment. For instance, a reactor constructed of carbon steel may have a service life of, say, two years and need replacement every two years till the project life of ten years (assumed for calculation of an economic viability). On the other hand, a glass-lined reactor would have a higher service life but would be much costlier than the reactor fabricated out of mild steel. The reactor (mild steel) needs perpetual replacement. This would be achieved by keeping some money aside. It is expected that interest accrued on this investment would be sufficient to meet the price of the reactor. Like in profitability estimation, here we assume that the interest rate remains constant in future. Please note that the variation in interest rate is not likely to be drastic. Further, the rate of inflation (in true sense escalation) is deemed to be zero. Optimistically, the inflation would be met through scrapped value of an asset, which is considered to be zero, for replacement calculation. Despite this limitation, the concept of capitalised cost is very useful in resolving the situation arising out of perpetual cost consideration. The interest needs to be accrued to replace the reactor cost $C_R$ can be computed as

$$C_R = P(1 + i)^n - P \quad (9.15\text{-}a)$$

$$= P\{(1 + i)^n - 1\} \quad (9.15\text{-}b)$$

where $C_R$ = cost of replacement

$P$ = principal to be kept aside to realise the interest equal to replacement cost using compound interest.

Therefore, $P = C_R/\{(1 + i)^n - 1\}$ (9.16)

The capitalised cost, $C_c$, by definition then becomes sum of original cost on an asset/equipment and the principal to be kept aside to realise the replacement through the interest.

$$C_c = C_0 + P$$

$$C_c = C_0 + C_R/\{(1 + i)^n - 1\} \quad (9.17)$$

where, $i$, is the interest rate. (The replacement cost can be based on escalation also). If $e$ is the fractional escalation in the price of an asset, then we have the capitalised cost $C_c$ as given below:

$$C_c = C_0 + P$$

$$= C_0 + C_R(1 + e)^n/\{(1 + i)^n - 1\} \quad (9.18)$$

One can compute the capitalised cost for the known service life, and the system or equipment with the lowest capitalised cost can then be selected. Alternatively, it is assumed that the capitalized cost would be the same for the other equipment. We then compute the value $n$ service life. If service life in reality exceeds $n$ computed, the alternative is deemed to be acceptable.

With the help of following numerical example we can illustrate this concept.

*Illustration*

A decision is required about selection of a reactor having two different materials of construction with totally different service life. The reactor 'A' costs ₹ 3 lakh and needs perpetual replacement after every two years. The other reactor B costs ₹ 5 lakh with service life of five years and needs perpetual replacement after every five years.

**Assumptions:**

Interest rate 12%

The annual rate of inflation (escalation) = 0.

For the reactor *A*, capitalized cost is:

$$C = 3 + 3/((1+0.12)^2 - 1) = ₹\ 14.8 \text{ lakh}$$

For the reactor *B* capitalised cost is:

$$C = 5 + 5/((1 + 0.12)^5 - 1) = ₹\ 11.6 \text{ lakh}$$

The second reactor has lower capitalised cost and hence may be selected.

If the escalation in price is at 6%, the capitalized cost for the reactor *A* is:

$$C_A = 3 + 3\ (I+0.06)^2/((1+0.12)^2 - 1) = ₹\ 16.25 \text{ Lakh},$$

and that for the reactor *B* is

$$C_B = ₹\ 13.78 \text{ lakh}$$

From the foregoing the importance of the interest concept is obvious. We shall see utility of this when we make estimate of the working result in Chapter 11 (Project Profitability).

## APPENDIX 9.1

A Quick Glance At Formulas Used With Interest Concept

Let $i$ = interest rate (fractional)

$P$ = present worth or principal amount

$F$ = future worth of $P$

$L$ = instalment or end of period payment or receipt in a

uniform series containing $n$ periods with equivalent to principal $P$ at interest rate $i$

$$F = P(1+i)^n$$

$$P = F/(1+i)^n$$

$$L = Pi(1+i)^n/((1+i)^n - 1)$$

$$= Fi/((1+i)^n - 1)$$

## REFERENCES

Dewett K.K., *Modern Economic Theory*, S. Chand and Company, New Delhi (1996).

Grant E.L. Grant Ireson W. and Leavenworth R.S., *Principles of Engineering Economy* 7th Edition, John Wiley and Sons, New York, (1982).

Peters M.S. and Timmerhous K.D., *Plant Design and Economics for Chemical Engineers*, 4th Edition, McGraw-Hill Inc. New York (1991).

***Interest in Very Interesting Concept in Project Economics.***

# 10

# Depreciation

## 10.1 INTRODUCTION

The concept of depreciation is very important in chemical project economics to assess realistically profit or cash accruals from any project. Many engineers misunderstand this concept because it is a 'notional cost' and no money is either spent (as in the case of interest payment) or received by the project owner while operating the project.

In order to appreciate this concept of depreciation, let us be familiar with some terminologies frequently used.

*Depreciation*

It is defined as a reduction in the value of an asset over a period of time. This loss of value could be the result of wear and tear arising out of use, or it could be due to obsolescence caused by newer technology or it could be merely by efflux of time. A vehicle loses its value over a period and this is mainly due to wear and tear. The introduction of cable network has lost the value for a videocassette recorder (VCR) thereby indicating that new technology makes the old one obsolete. Similarly, a mining lease loses its value as time passes irrespective of whether the same is put to use or not. At times, we may have a situation wherein both the above factors are responsible for the loss of value of an asset.

When the asset loses its value, the cost has to be reduced. Thus in the balance sheet, the capital cost of the asset is reduced. But the loss of value of an asset has also to be reflected in the accounts.

This loss of value under the heading is taken as 'depreciation' and is shown as expenditure in Profit and Loss account in the balance sheet.

*Appreciation*

As against depreciation the value of an asset may increase as the time passes. This is known as appreciation. For example, the value of land or a flat in metro cities appreciates.

*Service Life*

The period over which the asset remains useful, is known as its service life.

*Scrap Value*

The value of an asset at the end of its service life (to the owner) is known as scrap value.

*Market Value*

The value of an asset in the market depending upon the condition of an asset is known as its market value.

*Book Value*

The original value of an asset *less* depreciation is known as its book value. The book value would keep on changing from year to year and at the end of service life, it would be the scrap value.

Depreciation rate (straight-line method) is defined as:

$$\text{Depreciation rate (\%)} = \frac{(V_o - V_s)}{L} \times \frac{100}{V_o} \tag{10.1}$$

Where $V_o$ = original value
$V_s$ = scrap value
$L$ = service life

It means that the asset loses its value by constant amount every year.

Let us illustrate the above definitions with the help of an example.

*Illustration*

An asset has an original price say, ₹ 5 lakh . It has depreciated at the rate of 10%. The book value of the asset at the end of fourth year would be:

$$= 5\ (1 - 0.10 \times 4)$$
$$= ₹\ 3.0 \text{ lakh}$$

For the financier (banker), the book value of the asset would be ₹ 3.0 lakh at the end of the fourth year. Thus if the owner does not repay interest and loan, regularly, the banker can acquire the asset and hope to realise ₹ 3.0 lakh.

On the other hand, in real market, the same asset can fetch more or less amount depending upon its working conditions. Thus market value need not necessarily be identical to book value. Further, the rate of depreciation would depend not only on the nature of an asset but also on its use. A machine that is being operated in one shift (8 hours per day) will depreciate less in a year than that is being used in all the three shifts. Therefore, the rate of depreciation for 'plant and machinery' item should be different for one-shift and three-shift operations.

## 10.2 DEPRECIATION CONCEPT IN CHEMICAL PROJECT

The chemical project comprises various buildings, equipment, instruments, electricals, piping and miscellaneous fixed assets including vehicles, furniture & fixers and computers (used in office and not as part of instruments such as analytical instruments, process control, data acquisition system, and so on).

The buildings and civil work classified as 'factory buildings' would be subjected to hostile conditions of a chemical plant. On the other hand, the non-factory buildings, being away from the manufacturing facility are subjected to less hostile conditions. Therefore, we expect service life of factory buildings to be less than that of non-factory buildings. In other words, the depreciation rate for 'factory buildings' is expected to be higher than that for non-factory buildings.

The 'plant and machinery' is expected to subject to maximum wear and tear during the entire service life of a project. Therefore, the rate of depreciation is expected to be highest for this component of the project cost. The miscellaneous fixed assets would definitely depreciate at a lower rate than that for 'plant and machinery' but at a higher rate than that for factory buildings. Among miscellaneous assets, vehicles would be subjected to more wear and tear and, hence, would have higher depreciation rate. Computers would depreciate faster due to obsolescence.

On the other hand, land as well as the developed site would appreciate over a period of time and therefore, are not considered for depreciation purpose. Preliminary and capital issue related expenses and margin money, being direct monetary transactions, are not considered for depreciation purpose.

## 10.3 DEPRECIATION METHODS

In India, we follow two methods of computing depreciation, namely, one based on the Companies act, known as *straight line method* (SLM) of depreciation and the other, written down value method (WDV) based on Income Tax Act. We shall not discuss here whether Indian corporate world should follow two methods of depreciation or not. The pros and cons of the two methods mentioned, their impact on corporate world, project financier and the revenue department of Ministry of Finance, are excluded from the scope of this book. With the introduction of concept of minimum alternate tax (MAT) some economists may question the rationale behind the two methods of depreciation followed in the industry.

### 10.3.1 Straight Line Method (SLM)

In this method, the asset depreciates at a fixed rate uniformly over its service life. The depreciation rate, $D_{SLM}$ is expressed as per cent (%) per year of the original value of the asset.

$$D_{SLM} = [(V_O - V_S)/L] \times 100/V_O \qquad (10.2)$$

where $V_O$ = original value of the asset

$V_S$ = scrap value

$L$ = service life in years.

The asset depreciates at a constant rate and hence if a graph is plotted between the value of an asset ($V_A$) and the period in years, we obtain a straight line (Linear graph).

Thus we have,

$$V_A = V_O - (D_{SLM} \times V_O \times Y) \qquad (10.3)$$

It is seen that value of an asset is a linear function of number of years ($Y$) and fractional rate of depreciation $D_{SLM}$ ($D_{SLM}/100$). It implies that the value of an asset goes down at a fixed rate. This value of the asset is also known as *book value*.

The rate of depreciation, as explained, earlier would be different for different items of components of 'project cost.'

### 10.3.2 Written Down Value (WDV) Method

This method of depreciation deemed as accelerated depreciation method, is essentially used for computation of corporate tax. The rates of depreciation are fixed by the Income Tax Act and can be revised during the budget. In this method, the value of an asset decreases at a faster rate. The federal Government takes a compassionate view of the project profitability. It has well understood and appreciated, the efforts made by the project for the local development in the sense of social economics. Also, the state as well as the Central Government gets revenue from the project by way of statutory taxes or duties (such as octroi (by municipality), sales tax, excise, (VAT), project import duty, corporate tax, etc.). As a result of appreciation of the above and various hardships or struggles, the owner has to make during early life of the project, the income tax legislation permits higher depreciation to be shown as a notional cost or notional expenditure. This notional expenditure is subtracted from the gross profit *less* financial expenses to arrive at a taxable profit. Further, various concessions given by the tax authorities are also subtracted before the computation of taxable income. The corporate tax is then levied upon the same as would be obvious when we see the estimate of working results in Chapter 11.

If $D_{WDV}$ is the fractional rate of depreciation, expressed as fraction, by WDV method for the corporate tax purpose, we have the value of an asset $V_A$ at the end of any year, $n$ as:

$$V_A = V_O (1 - D_{WDV})^n \tag{10.4}$$

From the above, it is obvious that the value of an asset decreases at a faster rate in the early life than the actual decrease towards the second-half. This, in turn, gives benefit to the project owner by way of less taxation to be paid in early life of the project. Table 10.1 illustrates computations of depreciation by above methods.

**Table 10.1** Value of An Asset by Two Methods of Depreciation

| *Year* | *SLM method* | | *WDV method* | |
|---|---|---|---|---|
| | *Value* | *Depreciation* | *Value* | *Depreciation* |
| 0 | 100.00 | – | 100.00 | – |
| 1 | 89.66 | 10.34 | 75.00 | 25.00 |
| 2 | 79.32 | 10.34 | 56.25 | 18.75 |
| 3 | 68.98 | 10.34 | 42.19 | 14.06 |
| 4 | 58.64 | 10.34 | 31.64 | 10.55 |
| 5 | 48.30 | 10.34 | 23.73 | 7.91 |
| 6 | 37.96 | 10.34 | 17.80 | 5.93 |
| 7 | 27.62 | 10.34 | 13.35 | 4.45 |
| 8 | 17.28 | 10.34 | 10.01 | 3.34 |
| 9 | 06.94 | 10.34 | 7.51 | 2.50 |
| 10 | – | 6.94 | 5.63 | 1.88 |

The rate of depreciation by SLM method = 10.34% (Companies Act)
The rate of depreciation by WDV method = 25.00% (Income Tax Act)
The value of an asset (Plant and Machinery) = 100 units
Figure 10.1 exhibits the above results

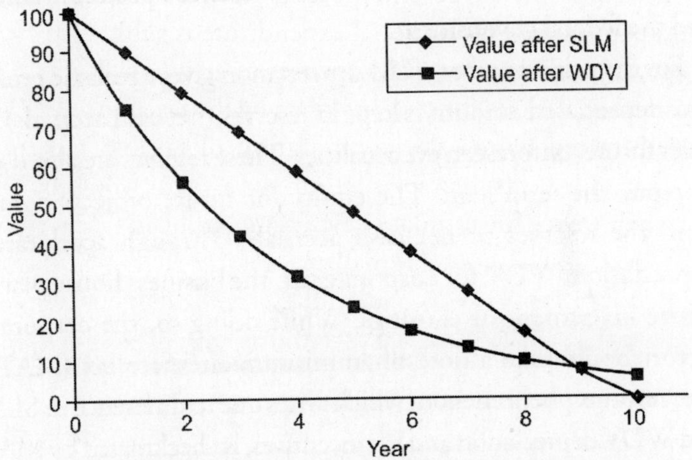


**Fig. 10.1** The Value of An Asset after Depreciation

The depreciated amount remains with the project owner, but for the corporate tax purpose it is deemed as expenditure.

The depreciation rates for both the methods will be different. The plant working in three shifts would have different rates than that working in one or two shifts. Further, continuous mode of operation would have different rates of depreciation compared to those of batch mode. In order to give boost to eco-friendly projects and energy conservation (ENCON) in projects, an incentive of 100% depreciation is given to effluent treatment plants and energy conservation plant. This results in tax savings, as 100% depreciation means all capital cost is written-off as expense. This is an indirect benefit. This depreciation benefit is also presented in the budget and hence is dynamic in nature.

## 10.4 APPRECIATION OF DEPRECIATION CONCEPT

The concept of depreciation is important to all concerned with the project. This includes the project owner, the project financer and the federal government.

For the project owner, SLM depreciation gives a realistic profit. The depreciated amount is kept in reserves (net cash accruals) to meet future, unforeseen eventualities. These reserves are also used to repay the term loan. The equity for future projects comes from the reserves or net cash accruals. Through accelerated depreciation, WDV for corporate tax, the business house plans, future investment or earnings. While doing so, the corporate sector should take a note of minimum alternate tax (MAT). The zero-tax phenomenon, which arises due to difference in SLM and WDV depreciation and tax incentives, is checkmated by MAT and corporate sectors are asked to pay minimum corporate tax on the profit worked as per Companies Act.

To project financier, the book value of all assets in the 'project' gives means to recover his money (loan) should the business collapse. The financier now knows how much he can recover.

To the government, through income tax act (accelerated depreciation and other concessions), the corporate tax yields additional revenue earnings.

It is seen that the concept of depreciation is important to all concerned with the project.

## 10.5 DEPRECIATION RATES

The rates of depreciation have been decided out of experience and have the legal sanction. The SLM rates are for the book value of the project cost components and they are based on Companies Act while the WDV rates are by Income-tax Act for corporate tax purpose. In principle, the rates can change, however a drastic change is not expected. Typical rates are given in Table 10.2.

**Table 10.2** Typical Rates of Depreciation (Three Shifts, Continuous Process)

| *Project Cost Components* | *SLM Rates (%)* | *WDV Rates (%)* |
|---|---|---|
| Factory Buildings | 3.34 | 10.00 |
| Non-Factory Buildings | 1.63 | 5.00 |
| Plant and Machinery | 10.34 | 25.00 |
| Miscellaneous Fixed Assets | 3.34 | 10.00 |
| Vehicles | 7.07 | 20.00 |
| Computers | 16.21 | 60.00 |
| Energy Conservation Plant | | 100.00 |
| Effluent Treatment Plant | | 100.00 |

The above rates are for illustration purpose only, and at the time of feasibility report preparation then prevailing rates should be considered.

## 10.6 THE DEPRECIATION SCHEDULE

The depreciation schedule is very important while evaluating profitability of a project. Let us see now, which components of project cost should be considered for depreciation purpose and how to prepare a new schedule of the project cost for computing depreciation.

The land and site development component, however, does not depreciate, on the company it appreciates. Therefore, it is not considered for depreciation purpose.

The factory buildings attract more depreciation than the non-factory buildings for obvious reasons. The factory buildings are subjected to harsher environment than those known as *non-factory buildings*, as a result wear and tear is more for the factory buildings.

The 'Plant and Machinery' component being subjected to

highest wear and tear, the depreciation rates are highest for this component.

The know-how and engineering component is directly linked to plant and machinery. The same is the case with expenses prior to commencement of production on foreign technicians and Indian personnel who one being trained abroad. Therefore, for depreciation purpose, they are clubbed together with the 'Plant & Machinery' component.

The miscellaneous fixed assets depreciate. It is obvious that vehicles would depreciate at higher rates. Computers also have higher rates of depreciation.

The contingencies and pre-operative expenses are linked to all above-mentioned components of the project cost. Therefore, they are allocated in direct proportion to their contribution up to the sum involving right from land and site development to miscellaneous fixed assets (MFA).

There is no depreciation for preliminary and capital issue related expenses. Margin money is also excluded from the calculations of depreciation. As explained earlier, both are financial transactions and do not form part of fixed assets.

Thus, we have now a revised schedule of the project cost components with allocation of contingencies and pre-operative expenses. The revised schedule has now only following components, namely (*i*) land and site development, (*ii*) factory buildings and non-factory buildings, (*iii*) plant and machinery, (*iv*) miscellaneous fixed assets, (*v*) vehicles, (*vi*) preliminary and capital issue expenses, and (*vii*) margin money. While carrying out allocation of contingencies and pre-operative expenses, the total project cost is not altered. Table 10.3 exhibits this exercise.

**Table 10.3** Allocation of Contingencies and Pre-operative Expenses

| | *Project Cost Component* | | *Allocation* | *Revised Cost for Depreciation* |
|---|---|---|---|---|
| (A) | | | | |
| 1 | Land & Site Development | X1 | X1 (B/A) | X1+X1 (B/A) |
| 2 | Building & Civil Works | | | |
| | A.2.1 Factory Building | X2 | X2 (B/A) | X2+X2 (B/A) |
| | A.2.2 Non-factory Building | X3 | X3 (B/A) | X3+X3 (B/A) |
| 3 | Plant & Machinery inclusive of Know-how Engineering and Expenses on Foreign Technicians and Indians abroad | X4 | X4 (B/A) | X4+X4 (B/A) |
| 4 | Miscellaneous Fixed Assets | | | |
| | A.4.1 Vehicles | X5 | X5 (B/A) | X5+X5 (B/A) |
| | A.4.2 The Other Assets | X6 | X6 (B/A) | X6+X6 (B/A) |
| | A.4.3 Computers | X7 | X7 (B/A) | X7+X7 (B/A) |
| | Total (A) | A | | AR |
| (B) | | | | |
| | B.1 Contingencies | Y1 | – | – |
| | B.2 Pre-operative Expenses | Y2 | – | – |
| | Total (B) | B | | |
| (C) | | | | |
| | C.1 Preliminary & Capital | Z1 | – | Z1 |
| | Issue Related Expenses | Z2 | – | Z2 |
| | C.2 Margin Money | | | |
| | Total (C) | C | | |
| | Grand Total Project Cost | A+B+C | | AR+C = (A+B+C) |

Based on the above rates, depreciation computations are done for all components listed in Table 10.2 after allocation, and total depreciation by straight line (SLM) method as well as by written down value (WDV) method are computed year by year to aid estimate of working results of the project under consideration (see Table 10.4).

**Table 10.4** Depreciation Computation

| *Year* | *1* | | *2* | | *10* | |
|---|---|---|---|---|---|---|
| | *SLM* | *WDV* | *SLM* | *WDV* | *SLM* | *WDV* |
| 1. Factory Buildings | S11 | W11 | S12 | W12 | S1,10 | W1,10 |
| 2. Non-factory Buildings | S21 | W21 | S22 | W22 | S2,10 | W2,10 |
| 3. Plant and Machinery | S31 | W31 | S32 | W32 | S3,10 | W3,10 |
| 4. Miss. Fixed Assets | S41 | W41 | S42 | W42 | S4,10 | W4,10 |
| 5. Vehicles | S51 | W51 | S52 | W52 | S5,10 | W5,10 |
| 6. Computers | S61 | W61 | S62 | W62 | S6,10 | W6,10 |
| Total | | $\Sigma S_{ij}$ and $\Sigma W_{ij}$ | | | $i = 1$ to 5<br>$J = 1$ to 10 | |

To readers may refer to the factory act and income-tax act for rates of depreciation. The budget also gives any changes or new introduction to depreciation.

***Appreciate Depreciation to Make Project Viable.***

# 11 Project Profitability

## 11.1 INTRODUCTION

Projection of the profitability of any new project over its lifetime is important for its realistic evaluation resulting, hopefully, in its implementation. For a chemical project, the life time is considered to be ten years for project evaluation purpose only. The profitability or net income arising out of any project could be positive (profit) or negative (loss). The profitability of a proposed project over its lifetime is presented in the form of estimate of working results. This is very much similar to profit and loss account accompanied by balance sheet in an annual report of an ongoing business (project). Here we shall consider how to estimate the working results of a proposed project under review so that its financial evaluation becomes possible.

For a proposed project, income is essentially generated from sales of product, by-products, or co-products. During the estimate of income, we do not consider interest earned on intermediate investments for the sake of simplicity and because it is not the objective of the project. It is further assumed that the market scenario is an ideal one thereby, product manufactured is sold in totality. In other words inventories of product, by-products, co-products, etc., are nil. This means capacity utilisation for the sales accruals is identical with that of capacity utilisation for the cost of production.

In the absence of information on futuristic policy of the government reflecting in GST, corporate tax, etc., we have to estimate the working of project based on scenario prevailing at the time of estimate. Further, there is no prior information on how prices of raw material and utilities would change in future and so are the product and by-product prices. Prices prevailing at the time of estimate are, therefore, assumed to remain unchanged. For salaries and wages component of cost of production, one may assume annual 10% rise on the salaries and wages of the workforce depending on the discretion of the owner of the project.

## 11.2 ESTIMATE OF WORKING RESULTS

It is always desirable to have an estimate of working results of the proposed project over its lifespan for evaluation, which is ten years before we make an investment decision after the project evaluation. It is necessary to comprehend meaning of various terms used in preparing an estimate of working result.

### 11.2.1 Sales

Sales are the income resulting from selling product, by-products and co-products and excess utility (power and steam), if any. The selling price includes GST. The prevailing market price of all the above products is considered for estimate of sales for project life span of ten years. There being zero inventory, capacity utilisation in the cost of production schedule (Chapter 7) would be identical to the quantities sold.

### 11.2.2 Gross Profit

Total sales realisation *less* gross cost of production yields gross profit.

Gross profit = Sales – Gross cost of production (11.1)

(The Elements of 'Gross cost of production' have been discussed in Chapter 7).

Since capacity utilisation varies from year to year, gross profit also varies from year to year.

Instead of Gross Profit as defined above, several Corporate accounts use the term EBITDA i.e. Earnings Before Interest, Tax (corporate tax), Depreciation, and Amortization. By amortization we mean distributing the cost of intangible assets over a period. It refers to repayment of the term loan with interest also. A company might pay say ₹10 Crores for purchase of a patent from Chemistry research laboratory of University. The project life is 10 years for economic viability calculation. The intangible asset (Patent in this case) is then amortized as ₹ 1 Crore per year. One may as well say it is one time expenditure in the first year. By doing so one may have a dip in Gross/Operating profit of the first year of a project. So this asset is amortized over a project life of ten years.

For business to make economic sense Gross profit or EBITDA has to be always positive.

### 11.2.3 Operating Profit

Financial expenses (the interest on term loan and working capital) and depreciation are accounted to get a realistic estimate of profit.

The financial expenses include interest for that particular year on various borrowings, mainly term loan and working capital. It does not include loan repayment.

By providing depreciation as per Companies Act, we keep aside some profit to make provision for major repairs, replacements, etc., for all depreciable assets to function. This would then give a realistic estimate of profit (please note that the depreciation is used as a notional cost).

$$\text{Operating profit} = \text{Gross profit} - \text{Financial Expenses} - \text{Depreciation} \quad (11.2)$$

Please note that the company has the flexibility of using WDV or SLM method of depreciation. However, for chemical projects, while carrying out the feasibility study, the SLM depreciation is considered in Eq. 11.2.

### 11.2.4 Profit for Corporate Tax

The computation of profit for corporate tax is a complex issue. The business can be through partnership firm or by a company formed and registered under the Company Act 1956. The chemical projects, by nature, are big enough to be companies and are generally listed in the stock exchange. In the past, big projects were in public sector having direct investment by the government. With the new economic scenario, the disinvestments programme is on, and in future we shall see the least holding by the government but companies would be listed for people to have equity stakes. Here, we shall not go into details of the law applicable to various firms or companies such as listed companies, the government owned companies and cooperative societies. However, we shall discuss in general, the principles underlying taxation.

The government takes a very compassionate view of the business activities. While earning revenues through corporate tax (income tax on business house or enterprise), it also wants to give benefits to business house in recognition of its contribution towards development of the region. This is done by allowing depreciation at higher rates and also by different method known as *written down value* (WDV) method of depreciation, and the rates given in Income Tax Act 1961 which may undergo amendments from time to time. The WDV rates of depreciation are different for project cost components, as seen in the Chapter 10.

In the operating profit, the realistic estimate of profit was achieved by subtracting SLM depreciation as per the Companies

Act 1956. While computing profit for tax purpose, we have to ignore SLM depreciation and consider depreciation by WDV method as per Income Tax Act.

From the gross profit, we subtract financial expenses and WDV depreciation. Further, loss from the previous year and various other benefits from Income Tax Act, such as tax holidays, export promotion, investment allowance as and when applicable, various deductions permissible under various section of 80 such as 80G, 80HCC, 80CGA, and so on, are also subtracted to calculate the profit before tax.

Thus we have,

Profit before tax or Taxable Income

$$= \text{Gross profit} - \text{Financial expenses} - \text{WDV depreciation} - (\text{Benefits under Income Tax Act}) \quad (11.3)$$

### 11.2.5 Corporate Tax

The income tax levied on business houses, (organisation/enterprise) is known as the Corporate Tax (also sometimes referred as the corporation tax). The corporate tax rate is decided by the Ministry of Finance and presented by honourable finance minister during the budget presentation to the nation. Let $X$ be percentage corporate tax, we then have,

$$\text{Corporate tax} = X(\text{Profit for tax})/100 \quad (11.4)$$

Profit after tax (PAT)

$$= \text{Gross profit} - \text{Financial expenses} - \text{Corporate tax} \quad (11.5)$$

### 11.2.6 Dividend

Dividend is the return on equity and it is paid out of the profit earned. The shareholders (equity holders) who invest their money look forward to have returns (in the form of dividend) higher than those obtained by the interest on fixed deposits in banks. The equity holder takes this view because he is risking his money by having investment into a project whose success is unpredictable. Higher is the risk rating of the project, higher is the expectation of dividend.

While paying dividend, care must be taken about futuristic needs of capital that is required to,

- overcome unforeseen maintenance requirements,
- repay the term loan as per agreed schedule with financial institutions,
- make provision for equity participation in new projects by way of expansion, diversification, backward or forward integration.

One way of doing this is to consider depreciation as the notional cost and keep aside SLM depreciation before declaring the dividend. In other words, profit for dividend can be computed as:

Profit for dividend

$$= \text{Gross profit} - \text{Financial expenses} - \text{Corporate tax} - \text{SLM depreciation} \quad (11.6)$$

From this profit, first dividend is paid to preference shareholders, then for the rest shareholders. The board of directors recommend dividend out of the net profit. The balance money is used to meet the futuristic needs. It is always desirable not to distribute the entire profit available for dividend. In the profit and loss account, dividend is indicated under 'Appropriations' and the balance is transferred to reserve funds. Lately tax on dividend is also introduced so that shareholders receive tax-free dividend. Like corporate tax, tax on dividend and cess thereupon if applicable, are presented in the budget. By nature, taxation is dynamic in nature depending on the policy of the government.

### 11.2.7 Net Cash Accruals

Net cash accruals of any project are computed after the allocation of dividend. The depreciation being the notional cost, SLM depreciation is added back to the profit after disbursing dividend to yield net cash accruals.

**Table 11.1** Estimates of Working Results

| Year | Production (Tonnes) | Capacity Utilisation (%) say | Sales (₹) | Gross Cost of Production (₹) | Gross Profit | Operating Profit | profit before Tax | Corporate Tax | Profit after Tax | Profit for Dividend | Devidend @ a% | Net Cash Accruals |
|---|---|---|---|---|---|---|---|---|---|---|---|---|
| 1 | $X_1$ | 65 | | | | | | | | | | |
| 2 | $X_2$ | 70 | | | | | | | | | | |
| . | . | | | | | | | | | | | |
| . | . | | | | | | | | | | | |
| | . | | | | | | | | | | | |
| 10 | $X_{10}$ | 90 | | | | | | | | | | |
| Comments | | | | | | | | | | | | |

Net Cash Accruals
= Profit for dividend – Dividend + SLM depreciation (11.7a)
= Operating profit – Corporate tax – Dividend
+ SLM depreciation (11.7b)

The net cash accrual essentially then becomes 'reserves'. Through this money, the project owner is supposed to repay the term loan and he can support future projects by way of equity and, so on.

*Comments:* The concept of depreciation for income tax/corporate tax purpose plays a very interesting role. In the early period of project working, the contribution of WDV–depreciation would be far higher than SLM depreciation (please refer to Table 10.1 of Chapter 10. As a result, despite operating profit being positive, profit for tax purpose may become negative. No corporate tax is then levied on negative profit (loss). However, the board of directors can still recommend some dividend. This would then mean that the business house pays dividend without paying any corporate tax to the federal government. Many business houses have taken legitimate advantage of such a situation by having continuous big projects under the same organisation. Recently, to overcome this apparent anomaly, the Ministry of Finance has introduced a minimum alternate tax (MAT). Details of computation of MAT and regular corporate tax having various benefits under Section 80 of income-tax act are excluded from the scope of this book because they keep on changing as we are in the process of liberalisation and globalisation. The readers are advised to a keep track of these aspects through annual budget presentation by our honourable finance minister.

The formal presentation of estimate of working results is given in Table 11.1. Appendix 11.1 illustrates the concept of depreciation in tax computation.

## SUGGESTED READINGS

Mehta, V.G. *Income Tax Ready Reckoner*, Shri Kuber Publishing House, Mumbai. (This is published every year after the budget is passed in the parliament).

*Application for Financial Assistance,* The Industrial Credit and Investment Corporation of India Ltd.

*The budget speech of the honourable Finance Minister* every year and thereafter statutory approvals with or without amendments by the parliament.

### Appendix 11.1 Computation of Corporate Tax

The analysis presented here assumes the cost of asset (Plant and Machinery) to be ₹ 100 and thta of profit before depreciation is ₹ 100.

The rate of depreciation (WDV) = 25 % (Income Tax Act)
The corporate tax rate = 35 %

| *Year* | *Profit before Depreciation* | *Depreciation (WDV)* | *Taxable Profit* | *Corporate Tax* |
|---|---|---|---|---|
| 1 | 100.00 | 25.00 | 75.00 | 26.25 |
| 2 | 100.00 | 18.75 | 81.25 | 28.44 |
| 3 | 100.00 | 14.06 | 85.94 | 30.08 |
| 4 | 100.00 | 10.55 | 89.45 | 31.31 |
| 5 | 100.00 | 07.91 | 92.09 | 32.23 |
| 6 | 100.00 | 05.93 | 94.07 | 32.92 |
| 7 | 100.00 | 04.45 | 95.55 | 33.44 |
| 8 | 100.00 | 03.34 | 96.66 | 33.83 |
| 9 | 100.00 | 02.50 | 97.50 | 34.12 |
| 10 | 100.00 | 01.88 | 98.12 | 34.34 |

Please note that in reality taxable profit is computed by subtracting WDV component of depreciation of all assets (Buildings, Plant and Machinery, MFA, Vehicles) from gross profit *less* financial expenses, less all benefits under Income Tax Act. The profit before tax would change every year due to different capacity utilisation and different financial expenses. The Table (in Appendix 11.1) illustrates how such a calculation is done for corporate tax purpose.

***Profitability is the Ability of A Project to Sustain.***

# 12 Project Evaluation

## 12.1 INTRODUCTION

Evaluation of ongoing or proposed project is a very important exercise for all concerned with the project. The project owner (promoters) and financiers/investors associated with the project take the view that the project is an opportunity to get better return (monetary benefit) on their investments. Therefore, their perception of an entire project is based on, primarily, a concept of return on investment (ROI). The capital investment and operating expenditure are deemed as cost of opportunity to earn money. On the other hand, the government and social economists are mainly concerned with returns in terms of sustainable social development through various aspects of projects. The news of new projects is deemed as a barometer of economic health and yardstick of social developments. As a result, the central or the state government, offer various incentives (carrots) to entrepreneurs/business houses in the form of capital subsidy (cash), free and reduced tariff on power, water, ease of norms for various emissions (gaseous, liquid, solid), corporate tax holidays, exemption from sales tax, excise, VAT system, project import duty, and so on. The prime objective of the project owner is to have returns in terms of money and social returns will follow. The real answer to returns on the investment lies in between the above two extremes.

While it is difficult to quantify social returns accurately, profits can be relatively easily projected for a proposed project over its lifespan. Therefore, in this chapter we shall concentrate on monetary returns (or profit). In other words, we take the view of an entrepreneur and exclude social returns from our scope of work while evaluating any project because a non-polluting healthy project always brings economic benefits to the community and the government.

Various financial parameters or ratios used in project evaluation do have some subjective elements. For instance, how much return one should have on the investment, will vary from one organisation to the other depending upon the perception of the cost of opportunity and the state of national economy. In corporate jargon, this is often termed as 'bottom line'. All project evaluation techniques presented here would tell us which projects should not be considered. The project evaluation exercise would screen all projects under evaluation and indicate which projects should be dropped, however it will not tell us ultimately which project should be considered for implementation. The final decision of the owner would depend on the risk analysis, the business acumen (intuition or the 'sixth sense') and the market assessment. Therefore a 'computer' cannot decide on implementation of any project but will assist 'human brain' to expedite implementation once a decision is made and to run the show efficiently and effectively.

Investment worthiness of a project from financial angle is assessed using different yardsticks and analytical procedures. The most popular and effective methods of project evaluation are break-even analysis, incremental analysis, ratio analysis and discounted profit flow technique.

We shall discuss these and illustrate with examples wherever possible.

## 12.2 BREAK-EVEN ANALYSIS

The Break-even analysis is a technique used by production management to evaluate the profit/loss of any project. It would reveal capacity of a project under consideration, at which all costs (*operating* or *variable* as well as annualised *fixed* capital related cost) are equal to revenue earned.

We have an estimate of a project cost of definite capacity based on the market demand-supply gap analysis (market survey report). Based on this capacity, a break-even capacity is computed. If break-even capacity is more than the assumed capacity of the project it is concluded that the project should not be considered due to non-viability. On the other hand, if break-even capacity is very much lower than the assumed capacity, the project is worth studying further. The final decision needs to be substantiated by way of other project evaluation criteria.

Following assumptions are made while carrying out the break-even analysis:

- All expenses can be bifurcated in fixed and variable costs.
- The market conditions are ideal. Whatever is produced is sold immediately. There is no inventory of finished products, by-products or co-products.
- The selling expenses are fixed as some % of sales.
- The following annualized (fixed) costs are not dependent on capacity utilisation, namely, interest charges on term loan, depreciation, salary and wages of plant and admin personnel, factory overheads and administrative expenses. The estimate of project cost is carried out for a definite capacity and then break-even analysis is done.

All the above fixed costs are added and are indicated by $F$ in Eq. (12.1) below.

The variable expenses, $V$, which are related to capacity, expressed as ₹ /T, would be as follows:

- Raw materials & chemicals consumptions
- utilities consumptions
- Packaging materials
- Sales expenses.

Let $X$ be the quantity of sales (units sold, also capacity), in tonnes (T) and $S$ be the selling price per unit, in ₹/T. The break-even analysis depicts that at break-even capacity, sales accruals match with variable ($V$) expenses, ₹/T and fixed ($F$) expenses. Thus we have,

$$S.X = V.X + F \tag{12.1}$$

The break-even quantity of sales, $X$, therefore is

$$X = F/(S - V) \tag{12.2}$$

$$\%\ \text{Break even capacity} = X100/(\text{planned capacity}) \tag{12.3}$$

It is seen from Eq. (12.2) that the break-even capacity is directly proportional to fixed annualised expenses and inversely proportional to the difference between sales realisation and variable cost expressed as ₹/T. The higher value of $(S - V)$ would result in lower break-even capacity. It is possible to have $(S - V)$ higher when either $S$ is very high or $V$ is very low for a given $S$. When $S$ is high, we may have 'monopoly' of a product or may be through formation of business cartel group of companies can have high $S$. A word of caution here in a sense that globalisation of industry/business may result in slashing import duties, thereby prevailing market price $S$ may go down. Also, there is a possibility of dumping of product by other countries. This would result in lower $S$ till anti-dumping measures are taken. The above factors would work advantageously for the owner by bringing down variable cost, $V$, through lower price of raw material. The other possibility of lower value of $X$ might be due to lower $F$. The lower value of $F$ means superior and cheaper technology requiring less capital investment and less manpower. This would then attract other players in the business resulting in more competition. Thus, it is seen that the project becomes more vulnerable to external factors. By and large very low break-even is not preferred.

Generally, as a rule of thumb, for a viable project, break-even capacity should be around 60–65% of the total plant capacity. Therefore, for a good project, we expect the break-even to occur in the very first year of production.

In the above analysis, linear relationship has been assumed between variable cost, $V$, and the capacity, $X$. Further, it is assumed that sales accruals are linearly dependent on the capacity. In real-life situation, the above assumptions may not hold true. For instance, one can sell the product at one price up to a certain capacity. Once the capacity goes beyond this, the selling price would be lower due to abundant availability of the product in market. The non-linearity might result in multiple break-evens.

In a multi-product project, say, manufacture of alkanol amines, namely, monoethanol amine (MEA), diethanol amine (DEA) and triethanol amine (TEA), the break-even would change depending upon quantity of various amines manufactured on demand basis.

The most important limitation of the break-even concept is its failure to highlight profitability beyond the break-even capacity. Therefore, this analysis may help the project owner in deciding-minimum production capacity of the plant. In case, a business is sailing through turbulent atmosphere, the break-even analysis can help the business house in deciding when to call it a day. No business house would like to sustain below the break-even capacity for a long period.

## 12.3 INCREMENTAL ANALYSIS

Many times an entrepreneur is faced with a dilemma of selecting a project among the various acceptable alternatives. They may have many business opportunities with different project costs.

Let us have a close look at the following project costs along with the respective profitabilities.

| | Project Cost (₹ in lakh) | Profit after Tax and Dividend (₹ lakh/Yr) | % Return on Investment per year (ROI) |
|---|---|---|---|
| (A) | 2,000 | 400 | 20.0 |
| (B) | 2,400 | 550 | 22.9 |
| (C) | 2,800 | 600 | 21.4 |

The minimum desired return is say, 20%. All the projects (A, B and C) satisfy the above criterion and hence none of these could be rejected.

Project A has the lowest investment, while Project B has the highest ROI and Project C has the highest total profit. Let us now have a close look at the above profitability. The question to be addressed is that how much extra benefit an entrepreneur would get if he moves from Project A to B and from Project B to C. It means that the yield on incremental investment should be considered. This analysis is known as *incremental analysis*.

Project A has the lowest investment. By investing extra ₹ 400 lakh in Project B, the profit obtained is 150 lakh/year. This would mean we could have 37.5% returns on this extra investment. On the other hand, if we invest 400 lakh more we can have Project C. The extra 400 lakh would result in 50 lakh extra profit thereby having 12.5% return on this incremental investment. Let us now compare the Project C to A, we notice ₹ 200 lakh/year extra profit on ₹ 800 lakh extra investment. Here the incremental investment would have 25% returns. Considering the minimum desired return to be 20%, one can say by incremental analysis the Project B looks more attractive when one has many business opportunities.

Thus, incremental analysis would tell us how to exploit an opportunity when many options are available.

## 12.4 RATIO ANALYSIS

Broadly speaking, with any chemical project following workforce is associated:

- Project promoters
- Term loan lenders (Financial Institutions)
- Public investors by means of share capital in equity.

Undoubtedly, all of them are interested in the project to perform and yield results (of course financial) beyond their expectations (positive).

The promoters of the project are interested in very good performance resulting in early payback on their investment. The financial institutions or project financiers are not only looking for good performance but also, payment of interest and repayment of the term loan on time as per the agreed schedule. The public investors in the stock market would like to earn money by way of selling shares and earning dividend on them as well. Thus there exists different perception to different group of people associated with the project. For easy understanding and appreciation, it was thought desirable that we should have appraisal of the project via ratio analysis wherein simple ratios are used to account performance of the project, its financial status and performance in the stock market. We have, therefore, three groups of ratios, namely,

- Performance ratios
- Financial ratios
- Stock market ratios

Please note that some ratios are important for ongoing project but not so for the feasibility of the proposed project. For example, stock market ratios are not for the feasibility purpose and so is the case with stock or debtor turnover ratio.

### 12.4.1 Performance Ratios

The performance ratios, as the name suggests, indicate how the project is performing or how it would perform. These ratios are primarily important to the owner of a project, but in general, more so to promoters of a project. The project financers (financial institutions) are also interested in the performance of a project. Their main concern is how promoter(s) is (are) going to service term loan by way of interest and repayment of capital. The shareholders being equity partners are, to some extent, also concerned with the performance of a project.

The return on investment (ROI) increases with risk. Having fixed deposit receipts in a nationalised bank can be deemed as a zero-risk venture wherein return is in the form of interest on fixed deposits. When any entrepreneur is promoting a project, he is looking forward to have returns on his investment which would far exceed the interest earned on practically 'zero risk' fixed deposit receipts.

#### *12.4.1.1 Payback Period*

The project has to earn money to pay interest on term loan and working capital, corporate tax dividend and even to repay the term loan and short-term borrowing of working capital. Therefore, the concept of the time when the project can recover the investment, assumes greater significance.

The payback period is defined as the time required to realise profit (Gross Profit) which is equal to total investment, i.e. project cost and working capital borrowing.

$$\text{Payback period} = \frac{\text{Project cost} + \text{Working capital borrowing}}{\text{Gross profit per year}} \tag{12.4}$$

Here, the profit per year is computed based on 100% capacity utilisation.

When the table of estimate of working results is prepared for ten years life of a project, one can have better estimate of payback period by matching profit and investment as defined above.

Sometimes, only depreciable investment in the project cost is considered, because non-depreciable project cost component (mainly land and site development) appreciates over a period. There is, of course, zero depreciation or appreciation for 'preliminary and capital issue' related expenses and for margin money. However the definition in Eq (12.4) would result in conservative estimate of the payback period. Often the working capital borrowing is neglected which should not be the case.

If one considers the operating profit, then the investment would be in terms of equity only. This is due to the fact that the term loan servicing through interest (financial expenses) and loan repayment through money available by keeping SLM depreciation aside would make 'real' investment as equity only. In reality the repayment of the loan is done through net cash accruals or reserves. Therefore through appropriate definition of investment and profit one can compute the payback period.

The payback analysis would immediately tell us how soon the investment could be recovered. However, it will not tell us what happens to the project after the investment is paid back. It would not depict the total profit over a notional service life of a project nor would it give the present value of return on investment beyond (or before) the payback period.

*Illustration*

Let us illustrate the above with the help of payback analysis of the two projects A and B. The project A being a speciality product project, its service life is five years and that of project B is ten years.

| *Project* | *A* | *B* |
|---|---|---|
| Investment | 50 | 50 |
| Profit/Year | 10 | 10 |
| Service life | 5 | 10 |
| Payback period, years | 5 | 5 |

In both the projects, payback period is identical. For Project A the investment is returned at the end of its service life. However, for the Project B the profit is double (the investment) at the end of service life.

The payback period analysis, being easy to carry out and comprehend, is used to screen plenty of opportunities a businessman has and is concerned about the recovery of capital investment. A rapid technological obsolescence might precipitate problems related to return of investment as in the case of projects related to information technology.

The cut-off figure for payback period be deemed as a rule of thumb to be reciprocal of weighted average cost of the capital. For instance, if weighted average cost of the capital is 25%, the payback period of less than four years is acceptable.

#### *12.4.1.2 Rate of Return (ROR)/Return on Investment (ROI)*

The rate of return (ROR) is also sometimes referred as return on investment (ROI). The rate of return as the name suggest is computed for every year. It is defined in a number of ways:

Rate of Return
= (Gross Profit)/(Investment)
= (Operating Profit)/(Investment)
= (Profit after Tax but before depreciation)/(Investment) (12.5)

(In all the above calculations the numerator refers to profit per year)

#### 12.4.1.3 Return on Equity

Return on Equity (per year)

$$= \frac{\text{(Gross profit} - \text{Financial expenses} - \text{Corporate tax) per year}}{\text{Equity}} \qquad (12.6)$$

The above computation is a bit complicated. For a quick conservative estimate, one can have gross profit at 100% capacity utilisation, and the financial expenses would be interest the during moratorium period. When a schedule of estimate of working results is prepared, it becomes very easy to see how much average return on equity could be obtained.

#### 12.4.1.4 Profit Margin

It is defined as the ratio of profit to sales.

$$\text{Profit Margin} = \text{(Gross profit)/(Sales)} \qquad (12.7)$$

Higher profit margin is always desirable. The profit margin is considered to be an index of overall efficiency of the project.

#### 12.4.1.5 Net Assets Turnover

It is defined as the ratio of sales to investment. This ratio may not be important for a proposed project but is important for an on- going project.

$$\text{Net assets turnover} = \text{(Net sales)/(Net fixed assets} + \text{net current assets)} \qquad (12.8)$$

A high ratio reflects ability of the project owner to make good use of resources at his disposal. For a highly capital-intensive project, such as petrochemical complex, this ratio is lower. However, in such situations it is interpreted together with other ratios. For a proposed project, current assets are not considered and, hence, one can consider the project cost as investment.

For an on-going project if ratio declines, the owner has to take the corrective measures to increase the sales. Interestingly, one can infer return on investment as

$$\text{Return on Investment} = (\text{Profit margin}) \times (\text{Net assets turnover}) \quad (12.9)$$

#### *12.4.1.6 Stock Turnover*

The stock turnover is the barometer of efficiency of 'sales' department. The lesser stock or inventory of product is a healthy sign of demand of the product.

$$\text{Stock turnover} = (\text{Net sales})/(\text{Stock}) \quad (12.10)$$

Strictly speaking, one can have in the numerator the cost of product sold in place of sales (Sales – Profit). On the other hand, the higher stocks (lower stock turnover) are a danger sign for the project. The higher inventory (stock) turnover means more profit. The higher inventory is always alarming. This ratio, also finds its utility for ongoing project rather than the proposed project.

#### *12.4.1.7 Debtor Turnover*

By the word debtor, we mean credits given to the buyer (accounts receivable). Credits to buyers of the product should be as low as possible because in future it may pose problems of recovery.

$$\text{Debtor turnover} = \text{Sales}/\text{Debtor} \quad (12.11)$$

#### *12.4.1.8 Average Collection Period*

There is a more appealing way of expressing the above 'Debtor Turn over ratio', and it is known as average collection period in days

$$\text{Average collection period} = \frac{\text{Sundry debtors}}{\text{Sales credit}} \times 365 \quad (12.12)$$

Thus all the above performance ratios would indicate to us how well the project is performing or in the case of a proposed project how well it would perform in future.

### 12.4.2 Financial Ratios

The financial ratios discussed below are not only important to project owner but also are important to the project financier. These ratios essentially reflect on the ability of a project to meet short-term and long-term liabilities. Of course, the interest of shareholders cannot be undermined here as well. Let us quickly review some important ratios.

#### *12.4.2.1 Debt to Equity Ratio*

The financing pattern of a project is straightway reflected in Debt : Equity ratio. As explained earlier, Debt means the the borrowed capital and 'Equity' means contribution of promoters and shareholders (for ongoing project reserves and surplus are to be added) put together in the project-financing pattern. Higher term loan (Debt) reflects the faith imposed by financial institutions in promoter(s) of the project. This reduces promoter's contribution. Very high Debt : Equity ratios (exceeding 3) are seen for mega projects of national interest say, a grassroots refinery. On the other hand, lower Debt : Equity ratio yields very high leverage of safety to the project financier.

The D:E ratio will tend to go down due to low-tax shield available on the same borrowed capital.

#### *12.4.2.2 Interest Cover*

The ability of a project to service the term loan by way of interest is reflected in the interest cover defined as

$$\text{Interest cover} = (\text{Gross profit})/(\text{Interest}) \qquad (12.13)$$

In reality, one should have in the numerator gross profit less tax in place of gross profit. This ratio refers to the performance of on-going project for any particular year. The higher ratio is a good sign for both the owner as well as the project financier. During turbulent days of business, the interest cover can be less than one also. At times it can be negative also (Loss = – ve profit).

The owner should carefully watch this ratio and corrective actions should be initiated to change the course of business. This ratio plays an important role for ongoing projects. For proposed projects this ratio would be always greater than unity.

#### 12.4.2.3 Debt Service Coverage Ratio (DSCR)

For ongoing project this is important. It is defined as:

DSCR = (PAT + DEP (SLM) + INT)/(INT + LRP)

PAT = Profit after tax

DEP (SLM) = Depreciation SLM method

INT = Interest on term loan

LRP = Loan repayment instalment (12.14)

For a normal company this is minimum 1.7 : 1. However, a higher ratio is desirable.

#### 12.4.2.4 Current Ratio

By definition, current ratio is the ratio of current assets to current liabilities.

Current ratio = (Current assets)/(Current liabilities) (12.15)

This ratio, like earlier, is also relevant to ongoing project (during its working). It reflects ability of the project to convert liquid assets easily into 'cash' to meet liabilities of the business. A critical appraisal of the ongoing business is required followed by result-oriented actions when the current ratio starts dipping down and, particularly so, when it becomes less than unity. A very high current ratio is a good sign. Ideally the current ratio, in the present context, is 2.

#### 12.4.2.5 Acid Test

The acid test is a true measure of the ability of a project to meet the current liabilities. In acid test we exclude stock or inventory and debtor while assessing the ability of a project to meet the current liabilities.

Acid Test = (Current assets excluding stock)/(Current liabilities excluding bank overdraft) (12.16)

The logic behind excluding the stock or inventory is that current liabilities need to be honoured as and when they become due, while the stock might take considerable time to realise into liquid cash. Similarly, the owner is not expected to pay a bank overdraft immediately.

The Acid Test ratio is also referred as 'Quick Ratio'. By 'Quick' we mean the ease with which assets can be converted into money. This, in turn, would depend on the nature of inventory also. The Acid Test ratio is nothing but a measure of liquidity and has emphasis on immediate conversion of assets into cash. The accounts receivables (debtors) may not be converted into cash at face value in short time. A quick ratio, 1 : 1 is considered to be good. It is project-specific.

### 12.4.3 Stock Market Ratios

These ratios are more important to shareholders at large than to a project financier. The contribution by shareholders is important in equity part of project financing and, therefore, one cannot underestimate the importance of stock market ratios. We present here some important stock market ratios.

#### *12.4.3.1 Earnings Per Share*

The earning per share is important to shareholders as they look forward to have more and more earnings. It is defined as:

Earning per share = (PAT – preference dividend)/(Number of ordinary shares issued)

PAT = Profit after tax (12.17)

#### *12.4.3.2 Price/Earning Ratio*

The market price of share is the barometer of people's reaction to the working of a project.

Price/Earning ratio = (Market price of share)/
(Earning per share) (12.18)

#### 12.4.3.3 *Cash Earning Per Share (CEPS)*

CEPS = (Profit after tax + Depreciation (SLM)
– Preference dividend)/shares (12.19)

#### 12.4.3.4 *Dividend Yield*

The dividend paid is important to shareholders.

Dividend yield = (Dividend per share)/
(Market price per share) (12.20)

The dividend yield for shareholders can change from year to year due to change in market price of share even if dividend is identical.

#### 12.4.3.5 *Dividend Cover*

This ratio reflects in the ability of a project to pay dividend.

Dividend cover = (Earning per share)/
(Dividend per share) (12.21)

The market reaction should always be based on sound fundamentals. The performance and financial ratios would indicate how well the project is performing. The market share price would react to the performance of the project.

Thus we see 'Ratio Analysis' can reveal how well the project is performing or in the case of a proposed project, how well it would perform.

### 12.4.4 Limitations of the Ratio Analysis

The main limitation of the above ratio analysis is the subjective nature. Is there any singular number for comparison? Each organisation has its own 'bottom line' drawn. Thus the standard for comparison would be a range rather than a single number. For example, Acid test ratio 1:1 is good but what happens if it is

1:0.5? Can we continue to operate the project or do we abandon the project?

Although current ratio and quick ratios are generally 2:1 and 1:1 respectively, it need not be accepted as standard norm. They could largely depend upon the constitution of each of the items of current assets and current liabilities. If the creditors are risking their capital by funding the project via higher credits, the current ratio will be lower (due to higher current liabilities).

There is built-in variations due to accounting methods practised by different organisations because accountants come from different schools of commerce. Therefore, to have meaningful inferences based on ratio analysis it is desirable to have experience.

The future projections of profit are risky. If we compare future projections of profit of two or more projects the associated risk would change from project to project. The risk associated with power project based on indigenous coal is less than that based on imported liquefied natural gas (LNG).

Another important fact is that in all the above analysis we have not considered time value of money.

Despite the above limitations, the 'Ratio Analysis' is popular among the project evaluators (appraisers) because the concept of ratio is understood easily.

In the above analysis, we have not considered the concept of 'time value of money'. It means what is the real profit to me as of today when we have say ₹ 100 lakh profit in the fifth year of the project life. We shall see in details in the following section, how to account for 'time value' of profit (money or cash) with the help of discounted profit flow (DPF) analysis/technique.

## 12.5 DISCOUNTED PROFIT FLOW TECHNIQUE (DPF)

The discounted profit flow technique, also known as *DPF analysis*, is a powerful tool in the hands of project appraiser or evaluator. By profit here we mean the gross profit. This technique is similar to the discounted cash flow (DCF) technique used by accountants.

All earlier techniques of project evaluation suffer from a major drawback of profit projection are for present and future without taking into account time value of money. The DPF technique takes into account 'time value' of profit and hence it is a realistic tool while screening various projects. The DPF technique calculates the present value of profit and investment. All profit projections are discounted for the zero date, i.e. the day, the plant is handed over to production personnel after successful commissioning of the same. All investment prior to this day, i.e. project construction activities, are counted in the forward direction to assign them the present value. In other words, DPF technique computes the present value of all futuristic profit projections and present value of all investments (project cost).

An estimate of working results yields gross profit projections over the service life of the project, say 10 years. Suppose, we have profit $P_1, P_2, P_3, ..., P_{10}$ for 10 years, a cumulative discounted gross profit for the present is then given by

$PV$ = Present Value

$$\frac{P_1}{(1+K)} + \frac{P_2}{(1+K)^2} + \frac{P_3}{(1+K)^3} + \ldots + \frac{P_{10}}{(1+K)^{10}} \qquad (12.22)$$

$$PV = \sum_{n=1}^{n=10} P_n / (1+K)^n \qquad (12.23)$$

where $K$ is known as the *hurdle rate of return* (expressed as a fraction). The project conception to commissioning journey is full of hurdles and therefore $K$ is known as hurdle rate of return, which the owner of the project would like to have. The factor, $1/(1+K)^n$, is known as discounting factor for $n$th year.

The investment prior to the date of evaluation is counted in the forward direction, i.e. future value. The present value of such investment is the today's worth of the investment made in the past. Though project construction expenditure is continuous, for the sake of ease of calculation we assume all expenditure incurred from the zero day to the end of fist year, as expenditure deemed to have occurred at the end of first year. All expenditure in the second year is deemed to have occurred at the end of second year, and so on, for the entire construction period. Generally, petrochemical projects are constructed in 2–2½ years and greenfield refinery and petrochemical complex project may take 3 to 4 years depending upon prevailing conditions at the site and size of the project.

The present value of the investment in the first year of construction period for total construction period being two years would then be $(1 + K)I_1$. Thus present value of investment during project construction period of two years would be

$$I_0 = (1 + K)\, I_1 + I_2 \tag{12.24}$$

Before discussing various profitability criteria based on DPF analysis, let us see the meaning of *K*-hurdle rate of return.

### 12.5.1 Hurdle Rate of Return (K)

The concept of Hurdle Rate of Return *K*, is similar to that of interest rate. The project owner always looks forward to earn money at a rate far higher than that of the interest rate of fixed deposits in banks. The reason is obvious because the owner has to overcome so many hurdles during the implementation of the project. Each and every person or organisation may value these hurdles at different rate. It is due to this reason hurdle rate of return, *K*, varies from one organisation to the other. Many times corporate managers call it as bottom line.

Let us see now whether we can assign some value to *K*. The project is financed by term loan from say Financial Institutions (or Banks) and equity coming from promoter(s) and shareholders.

The financial institute charges interest on the term loan. The equity holders are interested in having much more returns on their investment – definitely more than interest rate on zero-risk investment in fixed deposits in nationalised banks. The project owner decides how much dividend (return) he should give to all equity participants and this return might be two or three times the prevailing interest rate on fixed deposits.

It is possible now to calculate weighted average cost of capital (WACC) to the entrepreneur and suppose the hurdle rate of return is equal to this weighted average cost of capital. Thus we can now see two bounds for $K$, the lower bound would be the interest rate charged by financial institutions. The upper bound would be the choice of entrepreneur to have hurdle rate of return, $K$, which is equal to or greater than weighted average cost of the capital. When $K$ is considered as equal to return on equity, the profit is considered as operating profit less corporate tax.

### 12.5.2 Weighted Average Cost of Capital (WACC)

As seen earlier in Chapter 8 a project financing activity has two components namely, debt financing (D) and equity financing (E). The debt component is mainly term loan and to some extent debentures. While the interest on term loan is decided by the policies of the Finance Ministry through Reserve Bank of India (RBI) the project owner decides the interest rate on debentures. The interest on debentures will not exceed that on term loan. Therefore it would be safe (a conservative approach) to assume that the entire debt component is financed at the interest rate, $i_T$ of the term loan. In the equity, the promoters and share holders are looking for very high return on their investment. The return expected on equity ($r_E$) is definitely far higher than the interest rate on fixed deposits in nationalized bank (zero risk investment is in fixed deposits). This is because of the risk involved in business. The financing pattern for the project under consideration is known via Debt: Equity ratio (D : E).

Let $i_T$ = interest rate on term loan, and $r_E$ = desired return on equity.

The weighted average cost of capital (WACC) is then given as

$$\text{WACC} = (Di_T + Er_E)/(D + E) \quad (12.25)$$

The hurdle rate of return K, then can be given by

$$K = \text{WACC} \quad (12.26)$$

The above value of $K$ could be deemed as realistic value. One can have $K$ more than (WACC) also. When the above value of $K$ is used, the profit is gross profit.

The above method wherein we consider gross profit and pre-tax hurdle rate results in very conservative estimate of discounted profit. The more realistic way (desired for bankable document – detailed techno-economic feasibility report) would be the post-tax scenario. For this purpose, the profit and WACC or $K$ are redefined as,

$P$ = Profit after tax (PAT) + Depreciation (SLM) + Interest on term loan.

$$K = \frac{D}{(D+E)} i_T (1 - \text{Tax rate}) + \frac{E}{(D+E)} + r_E \quad (12.27)$$

### 12.5.3 Net Present Value (NPV) Analysis

In the preceding section, we have seen how to obtain present value (PV) of profit based on DPF analysis. We have seen how to estimate present value of project cost or investment (Eq. 12.23). The net present value of profit (NPV – P) is then given by

$$\text{NPV-P} = \left[ \sum_{n=1}^{n=10} P_n / (1+K)^n \right] - I_0 \quad (12.28)$$

The projects having positive values can then be considered for further evaluation. Further, the project having highest NPV-P would be recommended over others.

The major disadvantage with NPV analysis is that it yields a numerical figure having as high as nine digits (or even more). Unless one has feel for such numbers, it would be difficult to comprehend or appreciate NPV–P. This difficulty is resolved by having the profitability index (PI) as outlined is the subsequent section.

### 12.5.4 Profitability Index (PI)

It is defined as the ratio of present value of profit to present value of investment.

$$\text{Profitability Index (PI)} = \left[ \sum_{n=1}^{n=10} P_n / (1+K)^n \right] / I_0 \qquad (12.29)$$

The profitability index (PI) has to be greater than unity (1) so that NPV is positive. The projects with higher PI would be obvious choice.

### 12.5.5 Internal Rate of Return (IRR)

By definition, internal rate of return (IRR) is the value of hurdle rate of return at which NPV is zero.

Therefore we have,

$$\sum_{n=1}^{10} P_n / (1 + IRR)^n = I_0 \qquad (12.30)$$

The method involves iterative procedure but can be handled easily even on a programmable calculator.

If IRR > WACC, one can say project is attractive.

We shall illustrate the above aspects of DPF technique with the help of examples.

### 12.5.6 Economic Profit Analysis (EPA)

We define Economic Profit as:

Economic Profit (EP)

= (Gross Profit – Corporate Tax – Depreciation (SLM)) – Opportunity cost of funds (12.31)

Economic profit is deemed as the value created in excess of the normal return on the investment. This is super profit earned by a project.

The weighted average cost of capital, WACC (section 12.5.2), is the true measure of the cost of financing entire project and the normal return on investment. The project owner has to service term loan by way of interest and must also seek reasonably attractive return on equity investment. In this sense WACC is the true measure of the return on investment. Therefore we have,

Economic Profit (EP)

= (Gross Profit – Corporate Tax – depreciation (SLM )) – WACC × Project cost – interest on Working capital borrowing × (working capital borrowed). (12.32)

This is the barometer of creation of value for projects. Through WACC we give credit to equity holders (promoters and share holders). Well an enterprise might have its "bottom line" as desired return. This is thus subjective!.

The value creation for equity holders is possible if EP is positive. The project yielding negative EP is not recommended at all. Among various projects having EP value positive, the project having highest EP appears to be attractive. The calculation for the proposed project can be done for first year having 100% capacity utilization. This EPA analysis gives investor option to select a project from various other options available.

This is similar to **EVA analysis** of Stern Stewart & Co. The EVA is trademark of Stern Stewart & Co.

One can go further and have economic profit exclusively for share holders only as

Economic Profit (S)

$$= \text{Operating profit} - \text{Corporate tax} - r_E \times \text{Equity} \quad (12.33)$$

Wherein $r_E$ is fractional return on equity desired.

The term, operating profit, as seen from Eqn (11.2) includes financial expenses (interest) associated with project.

This is in true sense Economic Profit (S) after taking care of all stake holders.

It is possible to conduct similar analysis for ongoing project also.

The EPA analysis gives investor option to select a project from various other options available.

## 12.6 ILLUSTRATION

Following is the profitability projection expressed in ₹ crore for projects A, B and C for their service life of 10 years.

| *Year* | *1* | *2* | *3* | *4* | *5* | *6* | *7* | *8* | *9* | *10* | *Total* |
|---|---|---|---|---|---|---|---|---|---|---|---|
| A | 10 | 12 | 15 | 17 | 20 | 21 | 22 | 23 | 23 | 23 | 186 |
| B | 13 | 14 | 16 | 18 | 20 | 21 | 21 | 21 | 21 | 21 | 186 |
| C | 9 | 10 | 11 | 12 | 14 | 15 | 16 | 16 | 16 | 16 | 135 |

The project cost in all above cases is ₹ 40 crore. During the period of construction ₹ 24 crore were spent in the first year and ₹ 16 crore in the second year.

In all the above projects Debt: Equity ratio is 1.5 : 1.

The term loan is at the interest rate of 12%. The desired return on equity is 40%.

We shall now illustrate how to evaluate above projects based on the important ratio, payback period and DPF analysis.

### 12.6.1 Payback Period

The working capital requirement is neglected in the present analysis. The payback period can be computed from profitability projections and the average profit.

| *Project* | *Payback Period, Years (Average profit)* | *Payback Period Years (Actual profit)* |
|---|---|---|
| A | 2.2 | 3.2 |
| B | 2.2 | 2.9 |
| C | 3.0 | 3.8 |

It has been observed that the payback period based on average profit of 10 years is misleading and results in lower payback period than that obtained on the bases of actual cash flow profitability projections.

The average profit for project A and B, being the same, the resultant payback period is identical. On the other hand, one can see that in reality, the project B yields lower payback period than that for A.

### 12.6.2 Weighted Average Cost of the Capital (WACC) and Hurdle Rate of Return

The weighted average cost of capital in all above projects is calculated by substituting in Eq (12.25) that is

$$\text{WACC} = (1.5 \times 0.12 + 1 \times 0.4)/2.5 = 0.23 = 23\%$$

Therefore, the hurdle rate of return, $K = 25\%$ ( $K > \text{WACC}$).

### 12.6.3 Project Investment at the time of evaluation

We know by Eq. (12.24)

$$I_o = I_2 + (1 + K) I_1 = 16 + (1 + 0.25)(24)$$
$$= ₹\ 46 \text{ crore}$$

### 12.6.4 Net Present Value (NPV)

With the help of Eqs. (12.23) and (12.28), we have obtained the present value (PV) of the profit and net present value (NPV) as:

| *Project* | *PV of Profit (₹ in crore)* | *NPV (₹ in crore)* |
|---|---|---|
| A | 56.41 | 10.41 |
| B | 59.98 | 13.98 |
| C | 42.57 | –3.43 |

*Inference:*

Since NPV for the project C is negative, the project C should not be considered.

### 12.6.5 The Profitability Index (PI)

With the help of Eq. (12.29) we can compute profitability index as:

| *Project* | *PI* |
|---|---|
| A | 1.23 |
| B | 1.30 |
| C | 0.93 |

*Inference*

The profitability index for project C being less than 1, it is recommended that this project C should not be considered. (Since NPV is negative, PI is expected to be less than unity).

### 12.6.6 Internal Rate of Return (IRR)

The internal rate of return for a project can be computed with the help of Eq. (12.26) by trial and error.

| *Project* | *IRR (%)* |
|---|---|
| A | 30.15 |
| B | 32.22 |
| C | 23.09 |

*Inference*

The internal rate of return for project C is almost the same as WACC (23%) but it is lower than *K* (25%). Therefore, the project C is not recommended.

### 12.6.7 Other Inferences

The total profit in projects A and B is identical. However, the present value of profit for the project A is lower than that for B. It is seen that the project B has higher profit in the early years (first 4 years) than that for the project A.

Thus while selecting projects, it is desirable that the projects show higher profitability in early years compared to later period.

The projects with nearby values of NPV-P, PI&IRR need detailed and more accurate screening before the final decision is made.

## SUGGESTED READING

Peters M. S. and Timmerhaus K.D., *Plant Design and Economics for Chemical Engineers,* Fouth Edition, McGraw-Hill International Edition, New York, 1991.

Kuchhal S.C., *Financial Management* (1969).

IDBI *Manual of Industrial Project Analysis in Developing Countries,* Indian Edition, Industrial Development Bank of India (1980).

Grant E.L., Grant W. Ireson and Leavenworth R.S., *Principles of Engineering Economy,* Seventh Edition, John Wiley and Sons, New York, 1982.

***Project Evaluation and Risk Evaluation are Two Horses of the Chariot Wherein the Owner decides Destination.***

# 13 Product Pricing

## 13.1 INTRODUCTION

The success of any project depends on price of the product(s). In its simple form price is defined as

$$\text{Price} = \text{Cost} + \text{Profit} \quad (13.1)$$

When we buy an item/product we ask for its price. When we use the same as raw material for its value addition we say the same product costed us so many rupees. The concept of price or pricing is dynamic in nature and depends on so many factors, which are difficult to elaborate here. The most important factors among them could be as follows:

- Project economics considerations
- Market considerations

The market, in turn depends upon perfect and imperfect competition. In this chapter, we shall try to understand meaning of the above two factors.

## 13.2 PROJECT ECONOMICS CONSIDERATIONS

Here we shall see how to determine the price of a product of the proposed project based purely on economic considerations. The economy of scale plays important role in a chemical project. For instance, for a project having a capacity 1,00,000 TPA and 2,00,000 TPA, the manpower requirement will remain the same and, also, the investment will not double. We shall address this issue and understand the pros and cons of the same.

### 13.2.1 Proposed Project Product Pricing

In product pricing, transfer price and selling price are often used as synonyms. However, they are different. While the transfer price is purely derived from the fixed capital investment (project cost) and the operating cost(Expression13.2), the selling price is decided by the market considerations. Here, we shall use price as the transfer price. The relationship between the price, project cost (the fixed capital investment) and gross cost of production (the operating cost) is expressed as follows:

$$\text{Price} = \beta(\text{Project cost}) + \text{Gross cost of production} \quad (13.2)$$

The coefficient, β, depends on the desired return the owner would like to have on his fixed investment in the form of project cost and other project cost related expenses such as interest, dividend, loan repayment, etc. The profit concept is built in the above coefficient, β.

The desired rate of return from project investment has to be more than the interest rate the depositor will earn from a fixed deposit in a sound bank or from the government bonds. If returns from these financial instruments are more that from a project, there is no advantage in investing money in a project. Further, the promoter will not be able to repay his loan. A very important question, therefore, is how much more should be the rate of return because it depends on the industry, the product and the process.

In a speciality product the desired rate of return is higher even though the investment is less because technological risks are more. A speciality product has specific application. Another improved product may substitute the product. The formulation or the item where the product is one of the constituents, may itself lose market. Thus the lifespan of the product is uncertain. Secondly, if the manufacturing process is not very complicated it may be copied easily and a competitor may trigger a price war reducing profit margin. The new SHE regulations may find an objectionable component in the product formulation or the product itself that can terminate the product life. For example, hexane used as a solvent in the manufacture of spices by extraction is now being replaced by *iso*-hexane. Under the Montreal protocol the existing capacities of methyl bromide used as pesticide, are reduced as it was found to be an ozone-depleting product. Concentrates of spices are speciality products because their applications are for a specific purpose. They can be manufactured either by conventional solvent extraction process or by super critical extraction process. The first one is simpler while the latter yields purer product. Ultimately consumer's taste and preference is important. They may reject the purer product simply because it lacks familiar fragrance. On the other hand, commodity products, such as methanol, benzene, run low risks and hence the desired rate of return on these basic chemicals is relatively low. For example, methanol is a commodity chemical because it has a variety of applications from solvent to raw material for acetic acid, formaldehyde, propylene, gasoline and diesel, and so on. Their lifespan is much longer than the plant life. The process changes are also minor and not frequent. The chances of stealthily copying the process are now minimum. As a result we always have commodity products at lower price than speciality products

The gross cost of production takes into account all operating expenses at the production site as well as at operating site. We have seen earlier in Chapters 5 to 7 how to estimate project cost and gross cost of production. Let us see how to use the above Eq. (13.2) with the help of illustrations.

*Illustration 1*

What would be the price of product of a project costing ₹ 100 crore having capacity 20,000 TPA? The gross cost of production at 100% capacity utilisation, is ₹35,000/T. The desired return is 40%.

$$\underset{(₹/T)}{\text{Price}} = \beta\underset{(₹/T)}{(\text{Project cost})} + \underset{(₹/T)}{\text{Gross cost of production}}$$

Project cost = ₹ 100 crore.

Capacity = 20,000 TPA

The factor, $\beta = 0.40$ (40%)

Therefore,

$$\text{Price} = 0.40\ (100 \times 10^7/20{,}000) + 35{,}000$$

$$\text{Price} = (20{,}000 + 35{,}000)\ ₹/T$$

$$= 55{,}000\ ₹/T$$

While we are using the above expression, one can appreciate the concept of economy of scale.

### 13.2.2 Economy of Scale

As seen earlier in Chapter 6, uniqueness of chemical project is that there exists a relationship between the project cost and its capacity. In its simple form it is expressed as:

$$\text{Cost} = \alpha(\text{Capacity})^n \qquad (13.3)$$

Many times, $n$ is in the range of 0.5 to 0.9. In the absence of data, for estimate purpose we can take the value of $n$ to be equal to 0.75. Thus it is seen that for higher capacity the contribution of fixed investment (project cost) per unit production would be less. The gross cost of production expressed as per tonne of a product, will eventually be lower for higher capacity due to lower indirect cost such as salary and wages, administrative expenses, and so on. However, their contribution being less significant, for the illustration below, gross cost of production is deemed to be practically constant. Therefore, we have the transfer price of a product for higher capacity less than that at lower capacity as seen in Illustration 2.

*Illustration 2*

Calculate the price of the product for capacity 50,000 TPA. The rest of the data from the illustration 1 can be used.

The project cost for new capacity

$$= (\text{Project cost for old capacity}) \times (\text{new capacity/old capacity})^n$$
$$= 100 \times 10^7 \times (50{,}000/20{,}000)^{0.75}$$
$$= 198.8 \times 10^7 \text{ ₹}$$
$$\text{say, } = 200 \times 10^7 \text{ ₹}$$

Therefore,

$$\text{Price} = 0.4\,(200 \times 10^7/50{,}000) + 35{,}000$$
$$= 16{,}000 + 35{,}000$$
$$= 51{,}000 \text{ ₹/T}$$

Thus we see that when we increase the plant (project) capacity the price of the product goes down. In other words for the prevailing market price, the profit increases.

Thus there is always an advantage of economy of scale. The bigger is better. It should be noted that there is always an upper bound for capacity. This upper limit arises due to the following main considerations:

- For very large capacity, there might be constraints of availability and supply logistics of raw materials, utilities such as water and power.
- The technology might not have been matured yet to take advantage of the capacity. For example, there exists, as of today, no plant to manufacture 20,000 TPD methanol though plants having capacity 2,000 to 2,500 TPD are well established.
- The project cost at higher capacity may not be within the reach of the project owner. The financial and technical management of mega projects might dither the owner.

- It may not be possible to sell the entire production.
- The mega projects may precipitate environment related problems. The quantities of gaseous, liquid and solid emission at a single location could be so large that the project finds itself difficult to sustain environmentally. For example, $SO_2$ emissions at ppm level at stack in a sulphuric acid plant might be as per the local pollution norms. However, the mega project having three sulphuric acid plants each with capacity say, 3,000 TPD, may emit $SO_2$, which might not be acceptable at the site.

It is thus obvious that for any given project there is always an upper bound. The lower bound could be the break-even capacity.

## 13.3 MARKET CONSIDERATIONS

Often in a real world, price of the product is not only decided by economic considerations but also by the market scenario. The objective of any entrepreneur is to maximise the profit. The market often adds hurdles in achieving this goal. By and large market conditions are of two types, namely, perfect competition and imperfect competition. We shall here just introduce this concept. The detail discussions are excluded from the scope of this book. The readers are advised to refer any book on management or managerial economics (for example, Dwivedi 1995, Dewitt and Chand 1995). The imperfect competition is the result of monopolistic competition, oligopoly, monopoly and monopsony.

Market

Perfect Competition

Imperfect Competition
- Monopolistic
- Oligopoly
- Monopoly
- Monopsony

Let us understand meaning of all above market characteristics.

### 13.3.1 Perfect Competition

The perfect competition is also an ideal competition, and has the following characteristics:

- Large number of sellers and buyers exist mounting to homogeneous conditions. No one is in a position to control the market.
- The products supplied by all manufacturers are identical (rather difficult to distinguish).
- The buyers and sellers have total knowledge of the product and the prevailing market conditions.

Any manufacturer is free to enter the business of manufacturing the same product and quit the market as and when he pleases.

The above ideal scenario is seldom applicable to products of chemical projects.

### 13.3.2 Imperfect Competition

The real world thrives on imperfect competition as far as products of chemical projects are concerned. Let us comprehend the meaning of various forms of imperfect competition.

#### *13.3.2.1 Monopolistic Competition*

Under the monopolistic conditions, we have a limited number of manufacturers of products. Further, products are not homogeneous but are distinguishable by brand names, trademark appearance, services offered, etc. Paints, soaps, detergents, aerated soft drinks are some typical examples of products of monopolistic competition. Though prices of soaps are different but these are not radically different. The seller can have his own pricing policy. The demand of the product can change with the price. The market share changes with time, price and an introduction of better quality product. The hike in price of one brand may result in negative reaction of the market.

#### 13.3.2.2 Oligopoly

In oligopoly, there are less number of sellers than those in monopolistic situation. Every seller can influence price of a product of the other seller. The market share is comparable of all sellers. There is always interdependence of various project owners to fix the price. For example, manufacturers of mono ethylene glycol (MEG) will not decide the price of MEG independently. In our country MEG producers are not necessarily producers of polyester fibre. There is always a distinct possibility that all these few sellers may come together and form a cartel to dictate the price of MEG.

#### 13.3.2.3 Monopoly

It is the extreme case of monopolistic competition wherein only one seller of services or products and many buyers exist. Monopoly implies total control of the market power due to practically insignificant or no competition. Following are the main factors responsible for monopoly to exist:

*Control of the state or Central Government:* The government might totally control the business, as was the case with petroleum refining industry till recently.

*Patent protection:* The patent protection (for limited period) results in absolute market control of the product. Various catalysts used in chemical projects have patent protection.

*Superior technology:* The superior technology results in a superior quality product at lower price. This keeps competitors away.

*Availability of large financial resources:* If makes possible to set up new projects. The chemical projects are cost-intensive.

*Control of raw materials:* If one has absolute control over the raw materials cost benefits are obtained. For instance, the owner of methanol project can carry out forward integration by producing acetic acid via carbonylation of methanol, using CO from the syn gas. This eventually will produce acetic acid at lower price than that produced from alcohol thereby resulting in monopoly.

*Advantages of monopoly*

- The project owner can take advantage of economy of scale resulting in lower price of a product.
- The stable price makes buyer more secure so that he can plan more projects.
- The owner feels secured in business. This would give him more resources to invest in new projects and in research and development leading to more technical competence.

*Disadvantages of monopoly*

- Monopoly may result in manipulation of prices resulting in exploitation of buyers.
- The buyers feel insecured in their business due to raw material being not fairly priced.
- Complacency may set into business resulting in no progress. This may ultimately lead to collapse of the project

#### 13.3.2.4 Monopsony

In a business deal when there exists only one buyer and a large number of sellers, we have monopsony. For instance, to meet the requirement of nuclear-grade ion exchange resins for the atomic energy department one can have many suppliers. The same is the case with purchase of the defence department. The buyer decides the price of a product. This is almost opposite to monopoly practice.

Thus we have seen some important aspects of the market forces of imperfect competition. Therefore, while deciding the price of a product of any project, one has to look into not only the economic consideration but also into the market forces by way of competition.

## REFERENCES

Dewitt K.K. and Chand A., *Modern Economic Theory*, S. Chand and Co. Ltd, New Delhi, 1995.

Dwivedi D.N., *Managerial Economics*, Fourth Revised Edition, Vikas Publishing House Pvt. Ltd, New Delhi, 1995.

***Sustainable Development of the Society Rests on Affordable Product Price.***

# 14 Feasibility Report

## 14.1 PREAMBLE

The feasibility report of any project deals with financial feasibility or viability of the project under consideration.

The feasibility report is based on the pertinent details of the technology provided by the process licensor for battery limit plant. If the project under consideration is a Greenfield project, engineering department after considering all outside battery limit (OSBL) facilities prepares this report.

As we undertake the project conception to implementation journey, feasibility is carried out at various stages of implementation of a project, as outlined in the Chapter 1.

The project owner many times prepares a very preliminary report based on the order of magnitude estimate of project cost. If the project appears attractive, he engages services of project engineering contractor to prepare a preliminary feasibility report. This is based on budgetary estimate of various project cost components. The experience of project engineering organisation gives sound basis to a conceptually good idea. If the project looks financially attractive, the owner decides to take steps towards implementation of the project. While he is seriously discussing with the process licensor he might execute a memorandum of understanding (MoU), he would engage services of a reputed project engineering organisation to prepare a detailed techno-economic feasibility report. This report then forms the basis of various clearances the owner would like to have from the state and the central government. Further, this report is used as a bankable document in support of his application for term loan. It is, therefore, desirable that this report is prepared by competent project engineering company which can use its experience and wisdom to ensure the project cost to be reasonably accurate (+10% to –5%). No matter at what stage feasibility report is prepared, its contents remains the same. Let us now overview contents of the feasibility report.

## 14.2 CONTENTS

We present below outlines of the contents of a typical feasibility report.

### 14.2.1 Introduction

We should identify project owner, detailed engineering contractor who prepares the feasibility report and the process licensor. The type of project, namely, Greenfield/Grassroots or Battery limit project should be mentioned. Normal capacity of the project should be mentioned along with the feedstock. It is desirable to mention whether the feedstock is imported or sourced locally. The commitment to supply the feedstock is stated. For example, to manufacture 2-ethyl hexanol by LP- Oxo process using propylene as the raw material, one should have a firm assurance by way of a letter from nearby refinery or petro chemical complex to supply propylene continuously. The site location must be clearly identified by way of mention of state industrial development corporation (SIDC) area, or a village, with *taluka* and district place and the state. The location map would give a clear idea of the site location. If the location is in an industrially notified backward district, a statement with that effect should also be made. This will then reflect in all concessions offered to the owner. If the project is effluent treatment (ETP) or energy conservation (ENCON) project, a mention of the same should be made because such projects attract very high rates of depreciation (80 – 100%).

### 14.2.2 Executive Summary

The executive summary is prepared for people at very senior level to have a quick appraisal of the feasibility report. It should not exceed two pages. A typical format is presented in Appendix 14.1.

### 14.2.3 Market

In order to enable the project to perform year after year to the expectation, a sustainable market for the product is very important. Many times attractive projects at the level of conception, have failed due to lack of demand of products produced. This section discusses present demand-supply scenario along with projection for future. The prices of a product and by-products and prevailing statutory duties such as sales tax, excise, import duty (if any), are given.

The market search report is prepared by an organisation specialised in this job. Field and desk studies are conducted and market projections are made using the standard techniques. Utmost care must be exercised while forecasting a trend. Local availability of the product might spring up the demand even though import of the same was possible. The possibility of export of the product is also mentioned along with demand in countries of potential consumers. One should state the present and possible futuristic competition (competitors) within the country and from abroad.

In general, the project-engineering company constructing a project does not prepare the market search report. For this purpose, assistance of an organisation, recognised by financial institutions, is sought to prepare the market search report. This report is generally presented with the feasibility report. However, in the feasibility report a summary along with main findings of the market search report are included to make the document self-supportive.

### 14.2.4 Process (Technology)

It is desirable to state various processes available and explain in brief the rationale behind the choice of the process or technology.

A brief comprehensive description of the process is presented with the help of block diagrams and simplified process flow diagrams indicating all major equipments. The block diagram exhibits the overall material balance as well. The process description should include equipment number. For example, the feed stream is heated in a heat exchanger E1001, and so on. This facilitates understanding of estimate of cost of equipments (with 4-line specifications) as presented in Chapter 6. The description must be adequate to create technology feel among the project appraiser.

The process licensor offers know-how for the battery limit plant. The process description is limited to the battery limit plant. The detailed engineering contractor has to develop outside battery limit (OSBL) facilities – storage, utilities generation and effluent treatment plant. If a plant has exhaustive utilities systems, one may have a detailed description for the same. For instance, in methanol or ammonia plant, we have a co-generation system. Therefore its description is also presented along with steam utilisation diagram. Similarly, effluent treatment process is also described. Towards the end, consumption figures and specifications for raw materials and utilities and production of by-products/co-products are presented along with the main product to facilitate estimate of the cost of production.

### 14.2.5 Plant Site

The plant site is identified with the help of district and state map. The proximity of the site to port, national highway, railway station and airport is identified with approximate distances involved. The salient features of the site data are given along with seismic zone classification. Similar data are presented for housing colony also. Any culvert, small river and high-tension electric power lines passing through the project area are identified. A plot plan is also presented here.

### 14.2.6 Project Cost

An estimate of each and every component of project cost along with the rationale/basis is given. Here also, foreign exchange requirement is identified. The estimate is presented in a comprehensive manner (Chapter 5) with appropriate backups.

### 14.2.7 Plant and Machinery Cost

A reasonably accurate estimate (+ 10, – 5%) of the plant and machinery item is given along with the equipment list with 4-line specifications. Here the estimate is prepared, as discussed earlier (Chapter 6) based on in-house data and offers from the vendors. This estimate is for the entire plant, i.e. battery limit plant, OSBL facilities, effluent treatment plant. The entire estimate is presented in a comprehensive manner (See Table 6.1) identifying Indian Rupee component and foreign exchange component. The currency basket is identified along with foreign exchange rate.

### 14.2.8 Project Programme

The project implementation programme is given along with bar charts. Please note that network diagrams are not required at this stage.

### 14.2.9 Gross Cost of Production

The estimate of gross cost of production is given for ten years (Project Lifespan) identifying capacity utilisation. The estimate is prepared as discussed earlier in Chapter 7.

### 14.2.10 Project Financing

The proposed financing of the project is presented. The term loan component is identified along with promoters and shareholders contribution in the form of equity. The financial expenses are estimated.

### 14.2.11 Project Profitability

The estimate of working results for entire project life (ten years) of the project is given here. The depreciation schedule is prepared based on the companies' act (SLM depreciation) and the income-tax act (WDV depreciation). The estimates of gross profit, operating profit, corporate tax, dividend and net cash accruals are given for 10 years, as given in Chapter 11.

### 14.2.12 Project Evaluation

This chapter deals with the break-even analysis, ratio analysis and the evaluation of the project based on discounted profit flow Technique (DPF). The break-even capacity, payback period, weighted average cost of capital, internal rate of return are presented to highlight the financial viability of the proposed project.

The feasibility report concludes with a strong recommendation of the project. Thus, we see that the feasibility report contains all chapters described earlier with inferences and conclusions related to a specific project under implementation.

## 14.3 THE UTILITY OF THE FEASIBILITY REPORT

As stated above, the feasibility report is used to obtain all project related clearances.

It can be handy in case there is some project related public interest litigation.

This report is also used to obtain term loan from the financial institutions.

The report becomes very useful while selecting engineering, procurement and construction (EPC) contractor to construct the project.

During the construction period the feasibility report can be used for controlling the cost of project during very early period of the construction activities. With the help of the feasibility report we can identify equipments having long delivery schedule and identify the ones that are on critical path. By expediting detailed engineering and procurement of critical equipments, one can reduce the construction period.

The last but not least important utility of the feasibility report is to compare the estimated project cost and the actual cost realised. This progressive analysis of the project (during and after the construction is completed), would assist us in refining and improving our estimation techniques to make them to as near as possible to the actual cost thereby enabling corrective action for project cost overruns.

## Appendix 14.1 Executive Summary

| | |
|---|---|
| Project: | |
| Capacity: | main product: |
| | Co-product (s) |
| Process Licensor: | |
| Project Type: | Greenfield or Add-on |
| Project site: | |
| Raw materials: | |
| | Raw materials and sources |
| | Consumption |
| | Price |
| Gross cost of production: | ₹/T |
| Sales: | |
| | Selling price |
| | Total Sales |
| Project cost: | |
| Foreign exchange component | Details |
| Financing: | |
| | D:E , ratio |
| | Term loan |
| | Promoters |
| | Shares |
| Project evaluation: | |
| | Break-even capacity |
| | Payback period |
| | Weighted average cost of capital |
| | Internal rate of return (IRR) |

***Feasibility Report is the Horoscope of a Project.***

# 15

# Annual Report

## 15.1 INTRODUCTION

An annual report of an operating project (business) reflects the financial health of a project. It is a comprehensive and a statutory document summarising the actual working of a project during any financial year. It is not prepared for a proposed project, but it is prepared every year during the operating life of a project.

This chapter on Annual Report is not required for understanding of chemical project economics, which is more concerned with conceived, proposed and planned projects. However, since corporate planners can learn many things from annual reports, it was thought desirable to introduce basics of balance sheet, profit and loss account presented in the annual report of operating projects. The annual report is of considerable importance to all associated with the project, namely, owner, financier, shareholders, plant manager and operating personnel as well. The objective is not at all to see how to prepare and present the annual report with relevant back-up documents but to be familiar with its contents and its significance to understand the project performance. In this sense, we present here a broader perspective of the annual report.

In order to appreciate Annual Report it is necessary for engineers to understand commonly used accounting terminologies. We shall not go into details of practicing them.

$$\text{Assets} = \text{Shareholder's funds} + \text{Liabilities} \quad (15.1)$$

Assets are monetary values **owned** by a company/project (business) owner and liabilities are monetary values a company/project (business) **owes.**

Shareholder's funds are also known as **Net worth**.

Profit is income earned by the project on capital employed (deployed) and belongs to shareholders. Hence shareholders' funds include share capital and profit retained in the business. Profit retained in the business is also known as reserves.

Therefore, we have

Assets = Capital + Reserves + Liabilities. (15.2)

Liabilities = All dues of company (like Term loan, Working capital loan, interest due on term loan + interest due on working capital + accounts payable + corporate tax payable)

Reserves = Accumulated profits from year to year. (15.3)

## 15.2 CONTENTS OVERVIEWED

Let us see in a broader sense what a typical annual report contains. The annual report consists of the following:

- Report of Directors
- Report of Auditors
- Balance Sheet
- Profit and Loss Account
- Cash Flow Statement
- Annexures known as Schedules in support of above

We shall, briefly, discuss the contents of various chapters of annual report and understand utility of its contents.

Prior to report of directors, it is customary to provide a list of Board of Directors. The management team with the Managing Director and Vice Presidents – Operations, Finance and Human Resource Development is clearly identified. Auditors and financiers (bankers) are also stated. The works (plant) as well as administrative places are given along with their addresses.

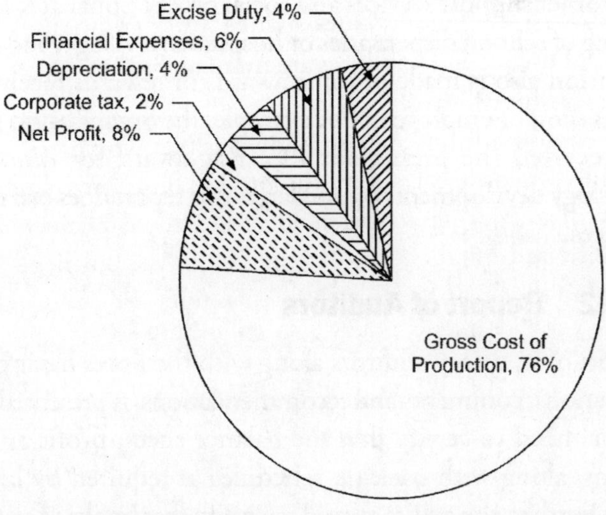


**Fig. 15.1** How the Rupee was Spent?

### 15.2.1 Report of Directors

The report of directors is a perfect blend of the performance of the project, perspective of the business and some information legally required to give to investors. It presents in brief the corporate financial results. Sales, gross profit, profit before tax, overview of profit and loss account resulting in disposable profit are briefly presented. A summary of disposable profit along with recommendation of dividend is presented. Wherever possible histographs, computer graphics are used to present the above. The report would tell us how money is spent via graphics as shown in Fig. 15.1. Operational highlights of the project, particularly the capacity utilisation, milestones achieved during production, efforts made to make project eco-friendly, energy conservation measures implemented, technology absorption, R&D efforts, active programme on 'responsible care', and so on which would project performance of the organisation as a progressive company, are presented in brief. A mention is made of customer support services and social promotional acts such as opening of school, dispensaries or hospital in a village, and so on. A mention also is made of some awards or rewards received by organisation or employees. For example, the organisation might have received the prestigious P.C. Ray award for innovative technology development. By and large, this report does not exceed ten pages.

### 15.2.2 Report of Auditors

A report of statutory auditors along with the notes having their observations, comments and recommendations, is presented. The auditors need to certify that the balance sheet, profit and loss account, along with back-up schedules as required by law, are given. Further, the auditors need to certify that books of accounts are kept properly and they had easy access to all financial data satisfying their queries. The auditors are required to express an opinion regarding the truth and fairness of the state of affairs as reflected in the balance sheet and of profit or loss, as shown in the Profit and Loss account.

### 15.2.3 Balance Sheet

A 'Balance Sheet' is a financial statement exhibiting how source of funds for the ongoing project (liabilities) and application of fund (assets) on the specified day during that financial year are balanced. This particular day is, generally, the last day of the financial year. As the name implies, it is the exercise of balancing assets and liabilities. All assets and all liabilities are quantified in terms of money (₹).

By definition, liability is the amount owed by the project to others. In this sense source of funds to a project is deemed as liability. The balance sheet exhibits what was the source of funds as on the last day of the year and how it was applied to create assets.

The accounting period is the period between two balance sheets and this period is the financial year. The accountants are thus required to assign values to various assets on the final day. The value of assets at times depends upon perception of the management. As a result, preparing the balance sheet is not an exact science, but is an art also in interpreting the financial status of the organisation. Every balance sheet must include the name of organisation or business house, and the date to which figures therein are referred to.

A typical format of balance sheet is presented in Table 15.1. The balance sheet is supported by the following documents.

- Statement of profit and loss account
- Statement of cash flow
- Various schedules as back-up
- Certificate from the authorised auditors

Let us quickly overview meaning of various statements in the balance sheet.

#### 15.2.3.1 Sources of Funds

There are two sources of funds for the project, namely, shareholders' and Loan funds.

*Shareholders' fund*

This includes share capital and reserves from the previous year.

*Loan funds*

The loan funds include secured loans in the form of debentures and term loan. The unsecured loans, e.g. fixed deposits from public or organisation are also included in loan funds.

#### 15.2.3.2 Application of Funds

The funds available are used to support investments in fixed assets, net current assets, and other miscellaneous expenditure.

*Fixed Assets*

Fixed assets, as the name suggests, include all assets required for running the business. By definition, fixed assets are the assets, which are tangible in the project and are purchased and constructed out of the funds. They are generally not converted into cash during the service life of a project.

Following components of the project cost are included here:

- land and developed site
- buildings
- plant and machinery
- miscellaneous fixed assets including vehicles.

*Current Assets*

The current assets have liquidity in a sense that they are easily converted into cash (ease of conversion is relative to fixed assets) during normal working of a project. The ease of cash conversion is referred normally as liquidity. The current assets include the following components:

- Inventories of raw materials, finished products, by-products, catalyst and others chemicals.
- Cash in hand and bank balance (This current asset is the most liquid asset).
- Sundry debtors (customers' account) to include outstanding money with customers who have not paid for the product they have purchased.
- Loan and advances given to staff and others.
- Interest accrued, but not received, on various accounts.

*Current Liabilities*

They include provision for unpaid taxes and duties, dividend, employee liabilities, interest due to secured and unsecured short-term loans, money that the project owner owes to suppliers, etc. (creditors).

While considering application of funds, we should consider the fixed assets and the net current assets (current assets less current liabilities).

We should also consider other miscellaneous expenditure that is not accounted under the above broad titles.

Thus, we have in the balance sheet,

$$\begin{aligned}\text{Sources of funds} &= \text{Application of funds}\\ &= \text{Fixed assets} + \text{Current assets}\\ &\qquad - \text{Current liabilities}\\ &= \text{Fixed assets} + \text{Net current assets} \qquad (15.4)\end{aligned}$$

The balance sheet is supported by various schedules giving details and break-up of these main figures. It is a normal practice to present working results for the current and previous year for comparison. For this purpose a different colour code is used.

### 15.2.4 Profit and Loss Account

The profit and loss account for the span of the financial year under consideration is presented along with appropriation (proposed) of the profit earned during that year. Like the balance sheet this account is also supported by various schedules, giving details of income and expenditure wherever, necessary of the current and the previous year.

The profit and loss account of the ongoing project is similar to what we have seen in the section on Estimate of Working Results, Chapter 11, for the proposed project.

The income of the project is not necessarily only from sales of products co-products and by-products, but it also includes interest received by way of investments from the reserves of previous year and income from sales of the fixed assets. The gross cost of production includes all operating expenditures. Gross profit, operating profit, profit before tax, corporate tax, profit after tax need to be presented. The utilisation of profit after tax, dividend, etc., is presented under the title 'appropriations'. The amount to be transferred to general reserves is indicated along with the balance that is carried forward to the balance sheet. A summary of profit and loss account is presented in Table 15.2.

### 15.2.5 Cash Flow Statement

Cash flow statement need to be prepared as per the listing agreement of local stock exchange. This includes the following:

- Cash flow from operating activities
- Cash flow from investing activities
- Cash flow from financing activities

## 15.3 INSIGHT INTO AN ANNUAL REPORT

Formidable inferences can be drawn from the annual report about the 'health' of the ongoing project. The proposed dividend can be deemed as the yardstick of the health of a project. Let us try to analyse some important information or data presented in the annual report and see its utility to various engineering groups within the organisation.

### 15.3.1 Sales Turnover and Capacity Utilisation

The relationship between sales turnover and capacity utilisation is rather complex. For instance, the increase in sales turnover need not be entirely due to increase in the capacity utilisation, but can also be due to increase in selling price of the product or sales of the stock from previous year. If capacity utilisation is below 100%, there is every reason to believe that something is wrong somewhere. One must analyse factors responsible for lower capacity utilisation and plan corrective action and implement the same by way of add on project or debottlenecking of the existing project. Some major factors responsible for lower capacity utilisation could be listed below with possible course of action.

*Improper Absorption of Technology*

The effective absorption of the technology could be achieved by selecting qualified people from the reputed institutions. Refresher courses for plant personnel often help in assimilation of the technology.

*Inferior technology*

The updating of the existing technology can be achieved, if possible, through Research and Technology development activities at the owner's R&D Centre. The 'quantum' spent on R&D activities as percentage of sales indicates the commitment.

*Availability of Cheaper and Equally Good Product(s) Due to Liberation of the Trade*

The entrepreneur cannot do much when cheaper and better quality products are available due to liberalisation of trade. Instead of wishing to have trade barriers by way of import duties, he should concentrate on how to match price of his product with that of imported one. If unable to do this, perhaps switching over to new product line is feasible.

Here is a challenge to engineers in technology cell how to reduce the cost of production by lower consumptions of raw materials and utilities. This could be achieved by sustained research and development efforts.

*Competition*

The cut-throat competition in imperfect market might result in reduction in production. Better quality, better packaging for consumer products and awareness drive might perhaps improve sales.

*Frequent Breakdowns Due to Non-availability of Raw Materials/ Utilities*

The corporate planning department can now explore possibility of a co-generation unit or captive power plant, improve supply chain logistics, and so on. The resourcing from neighbouring countries or even distant overseas supplier may be the answer.

*Strained Labour Relationship*

A realistic and compassionate approach by human resource development department can solve this problem.

Thus, we see how problems related to production capacity utilisation can be resolved. These are some of the important factors responsible for lower capacity utilisation. There can be other factors also.

### 15.3.2 Cost of Production

The sensitivity analysis of elements of cost of production would bring out importance of raw materials and utilities. The economic policies of the state and central government by way of import duties, excise and sales tax have impact on the raw material prices. The consumption of raw materials and utilities may be brought down by sustained R&D efforts. Sometimes it may not be possible to do that unless a technology breakthrough is achieved.

### 15.3.3 Corporate Planning

The power consumption may necessitate a co-generation unit. Therefore, engineers in the planning department may plan such a project by having natural gas discovered in nearby area.

In the effluent treatment plant, the emphasis may be on water recycle and recovery of wealth (value added by-products) from the waste. The water recycle from effluent treatment plant would not only conserve water but may reduce water bill paid to the local state industrial development corporation. The people working in corporate planning department might initiate action plan to take care of the above.

It is possible to recover valuable chemicals from the waste stream and have value-added products. For example, one may recover butyric, valeric and caproic acid (BVC acids) from the aqueous waste stream originating from cyclohexane oxidation plant to manufacture cyclohexanol and cyclohexanone.

By analysing annual reports of other companies, we can derive the benefits. If we are planning a project to manufacture $H_2$ for captive (in-house) consumption based on various raw materials such as naphtha, natural gas or LPG, one can see from other balance sheet what is the price of the above-mentioned feedstock and how the government policies have affected their prices. In his address to the shareholders, the chairman might have made reference to the ever-increasing price of naphtha causing impact on the cost of generation of $H_2$, thereby affecting profits. This would initiate us to look into alternative cheap and stable source of the raw material, say natural gas.

If we are planning a project to manufacture phenol and the annual report of the present manufacturer indicates difficulties in selling acetone; a co-product in phenol project, we have to think of an innovative approach. We can simultaneously plan forward integration and think in terms of manufacture of *bis* phenol-A. If propylene is not readily available, instead of importing propylene why not think of hydrogenating acetone to iso-propanol followed by dehydration of the same to propylene. Thus we can take care of co-product acetone in phenol project.

### 15.3.4 Research and Development

The fraction of turnover spent on R&D activities would clearly indicate the commitment of an organisation towards development and the self-reliance. More you spend on R&D more rewards are expected, as this would be market-and need-based effort. The stress on indigenous development of technology should be emphasised. When such an attempt is made for forward or backward integration, engineers from corporate planning department would continuously assess economic viability of such efforts in R&D resulting in economically viable process.

### 15.3.5 Responsible Care

Accreditation of a project to ISO14000 (2000) or part of it would clearly indicate how serious the management is towards a Safety Health and Environment (SHE), management issues. This would not only change outlook of the local project-affected people but also enhance the image among customers from the developed countries. This would enable the owner to have export promotion.

### 15.3.6 Project Financing

The annual report of any organisation is an indicator of the health of the organisation. The shareholders would be impressed if the project is performing well. This inturn, would give right signals to new equity participants by way of shares. The group of promoters with proven track record would not find any difficulties to raise the equity funds in the market. In doing so the promoters might even have public issue at an early date before funds from financial institution are taken. This would then reduce pre-operative expenses through reduction in interest on the borrowed capital. As a result, there will be reduction in the project cost. As explained earlier in Chapter 5, it is thus possible to reduce project cost by timing public issue.

The impressive working results, as seen from the annual reports, year after year would make commercial bankers, financial institutions more comfortable while sanctioning term loan. This is mainly due to reduction in the risk associated with promoters.

The financial institutions then would not hesitate to give term loan even at higher Debt: Equity ratio. Thus corporate planning managers would have smooth sailing to finance the proposed projects.

Thus, we see that the annual report is very useful to all concerned with the project. We recommend at this stage to have a look at any available Annual Report from a chemical company.

**Table 15.1** The Balance Sheet (Format)

| *Name: MAMOK LTD*<br>*Period: April1, 2003 to*<br>*March 31, 2004* | *Present Year* | *Previous Year* |
|---|---|---|
| **1.0 Source of Funds** | | |
| 1.1 Shareholders fund | | |
| Capital | | |
| Reserves and surplus | | |
| Total | SF | |
| 1.2 Loan fund | | |
| Secured loans | | |
| Unsecured loans | | |
| Total | LF | |
| Source of fund | = (SF) + (LF) | |
| **2.0 Application of funds** | | |
| 2.1 Fixed Assets | | |
| Gross block (all fixed assets) | | |
| Less: Depreciation | | |
| Project work in progress | | |
| Total | FA | |
| 2.2 Current assets | | |
| 2.3 Current Liabilities (less) | | |
| Net current assets | NCA | |
| Application of fund | = (FA) + (NCA) | |
| In the balance sheet, | | |
| Source of fund | = Application of fund | |
| (SF) + (LF) | = (FA) + (NCA) | |

**Table 15.2** A Typical Format of **Profit** and **Loss Account**

| | *Present Year* | *Previous Year* |
|---|---|---|
| Income | | |
| Expenditure | | |
| Profit before depreciation | | |
| Profit before tax | | |
| Provision for tax Net Profit | | |
| Appropriations | | |

The 'Annual Report' of any company preferably of a chemical project, is recommended for further information.

***An Annual Report Reflects on Sustainability of the Project.***

# Index


## A

Accounting period, 289
Acid test, 253
Add-on project, 8, 9-11, 183
Admin.expenses,180
Airport, 58
American Association of Cost Engineers(AACE), 75
Annual report, 285-298
Annualized cost, 213, 214
Application of funds, 289
Appreciation,220
Aromatics, 1
Auditor's report, 285

## B

Backward integration,10
Balance sheet, 297, 288
Bankable document, 69, 108, 190
Basic engineering package, 84, 92, 95, 127,169
Battery limit plant, 34, 81, 126, 169
Battery limit project, 9
Biological Oxygen Demand (BOD), 36
Book value, 220
Borrowed capital,184, 188
Break-even analysis, 242
Break-even capacity, 243
Budgetary estimates, 131, 142
Buildings and civil works, 87, 90, 103

## C

Capacity utilization, 292
Capitalised cost, 215-217
Captive power plant, 52, 171, 172
Carbon black, 51
Cash earning per share, 255
Cash cost, 120
Cash flow, 292
Catalyst
  Recovery of , 27
CE Plant cost index, 138, 153, 158
  (*See also* Cost index)
Chemical Engineering plant cost Index (USA), 158
Chemical oxygen demand, 36
Chemical plant utilities
  applied, 21
  basic, 21
Chemical Projects classification of, 11
Chemicals
  commodity, 11
  specialty, 11, 12
CIFprice,120, 138
Civic amenities 57
Civil engineering, 98
Common Effluent Treatment Plant (CETP), 54
Communication 55
Communication parameters,55
  (*See also* Parameters)
Competition
  Imperfect , 273
  monopolistic, 273
  perfect, 273
Composite index, 157

Compound interest, 204
Computer-aided cost estimate, 165
Contingencies, 102
Corporate planning, 294
Corrosive environment, 87
Cost
  Annualized , 213-14
  Capitalised , 215 - 217
  project, 32-39, 77-123
  (*See also* Project cost)
Cost capacity relation,153,155
Cost estimates
  computer-aided, 165
  definitive,142
  electricals , 139
  equipment , 129
  installation,149
  instrumentation ,139
  piping, ,139
  parametric,132
  transportation ,148
Cost index,
  CEplant, 138,153,158
  Nelson-Ferrar Refinery
  Construction,158, 159
  VATAVUK air pollution
  control, 135
Cost inclusive of Insurance and
  Freight (CIF) 120, 130
Cost of production, 167-182 , 294
  elementsof,169-175
  factory overheads, 175
  gross, 177
  normative, 178
  packaging, 174
  raw materials,169
  salary and wages,175
  schedule,179
  utilities, 170
Cost scale-up, 153
Cryogenic fuel, 3
Cumene process, 17
Currency basket, 79, 122, 139
Current assets, 116, 122, 290
Current liabilities, 122, 290
Current ratio, 253
Customer's account, 120

**D**

Debottlenecking, 10
Debtor turnover, 251
Debt: equity ratio, 190-191, 252
Debt: service coverage ratio, 253
Deep shaft technology, 37
Definitive Estimate, 142
Depreciation, 219- 230
  computation of, 230
  definition, 219
  In chemical projects, 221-222
  methods, 222
  rates, 226
  schedule, 227
  SLM,
  Straight line method (SLM) 223
  Written down value(WDV)
  method, 223-224
Desalination, 52
Detailed/definitive cost etimate,129
Detailed engineering, 93,95
Director's report, 286
Discounted cash flow technique, 257
Discounted profit flow
  (DPF) 204,
  technique, 256-258
Distillation column system, 94
Diversification, 10
Dividend, 235-236
  cover, 255
  yield, 255

## E

Earnings per share, 254
EBITDA , 233
Economic Profit Analysis (EPA),
    262
EVA Analysis , 263
Economy of scale, 270
Effluent treatment plant,
    36,83,146,
Effluents, 2
Electricals, 141
Electrical engineering, 98
Energy conservation
    (ENCON) concept,7, 25, 31, 225
Engineering, 4
    civil, 98
    detailed, 93
    electrical, 98
    instrumentation, 99
    mechanical, 96
    piping, 97
    process 96
Engineering Procurement and
    Construction services, 94
Environment management system,
    53
Environmental clearance, 67
Equipment
    Cost estimate, 129
    imported, 138
Equipment cost-capacity
    algorithm ,135
Equity, 184-188,190,191
    participation, 26
Escalation, 135
Establishment charges, 107
Estimation by considering time
    factor, 135
Estimates, 70-76
    budgetary, 131-138, 142
    definitive,142
    miscellaneous items, 148
    order of magnitude, 129, 142,
    152, 162
    relative errors, 155
    repairs and maintenance, 176
    types of, 74
    working capital, 117
    working results, 232, 237
Expansion project, 10
Expenditure Coefficient (EC), 60
Expenses
    financial, 109,
    mortgage and legal, 108
    on foreign technicians
    &training of Indian technicians
    abroad, 99
    preliminary, 113
    pre-operative, 229
    public issue related, 113
    start-up,108
Extraction turbines, 171
Engineering Procurement
Construction (EPC), 151

## F

Factory act and Petroleum act, 82
Factory buildings, 83, 87, 227
Factory overheads, 175
Feasibility report,14, 108, 277-284,
    techno-economic,128
    utility of, 283
Fenton chemistry, 173
Financial
Expenses during the period of
    construction, 109
    (*See* also Expenses)
    institutions, 189
Firewater, 83
Fixed assets, 290

FOB Price 120
Formaldehyde from methanol
    manufacturing of, 141, 144
Formation of Cartel, 136
Forward integration, 9
Free-on-board (FOB) price, 120, 130
Fund flow statement, 111
Funds
    application of, 289
    sources of, 289

**G**

Globalization, 137
Goods and Services Tax (GST) 54, 126, 127, 150
GST on imported items 126
Greenfield project, 8, 78, 183
Greenfield project cost, 80
Gross cost of production,30, 177
Grossprofit, 41, 232
Guesstimate, 70

**H**

Harmonised System Nomenclature (HSN) 127, 151
Hazard analysis (HAZAN), 15, 22, 67
Hazard operability studies (HAZOP) analysis, 13,22,67
Housing /Hotels 56
Heat pump concept, 144
Hurdle rate of return, 257-260

**I**

Imperfect competition, 273
Incineration, 36
Income Tax Act, 1961, 234
Incremental analysis, 244
Index
    cost, 157
    location, 160
    plant cost, 161
    profitability, 261, 265
Indirect costs, 167
Industrial infrastructure, 56
Inflation
    factors influencing,136
In-process stock,119
Installation,149
Instalments,210
Instrumentation engineering, 99
Insulation,
    cold, 150
    hot, 150
Insurance, 108,150
    Interstate GST, 151
Integration,
    backward, 10, 28
    forward, 9, 28
    horizontal, 10
Interest, 201-218
    compound, 204
    cover,252
    during construction,110,111
    rates, 204
    simple, 203
Internal rate of return (IRR), 261, 265
International monetary fund, 189
ISO
    accreditation, 66, 296

**K**

Know-how and engineering, 91, 103
Know-how fees (licensing fees) 91

**L**

Labour 57
Land location, 63

Land and site development, 81, 103,
  Estimates of, 86
Land requirement estimate of, 84-85
Liquefied natural gas (LNG) , 3
Loan repayment, 205
  options, 206-209
Location index, 160
Low sulphur heavy stock (LSHS), 147,173

**M**

Material take-off (MTO), 142
Maintenance Spares, 119
Man-hours required, 93
Manufacturing facility, 24
Margin money,104, 114
Market
  considerations, 272
  potential, 14
  search report, 108,279
  value, 291, 220
Mechanical engineering, 96
Meteorolog ical data, 66
Methanol from natural gas,140, 143
Minimum alternate tax (MAT), 222, 226, 238
Miscellaneous fixed assets,101,104, 230
Monitor this way, 178
Monopoly, 274
Monopolistic competition,273
Monopsony, 275
Montreal protocol, 269
Moratorium period, 209
Mortgage and Legal expenses, 108,

**N**

Nelson-Ferrar refinery construction cost index, 159
Net assets turnover, 250
Net cash accruals, 238
Net present value analysis, 260, 265
Nominal and effective interest rates, 204
Non-factory buildings, 83, 87,90,221,227
Non-vehicle components,101

**O**

Octroi, 151
Oligopoly, 274
Ongoing business, 192
Operating expenses, 167
Operating profit, 233
Order of magnitude (quick) estimates, 152
Outside battery limit-facilities (OSBL), 32,81, 88,126, 169, 172
Cost estimates,145-147
  utilities,145
Owner's capital, 184
Oxirane
  process 22

**P**

Packaging, 174
Packaging Material 119
Packing and forwarding,148
Painting and insulation,149
Parameter
  communication, 55
  cost capacity correlation,134
Parametric cost estimation,132
Payback period, 247, 264
Per-diem rate, 100
Perfect competition, 272, 273
Performance ratios, 247
Periodic payments, 210
Piping engineering, 97
Piping, instrumentation and electrical cost estimate, 139

Plant and machinery cost,124-165
  elements of,126
Plant
  model, 90
  cost in India, 162
  cost index, 158
Plant and machinery, 90, 103
Plant of different capacity, 153
Power law model, 153
Preliminary and capital issue
  related expenses, 104, 113
Preliminary process flow diagram,
  128
Pre-operative expenses, 80, 104
  elements of, 105
Pre-project activities, 6-8
Present value, 257
Price and cost difference, 13
Price parameter equation, 132-133
Process
  engineering 96
  evaluation, 39
  flow diagrams, 142
  licensor, 18
  selection, 17-42
  selection coefficient, 41
Product
  inventory, 1 119
  market, 50
  market considerations of,
    272-275
  pricing, 267 -275
Productivity coefficient, 62
Productivity factors, 55-58
  evaluation of, 61-62
Profit and loss account, 291
Profit after tax, 235
Profit before tax, 235
Profit for corporate tax, 234, 235
  gross, 232
  operating, 233
Profit margin, 250
Profitability coefficient, 41
  factors, 59,
  evaluation of, 59-61
  index, 261,265
  parameters, 18,29
  project, 231-239
  (*See also* Project profitability)
Project
  capital outlay, 12
  classification,11
  commissioning, 13
  conception, 14
  financing,183
  types of, 8-10
  office cost, 106
Project cost,32-39,77-123
  overrun, 77
Project
  economics, 267-271
  engineering, 4,16 evaluation,
  240-266
  financing,16, 183-200, 296
  import duty, 151
  life span, 179
  office cost,105
  profitability,47,231-239
Promoters, 185
Proposed project product pricing,
  267
Prosperity factors, 45
Proven track record, 25

## R

Raschig process, 17
Ratio analysis, 246-255
  limitations of, 255
Rate of Return, 249
Raw materials, 19, 118, 169
  source of, 50

Reactive distillation,23
Reactor
specifications, 130
four-line specifications, 131
Reliability of Power and Water Supply 56
Report of Directors, 287
Report of Auditor, 288
Research and development, 295
Reserve Bank of India, 115
Resources, use of, 46
Return on equity, 250
Return on investment,240, 249

**S**

State GST (SGST),150
Safety,Health and Environment (SHE), 7, 22, 25, 136
Sales turn over and capacity utilisation, 291
Schedule, 179
Scrap value, 220
Service life, 220
Service Accounting Codes (SAC), 94
Similarity principle, 131
Simple interest, 203
Site
clearance, 67
evaluation, 58
Site selection, 15, 45-58
Site specific discharge standard, 66
Six-tenth rule, 134
Soft loan, 189
Soil survey report, 65
Sources of funds, 289
Spares, 148
Spread sheet concept,122
Start up expenses 108
Statutory duties and taxation,54
Stock turnover, 251
Storage facilities, 146
Straight line method (SLM), 222, 223
Subsidy,183

**T**

Tandon Committee, 115
Technology Innovation, 136
Technology search and evaluation, 14
Term loan (Debt),114
repayment, 209
Timefactor, 135
TQM , 7, 25 136
Turnover
debtors, 251
ratio, 156
netassets, 250

**U**

Utilities 118

**V**

Venture capital, 198
Venture capitalist, 198-200

**W**

Weighted Average Cost of Capital (WACC), 259, 260
Working capital, 114
Written Down Value (WDV) method, 222, 223